make it
YOUR
BUSINESS

FUEL^{RCA}

FuelRCA Collection
RCA Library
Kensington Gore
London SW7 2EU

fuel.rca.ac.uk

Lucy Martin   Bella Mehta

make it
YOUR
BUSINESS

*The Ultimate Business Start-Up
Guide for Women*

SPRING HILL

Published by Spring Hill

Spring Hill is an imprint of
How To Books Ltd
Spring Hill House
Spring Hill Road
Begbroke
Oxford
OX5 1RX
Tel: 01865 375794
info@howtobooks.co.uk
www.howtobooks.co.uk

First edition 2006
Reprinted 2007

British Library Cataloguing in Publication Data
A catalogue record of this book is available from the British Library

Cover Design by Mousemat Design Ltd

Produced for How To Books by Deer Park Productions
Designed and typeset by Mousemat Design Ltd
Printed and bound by Bell & Bain Ltd, Glasgow

NOTE: The material contained in this book is set out in good faith for general
guidance and no liability can be accepted for loss or expense incurred as a result of
relying in particular circumstances on statements made in the book. Laws and
regulations are complex and liable to change, and readers should check the current
position with relevant authorities before making personal arrangements.

ISBN: 978-1-905862-00-9

CONTENTS

ABOUT THE AUTHORS

Lucy Martin (39) is a mother of three, ex-city lawyer, founder of childcare agency Gina's Nannies, writer and columnist.

The daughter of a barrister and an accountant, Lucy grew up in Belgium and Surrey, and gained a first from Oxford University in French and Russian. She went on to study law and qualified as a solicitor in 1992 but became disillusioned with her legal career - feeling she was working below her potential and held back by a glass ceiling.

In 2001 Lucy left law to set up Gina's Nannies (named after her second daughter), which now provides childcare to families across SW London, as well as an all-round consultancy service on childcare options, costs and practicalities.

In response to the lack of information and support for female business start-ups, Lucy set up Wimbledon Women in Business. Its immediate success (40 member businesses within 8 months) was further evidence that women had specific needs when it came to networking and business support. Through WWIB Lucy met coach and co-author-to-be Bella Mehta, and the idea for their book was born.

Bella Mehta (35) is a mother, organisational consultant and career coach.

Born in Bangor, North Wales, Bella is the middle daughter of parents who met in Baroda, India, and immigrated to the UK in the sixties. Both her mother and father are ophthalmologists, her older sister is a consultant anaesthetist, and her younger sister is an optometrist. Bella studied music, biochemistry, information management and humanistic psychology.

She worked as a piano teacher, shop assistant, waitress, secretary and barmaid to help fund herself through university. After graduating she worked for the Commonwealth Development Corporation before joining a weekly science journal, rising quickly to Managing Editor.

Bella subsequently completed a Masters in Information Management at Sheffield University, and joined Deloitte Consulting where she was on the Fast Track programme for future partnership. As a consultant, she worked for many large public and private sector organisations, and she began to observe how completely different the world of work was for men and women. In 1999 Bella started training at the Metanoia Institute in Transactional Analysis Counselling, and then set up a company called Enspiral, focusing on project management, facilitation, coaching and training.

She has a Diploma in Humanistic Psychology from the Institute for the Development of Human Potential (one of the oldest accrediting bodies in Europe for coaching and facilitation).

Bella is currently Chair of Wimbledon Women in Business and also works closely with a local school which is a specialist Business and Enterprise school for girls.

ACKNOWLEDGEMENTS

We would very much like to thank the following businesswomen who we have quoted or featured as case sudies

Abi Davies, Aromatherapist (abi.aromatherapist@virgin.net)
Alice Wood, Virgin Consultant (alice@alicewood.com)
Amanda Hazell, Making Moves (www.makingmoves.co.uk)
Amar Basra, Division for Lifelong Learning, University of Bath (a.k.basra@bath.ac.uk)
Anita Roddick (www.anitaroddick.com)
Annie Stevens, Annie Stevens Design (www.anniestevens.co.uk)
Antonia Rolls, Artist Extraordinaire (www.antoniarolls.co.uk)
Brenda Burling, Cheshire Day Nursery Group (brenda.burling@ntlworld.com)
Britt Armstrong-Gash & Kelly Chandler, The Bespoke Wedding Company (www.thebespokeweddingco.com)
Carla Boulton, Naughty Mutt Ltd (www.naughtymutt.com)
Carol Daniels, The Gender Sensitive Consultancy (cdaniels@odpnetwork.fsnet.co.uk)
Carol Goodsman, Alice Carroll (www.alicecarroll.co.uk)
Caroline Lashley, The Editors Office (www.theeditorsoffice.co.uk)
Catherine Green, CG Scubbers (www.cgscrubbers.co.uk)
Charlotte Fuller (www.fullerpr.co.uk)
Claire Alexander, Ad Hominem (clairealexander@blackmoss.net)
Claire Owen, Stopgap (www.stopgap.co.uk)
Debi Harris and Jo Dew, Porous Designs (www.porousdesigns.com)
Denice Purdie, Purdie's Scottish Soap Company (www.thescottishsoapcompany.co.uk)
Diana Colquhoun and Julia Linford, Flower Power (julialinford@aol.com)
Diana Sterck, Chief Executive, Merton Chamber of Commerce (www.mertonchamber.co.uk)
Eileen McKay, The Leemac Clinic (myclinic@btinternet.com)
Elaine Barbook, Promise Design (Elaine@promisedesign.co.uk)
Ellen Kerr, Enterprise Development Relationship Manager, Business Link for Greater Merseyside (ellen.kerr@gme.org.uk)
Emma Reid, Grey Sells (emma.reid@greysells.co.uk)
Eugenie Harvey, We Are What We Do (www.wearewhatwedo.org)
Fiona Price (www.fiona-price.co.uk)

Freya Bletsoe, Homefinder UK (www.homefinderuk.com)
Genevieve Taylor (www.thehomegourmet.co.uk)
Gill Fennings, Her Business (www.herbusinessuk.co.uk)
Gita Patel, Stargate Capital Trapezia (www.trapeziacapital.co.uk)
Geetie Singh, Sloeberry Trading (www.sloeberry.co.uk)
Halifax Bank of Scotland's Women in Business Team
    (www.bankofscotland.co.uk/women)
Helen Fell (helenfell@onetel.com)
Helen Furze and Paula Rogers, Furze Rogers Recruitment
    (www.furzerogersassociates.co.uk)
Jackie Abey and Jill Smallcombe, Abey Smallcombe (www.abeysmallcombe.com)
Jackie Frost, Jackie Frost Photography (www.jfphotography.co.uk)
Jane Geldart (www.daisyjaneflowers.co.uk)
Jenny Cook, Institute for the Development of Human Potential
    (www.idhp.org.uk)
Jenny Watson, Chair, Equal Opportunities Commission (www.eoc.org.uk)
Jo Haines, Cake Magic
Jocelyn Ashton, Building Blocks Nurseries (www.buildingblocks-
    wimbledon.co.uk)
Josu Shepherd (www.jakabel.com)
Judy Bell, Shepherds Purse (www.shepherdspurse.co.uk)
Julie Weeks, Womenable (www.womenable.com)
Justine Dalby, Premium Sourcing (www.tcseurope.co.uk)
Karen Mattison, Women Like Us (www.womenlikeus.org)
Katherine Watkins, Chartered Physiotherapist (www.watkinsphysio.com)
Kelly Stevens & Sarah Steele, The Women's Networking Company
    (www.thewomensnetworkingcompany.com)
Leila Wilcox, Halos n Horns (www.halogb.co.uk)
Lin Taylor, Stars Stripes and Snowflakes (www.starsstripesandsnowflakes.com)
Linda Lloyd, Homeopathy Resource (www.homeopathyresource.com)
Lisa Thefaut, Business Links Coordinator, Ursuline School, Wimbledon
    (www.ursulinehigh.merton.sch.uk)
Liz Jackson, Great Guns Marketing (www.greatgunsmarketing.co.uk)
Liz Nelson (liz@stargatecapital.co.uk)
Louise Cooper, Gingham Hearts (louisecooper@ginghamhearts.plus.com)
Louise Ladbrooke, Bees Knees Nurseries (www.louiseladbrooke.com)
Lynne Embleton
Mary Corrie, City Organiser (www.cityorganiser.com)
Mary Tyler, Davidson Hall Executive Search (www.davidsonhall.com)
Nicola Horlick, Bramdiva (www.bramdiva.com)
Nina Sian, Slough Enterprise Gateway (www.sloughenterprisegateway.co.uk)
Paula Lamb, Mrs Fix It (ipolonio@aol.co.uk)
Rebecca Exley, Rebecca Exley Groundwater Ltd (rebeccaexley@aol.com)
Ruth Bradbrook, An Turus (www.an-turus.co.uk)
Sally Robinson, Ample Bosom (www.amplebosom.com)
Sandy Eifion-Jones, SEJ Consultancy (sandy.eifionjones@btopenworld.com)
Sara Carter, Professor of Entrepreneurship, Stirling University (www.stir.ac.uk)
Sarah Holland (www.lifesupport.co.uk)
Stella Thomas, Global Water Fund (www.globalwaterfund.com)
Stephanie Butland, haveyouthoughtabout.com (www.haveyouthoughtabout.com)
Stephanie Upton-Prowse, Style Studio (www.style-studio.co.uk)
Sue Botterill, Mymag (www.mymaguk.com)

Susanna Riviere (www.susanna-riviere.co.uk)
Teresa Owen and Martin Abel, Fairwind Trading (www.fairwindonline.com)
Val Howard and Mary Fitzhenry, Safesitters (www.safesitters.co.uk)
Veronica Sarkhel (veronicasarkhel@yahoo.co.uk)

We would also like to thank the following people and businesses who we talked to during the course of this book, or who provided insights and background information.

Allison Pearson, author of *I Don't Know How She Does It*: The Life of Kate Reddy, Working Mother (Knopf, 2002)
Announce It (www.announceit.co.uk)
Antonietta Beecheno, AB Marketing (www.abmarketingservices.co.uk)
Cate Newnes-Smith, Mountain Top (www.mountain-top.co.uk)
Chey Garland and Michael Grey (www.cjgarland.co.uk)
Henrietta Laitt (henrietta@resultsforsuccess.com)
Innocent (www.innocentdrinks.com)
Jenni Talman (www.justhealthpr.com)
Judi James (www.judijames.com)
Karen Skidmore (www.candocanbe.co.uk)
Lucy Kane, Time and Leisure Magazine (www.timeandleisure.co.uk)
Mandy Haberman (www.mandyhaberman.com)
Mandy Muckalt, Roots for Success (www.rootsforsuccess.com)
Militza Ortiz, Jewellery Designer (militzaortiz@aol.com)
Natalie Dagnall (Natalie@lifewize.co.uk)
Oxford Entrepreneurs (www.bouncewithit.com)
Polly Toynbee, Guardian Journalist and author
Richard Martin (richard.martin@speechlys.com)
Sahar Hashemi, founder of Coffee Republic and co-author of *Anyone Can Do It*: Building Coffee Republic from Our Kitchen Table (Capstone, 2005)
Sophi Tranchell, Day Chocolate Company
Stephanie Calman, author of *Confessions of a Bad Mother*: In the aisle by the chill cabinet No-one can hear you scream (Pan, 2006)
Toyin Dania, Wandsworth Youth Enterprise Centre (www.wyec.org.uk)
Vicky Alkalai, founder of The Plastic People

Special thanks to Julia McCutchen of Firefly Media, for advice, encouragement and coaching, Professor Sara Carter of Stirling University for allowing us to use the text of her speech, Salema Gulbahar of London Development Agency/Prowess, Elizabeth Parks for accountancy advice and to Martin Abel of Fairwind Trading Online (www.fairwindonline.co.uk) for useful information about cashflow and running a shop. Thanks also to Stephanie Upton-Prowse of Style Studio (www.style-studio.co.uk) and Adre King of K&G Image Consultancy (www.kgimageconsulting.co.za) for styling advice for the cover. Finally, thanks to members of Wimbledon Women in Business (www.wwib.org.uk) for support, friendship and stories. Lucy would like to particularly thank Victoria Burmester and Jenny Scott for their support and enthusiasm. Bella would particularly like to thank Andy Sturt and Liz Veecock for their support, insight and encouragement.

INTRODUCTION

WHY THIS BOOK?

We have written this book to show you how straightforward, empowering and satisfying business ownership can be. That's not to say it has been an easy ride – we have certainly had plenty of challenges, doubts and difficulties along the way – but several years down the line we are looking back on an exciting and fulfilling journey – and it isn't over yet.

Women set up businesses in a variety of circumstances, and for many reasons, but a universal driver is the prospect of more freedom and control over their working lives, home lives and environment, not to mention having fun and making a profit at the same time.

The majority of self-employment books to be found on the shelves today are written by men, for men, about men, and when we were looking for help and inspiration, they could easily have put us off. They may well provide you with the intellectual tools to write a masterful business plan or learn the intricacies of double-entry book-keeping, but there is a lot more to be discovered and understood about business ownership than facts and figures. All entrepreneurs need to find out about business plans, billing and record-keeping, but we place equal importance on finding out, for example, what life will be like as a woman business owner, how to overcome psychological barriers to self-employment, such as the 'little old me syndrome', how to stay focused and how to achieve your ambitions and financial targets without sacrificing what is important in your life.

It may feel like a big financial and personal risk to set up your own business; this book shows you how to minimise these risks, and still aim high. We cover everything you need to know, from what to have on your business card to filing annual accounts, and from negotiating a contract to what to wear to a networking event. More than that, it addresses the lifestyle issues that are important to you as a woman, and how to make setting up and running a business a deeply satisfying and rewarding experience on many levels.

WOMEN AS ENTREPRENEURS

Despite media images to the contrary, there are no standard characteristics of a woman business owner. Almost anyone can start up a business with children or without; with qualifications or without; with a corporate career behind you or no training at all. You could be thinking about a home-based business or planning a global empire; leaving a glittering career; nursing your wounds after an encounter with the glass ceiling; or re-evaluating your priorities after an illness or life change. Most women we have spoken to started up businesses in their thirties or forties. They span the full diversity of backgrounds, cultures, ages and physical abilities that we see in the world around us. They are self-motivated and driven by a strong desire for their career to be meaningful and for work and life to be balanced.

As women, we have natural advantages to succeeding in business. Networking, communication, sensitivity, co-operation, multitasking, community concerns and authenticity all come easily to us.

Women at work are often disenchanted by patriarchal practices, lack of integrity and genuine friendship, or just a feeling that work–life balance is not as good as it could be.

The problem is not just that we cannot get to the top of these organisations, but often that we don't want to. We look to self-employment for financial rewards and the flexibility to make work compatible with family or other interests, and are driven to set up a business that 'makes a difference' and solves our existing employment issues.

Making the decision to be a business leader is a big leap for anyone, but as women, we have a great deal to gain from creating a working environment where we are happy and productive and can use our female attributes to their best effect. The results speak for themselves – just look at the formidable successes of The Body Shop, Ann Summers, LK Bennett, Coffee Republic and JoJo Maman Bébé.

The prospect of independence, money, power and success and the thrill of seizing an opportunity provide a strong incentive for all entrepreneurs, male and female. Women seek these rewards just as much as men do, but are prone to downplay their drive for success and to attribute positive outcomes to luck. The 'impostor syndrome'[i] as it is known, is common to a lot of high-achieving women with degrees, professional success and promotions under their belts, who routinely dismiss their success, attributing it to contacts, timing or having fooled others – consequently living in fear of being 'found out'.

Reading this book will help you to separate feelings from facts, to stamp out the fear of being found out and to set free your 'inner tycoon'.

MOTHERS AS ENTREPRENEURS

Motherhood should not be seen as a barrier to self-employment, but rather as a qualification that opens the door to it. Having children teaches us to be multitasking experts, peacemakers, providers, accountants and leaders and to meet several inflexible deadlines each day. Becoming a mother is a huge life event where you discover more about who you are and what is important in your life. What many mothers want is a career which allows them to go to the school sports day and see friends or go to the gym.

There is still huge pressure on women to do the bulk of childcare despite the media love affair with 'house husbands' and 'new men'. Research from women's organisation Prowess shows that women in the UK are responsible for 80 per cent of childcare and caring duties, and most male-run organisations do not offer the flexibility that childcare arrangements demand. Most women alter or interrupt their career path around having children, and most men don't. We deal with the issue of motherhood, childcare and guilt in Chapter 1.

DEFINING SUCCESS

Setting up and succeeding with any business venture will test your resilience, push at the boundaries of your comfort zone, and require deep-rooted commitment. While it may involve hard work and personal growth, it does not have to be stressful, and the rewards can be sweet. Beyond the fortunes for the one-in-a-thousand business owner who makes their millions, there are plenty of financial, professional and personal rewards for those who are prepared to give it a go. Being self-employed, you are free to define what success and fulfilment mean to you. Success might mean a highly profitable, expanding company, or it may mean a small, stable organisation that fits around family life and provides an income, professional independence, personal growth, or a community/political contribution. It can be what you want it to be.

HOW TO USE THIS BOOK

Use this book in a way that works for you. Chances are you won't have several solid days to read, absorb and take notes on its contents. The book is not a course that should be undertaken stage by stage, but we would advise you to start by reading the first two chapters. These will take you through some essential personal and practical considerations before you move ahead. It may be that you have already set up your business and are looking for guidance on specific topics, which you will find in Chapters 3–6. In any event you will benefit from going back to basics, because it is there that we lay the foundations of our success or failure. The final chapter explores the historical, political and social context in which women are setting up businesses.

Whatever your future in business holds for you, and whatever path you take, you are sure to face some interesting truths and make some inspiring discoveries about yourself.

1

MAKING THE DECISION

Running a business may be the burning ambition you have had in the back of your mind since childhood, an opportunity ripe for the picking, or it may be a hazy vision you can't quite grasp. You may already have a name or concept for your business, but no idea where to take it from here. Perhaps you are just toying with the concept of business ownership, franchising or partnership and want to decide if it is for you. At the end of this chapter you will be able to answer the question 'Is running a business for me?' with a 'yes', 'no' or 'maybe later', and you will have the tools to build a solid foundation for success if you go ahead. By examining your motives, circumstances and your personality, you will be able to work out how viable your goal really is and begin to shape your vision into reality.

WHAT'S YOUR IDEA?

We believe that women can do most things that men can, and that definitely includes running a successful business. Women have traditionally had a high profile in lifestyle and design-type businesses, but also have a presence in finance, construction, manufacturing and professional service businesses. Take a look at the list of businesses run by women in Table 1 and see if that inspires you.

For some people it's the actual business idea that is the most important thing.

Bella was inspired to coach by people who had coached her.

I'd previously worked within organisations on large projects where I was managing a team and being coached to do that well. I was also studying counselling and realising that being a deep thinker and highly sensitive to other people were great assets. At work, I saw how personal relationships were crucial to success, and how changes in behaviour of any team member (myself included) could make life better for all of us. I set up my business to focus on the 'inner life' of employees, my own development, and to support women, men and organisations to make work a fulfilling part of life.

At work, I saw how personal relationships were crucial to success, and how changes in behaviour of any team member (myself included) could make life better for all of us.

For others, like Lucy, the important thing was the urge, or need to run a business – to have ownership and control of her work.

At 35 years old I suddenly felt I was simply too old to be bossed around by managers who I felt did not appreciate the skills I had to offer, and could not offer me any worthwhile career prospects at the firm. What I was good at and passionate about and what I was doing seemed to be poles apart. Business ownership was the glittering prize which I believed would give me the chance to do something brilliantly, to control its shape and direction, and to reap the rewards directly. I had decided to set up something on my own a long time before I thought of setting up a nanny agency.

If you belong in the first category like Bella, you need to make sure you are the type of person who will enjoy all aspects of running a business, no matter how passionate you are about your idea. If you belong in the second category, you need to find a business that fits with your life and who you are. As **Eugenie Harvey,** co-founder of the 'We Are What We Do' movement, told us: 'You have to be passionate about what you do, or you won't be able to survive the low points.'

You have to be passionate about what you do, or you won't be able to survive the low points.

Most of us don't allow ourselves the luxury of enough thinking time, but giving yourself permission to take a break and think about your life really does pay off. **Britt Armstrong-Gash,** co-founder of The Bespoke Wedding Company, took six months off from her demanding job as a research assistant in the City of London to decide what she really wanted to do with her life, and came up with three possibilities: writing, make-up artistry and wedding planning.

Writing really appealed at first, but I discovered I'm too much of an extrovert to work on my own. I knew I had the skills to be a wedding planner from the jobs I'd done, from organising my own wedding, and from helping friends with theirs. I can research like a demon, which is handy when looking for things for weddings. I found myself a business partner (this being an absolute requirement I had decided). Et voilà – The Bespoke Wedding Company was born. Now I organise weddings, write most of the press releases and web content, and I qualified as a make-up artist, so occasionally I do the bride's make-up too. Life is good.

Most business manuals emphasise the need for starting with a big vision and a detailed business plan; but there are hundreds of successful businesses that began as hobbies at the kitchen table. With the right support, these fledgling projects can move up to the next level when the time is right. **Vicky Alkalai** of The Plastic People Company, who supplies decorative fairy lights to high-street shops such as Debenhams and River Island, started her business from her tiny one-bedroom flat. She made the lights originally for herself and friends, and discovered that they sold well at her local market. She approached the government agency, Business Link, for help in setting up a business, and secured funding of £100,000 for further business expansion.

It may be that an idea that has come to you on your travels or through other experiences in your life. The chain of Coffee

Republic shops was conceived when the founder, **Sahar Hashemi**, missed New York coffee shops on her return to London, and realised there was a big gap in the UK market. Your business doesn't have to be new or unique. It can be a franchise of a well-known operation, such as the Body Shop or party-plan business such as Virgin Vie or Color Me Beautiful. Franchises are a great way to be your own boss, while also having support from a larger organisation and from colleagues. Most franchise openings come with opportunities for training, networking and other practical support.

Alice Wood's background was in women's magazine publishing. She became a Virgin Cosmetics consultant when her children left home for university.

I enjoyed publishing, but realised a few years ago that I wanted a fresh change of direction. I'd always been interested in cosmetics and skincare and loved learning about make-up. I was invited to a Virgin party and was so impressed that I decided to become a consultant. I had never been involved in direct sales before so it was a massive learning curve, but I wasn't alone. One of the great things about Virgin Cosmetics is that there is a very professional and supportive culture, and an excellent mentoring network. I think the training I've received from Virgin would be valuable to anyone in any profession. And I find myself using some of the motivation techniques I've learned on my children! Four years on, I've made so many new friends, become a manager and expanded my Virgin business to Spain. Our company encourages women to help other women by sharing their knowledge and being supportive to each other.

It could also be that you are setting up a business to continue what you are doing now as an employee or for friends for free. In these cases you will already have many of the skills and the experience you need. Graphic designer **Elaine Barbrook** set up Promise Design to work around her children's school hours after 15 years in a high-profile corporate career. 'I realised that my family life couldn't take the pressure of my husband and I both working such long hours. Setting up my own design business was a logical step to take, as I always loved what I did, just not what it did to me…' Party planner **Louise Cooper** set up Gingham Hearts when she received glowing feedback from parents attending her children's parties. She started helping out friends with their parties for free, and gradually realised that she had a talent people would pay for. She quickly built up a reputation for outstanding customer service, as she treats each party as if it were her own. She now regularly organises large events for clients as prestigious as the Houses of Parliament and National Trust.

Women have set up and run all of the businesses shown in Table 1 (not all at once):

Table 1: Some of the many businesses run by women

Accountant	Doctor	Internet shop	Private detective
Alternative therapist	Driver	IT programmer	Proofreader
Antiques trader	Electrician	Jeweller	Project manager
Author	Entertainer	Journalist	Psychotherapist
Architecture	Events organiser	Management	Public relations
Artist	Fashion consultant	consultant	Publisher
Beauty therapist	Fashion designer	Market stall	Recruitment agency
Builder	Financial services	Marketing	Researcher
Cards	Florist	Massage	Restaurant
Catering business	Framing	Midwife	Sandwich bar
Childminder	Furniture	Nanny agency	Shoe/clothes shop
Cleaner	Garden design	Nursery	Solicitor
Cleaning agency	Gardener	Nutritionist	Spa/Salon owner
Coach	Gifts	Office services	Specialist advisor
Coffee shop	Graphic designer	Optician	Specialist shop
Construction worker	Grocers	Painter	Stationery
Counsellor	Hairdresser	Party-plan	Take-away
Dancer	Health practitioner	franchises	Teacher
Dating agency	Holiday consultant	Personal assistant	Technology
Decorator	Home wares	Personal stylist	consultant
Delicatessen	Hotel/B&B	Personal trainer	Trainer
Dentist	Insurance	Photographer	Virtual assistant
Designer	Interior design	Plumber	Wedding planner

HOW DID YOU GET HERE?

It's worth spending some time reflecting on how you got to this point in your life. Knowing how you got here will be useful when you plan the journey ahead, and all the experiences you have had are relevant when you start up your own business. If you are privileged enough to have had a good education and a professional career, you are likely to be better equipped than a school leaver with no employment experience, but if you are a creative self-starter, love hard work and learn quickly, you have your own natural advantages. Use the questions in the box below to review your current situation. Note down your answers to each question. The best way to do this exercise is in a conversation with a friend or coach.

All the experiences you have had are relevant when you start up your own business.

What is your current situation?

Family of origin
- What did your parents/carers do? Do they or did they have an entrepreneurial streak?
- Has anyone they know set up a business, and what happened?
- What would they do/think of your business idea?
- How important is their opinion? What will the consequences be of you doing something they disapprove of?

Current friends/family
- Do you have business-minded people around you?
- Are you supported emotionally/practically by family and friends?
- Are you planning to work from home and have you discussed the implications of this with your family?

If you have children
- How does setting up a business fit with your parenting role, practically and emotionally?
- Do you need help with childcare?
- What will happen during the school holidays?

Finance

- What financial commitments do you have?
- How dependent is your household on your salary?
- How well do you manage your money?
- How good are you at keeping records?
- What are your financial requirements and expectations for the future?
- Roughly how much will your business cost to set up?
- Roughly how much do you want to earn?
- How quickly do you need money to come in?

Education

- What kind of education did you have?
- How did you get on at school – were you a hard worker/selling tuck in the playground?
- What did you like/dislike about school?
- What skills and qualifications do you have?
- Do you need more training or qualifications to do what you want to do?
- Are you prepared to spend the time and/or money required to achieve that?
- How did you get around any difficulties at school/college?

Employment

- What jobs have you done? (Include work experience, involvement in a family business, holiday jobs, etc.)
- What did you excel at? What did you never quite grasp?
- What did you learn about management/leadership that you can use in your own business?
- What did you like/dislike about work?
- How comfortable are you with talking about what you do?

People

- Who do you get your inspiration from?
- What type of business person do you aspire to be?
- What kind of people do you want as your clients and co-workers?
- What characteristics in people do you most like/dislike?

Passions, hobbies and energy

- What did you enjoy doing as a child, teenager, adult?
- What are you passionate about now and why?
- What are your hobbies?
- What is the best part of your day?
- What do you have energy for/what energises you?

The bigger picture

- What are your core beliefs and values?
- What do you think other people value about you?
- What kind of environment do you like to live and work in?
- What, more than your skills, do you bring to the world?

Your past or current situation should not be a barrier at this early stage – if you don't have the support or skills you think you need, then you can find these, and we'll tell you how later on in this book. Make a note here of any areas listed above which you feel are barriers to becoming a business owner, so you can check you have dealt with your concerns before making a decision.

My concerns are:

-
-
-
-

Bella: My parents were entrepreneurial, as is their culture (Indian Hindu). At one point my mother was going to build a factory in our back garden just next to my father's business. I always had Saturday jobs and summer jobs as a student, and looking back that was a great experience – not just to introduce me to lots of different people and environments, but also because I learnt about finding work, earning money, managing my schedule and so on. All my life experiences have been helpful, but I'm glad I had twelve years of full-time employment before I set up my business. By then I knew a lot about my business area, I had developed my management, communication and leadership skills, and generally just 'grown up'. I'd been lucky enough to work for employers who sent me on lots of training courses, but I also spent my own time and money on part-time and evening courses whenever I could, from counselling to car mechanics, and editing to speed typing. On the personal side, I was single when I set up, although, unknown to me, about to meet the man I would settle down with. Now that we have a toddler, I appreciate how well self-employment suits me and my new family.

Lucy: Having trotted obediently from public school to Oxford, to law school, to a City law firm, it caused a bit of a shock to everyone when I left all that behind to set up a business. But when I look back on my experience as a whole, I was never as conventional as I appeared to be. At school and university I worked hard (I still stay up all night to get something done properly), but also made unusual choices and fought the system where I felt that what was being asked was unfair, unreasonable or pointless. At work, I was a champion for female-friendly working practices, and was always suggesting ways in which systems could be improved and made more efficient (very frustrating). Being my own boss gives me the chance to put my best ideas and extensive training and education into practice, and also to work hard to stay top of the class…

WHAT IS MOTIVATING YOU?

Women set up businesses for a huge variety of reasons and in many different circumstances. For example, you might be employed, unemployed, retired, a new mother, a mother of older children, or you might have come into some money or freedom through savings, inheritance, redundancy or luck. Something may have led you to reassess your life at this point, and to question what it is you really want. If you have been in employment you may have met a glass ceiling, unfriendly work practices, or perhaps you just don't enjoy your job. Whatever your situation, there is likely to be a combination of 'push' factors (propelling you out of current jobs and situations) and 'pull' factors (which attract you to self-employment).

Women with children often say they are unfulfilled in their careers, and want to do meaningful work that fits around family commitments. In general, push factors seem to be a more important influence for women than for men – women are more likely to leave a job they don't like.

Tick the factors in the boxes below that apply to you. Feel free to add your own in the spaces provided.

> *In general, push factors seem to be a more important influence for women than for men – women are more likely to leave a job they don't like.*

Table 2: Push and pull factors propelling women into self-employment

Pull factors: What you want...	Push factors: What you don't want...
☐ To be your own boss	☐ Lack of challenge
☐ Control over your working life and working practice	☐ Financial problems
☐ To make a difference	☐ Unemployment
☐ To make the most of a great idea	☐ Not being promoted
☐ To get something more out of work	☐ Not being paid enough
☐ A change of lifestyle	☐ 9–5 grind
☐ To work with different people	☐ Evenings and weekends taken up by your job
☐ To earn money	☐ Travelling and commuting
☐ Flexibility, especially over working hours	☐ Glass ceiling
☐ To fulfil family commitments	☐ Being housewife/full-time carer
☐ A new challenge	☐ Struggle to combine employment with motherhood, e.g. lack of flexibility at work/no suitable childcare
☐ Achievement	☐ Don't enjoy work culture
☐ Status	☐ Don't enjoy job
☐ To put something more into community/world	☐ Don't want someone else (employer) to have all the benefit of your hard work
☐ 'I could do it better than they do'	☐
☐ Power	☐
☐ Personal growth	☐
☐	☐
☐	
☐	

Remember, your pull factors do not have to be high-minded or lofty, but equally you can set your sights as high as you choose. You may want to win next year's Business Woman of the Year Award, or you may just be looking to work closer to home. It's all perfectly acceptable, whatever the big macho business books tell you.

Bella's decision was part of a big overall life change when she hit 30, and involved both push and pull factors.

> *Two weeks before my birthday a ten-year relationship ended, and I moved out of the flat we had bought together … at the same time as a job change. Even with the chaos in my life, which coincided with the horror of the 9/11 bombings, I felt calm and positive about the future, and decided to become self-employed. I had previously worked in large organisations, and there were lots of things I didn't like about the company culture. It's impossible to be a woman and not experience some degree of unfairness in an office environment. Even though I was climbing the slippery ladder successfully, I just didn't want to be like the managers where I worked. The majority of them were overworked, endlessly travelling, divorced, unfaithful, single or childless and seemed to be constantly looking over their shoulders. I found myself wading through politics and lack of transparency. I do know people who thrive in those environments but it wasn't for me, and turning 30 forced me to face that. Further down the line the pull factors have become more important. I like working from home and controlling my working hours, and I like putting health, ethics and community at the centre of my business.*

Lucy found that the push factors which she had ignored for years as a city lawyer were given new life by the pull factors which arrived in 1998 in the shape of her first daughter Stephanie.

> *Until then I was happy plodding away at my job as a lawyer, and doing my bit at work for women where I could. But as a mother, I suddenly knew that (a) plodding wasn't enough anymore and (b) I just needed*

to be nearer home. I felt very disappointed with the childcare options available. I knew that if I was going to go back to work, it needed to be to do something really worthwhile.

I knew that if I was going to go back to work, it needed to be to do something really worthwhile.

Leila Wilcox launched Halos 'n' Horns to provide chemical-free, safe, affordable toiletries for children, inspired by her own experience as a mum.

CASE STUDY

My son's eczema condition kept on flaring up after his bath, despite the fact that I only ever used organic or so-called skin-friendly products. I was concerned and upset to see him so uncomfortable, and did some research. When I actually found out how many harmful chemicals were in the supposedly additive-free products, I was totally shocked. That's what gave me the idea and determination to make safe, affordable skincare products for children. I'm an unmarried mum, and I got pregnant quite young, but I was totally determined not to be a single mum on benefits, or to work my heart out for £20,000 in a dead-end job. If I was going to do something I wanted it to be worthwhile for me and my son, and to make a difference in the wider world.

Some women are propelled into change by factors beyond careers, children or daily life: **Eugenie Harvey**, who we met earlier, told us:

CASE STUDY

I was at a very low point in my life, feeling like I'd hit rock bottom. I knew that my job no longer suited me, I was single and sorry for myself, and was spending more time in the wine bar than in the gym. My sister had just had her third baby and was wonderfully happy, while I was on the other side of the world, feeling like Bridget Jones. Thankfully something snapped in me one morning and I woke up thinking 'you need to pull your finger out!' and I knew I had to change something to be happy. Very soon after, a speaker from a charity called to speak at one of my firm's events. I was inspired by what they were doing, knew I could help them, and eventually made the decision to resign from my well-paid job to work for the charity Community Links, out of which we grew the We Are What We Do movement. Although this was a charity rather than my own business, I found my entrepreneurial spirit for the first time in my life – I suggested that I pushed ahead with one of their projects, to write a book to give people ideas about all the small things they could do to change the world, like turning off the tap while they're brushing their teeth. For the first six months, I lived off my savings and worked phenomenally hard, but what was different was that I was actually enjoying what I was doing. The book Change The World for a Fiver *sold 130,000 copies in its first year and is about to be launched in six other countries across the world. The profits from the book largely go back into the organisation and the salary I get is nothing like what I would have made in my old career in financial PR, but it's great to do something that means so much to me. On the personal side, I'm in a committed relationship now which is particularly solid because it is founded on me being the person that I want to be. None of this would have happened if I hadn't decided to go for it three years ago.*

CASE STUDY

For **Ruth Bradbrook,** co-founder of An-Turus, offering outdoor personal development journeys, the pull factors were compelling, if somewhat unusual:

I had been competing in triathlons at a high level for some time, and training while in full-time employment was a bit difficult, but I still came fifth in my age group in the world championships, and ninth in the New Zealand Coast-to-Coast race. I wanted to go a stage further with my training, and found that going freelance gave me the flexibility to take my training to the next level.

Ever one to take on a challenge, Ruth, based in Bristol, runs An-Turus with her business partner, Nick, based in Inverness.

Women set up in business for all sorts of reasons, but that is not to say that all reasons are good reasons. You will save yourself time and some costly mistakes if you can avoid falling into some common traps.

The wrong reasons to set up in business

- Pressure from family or friends — are you doing this because someone else thinks you should? Or because it would suit them rather than you?

- Can't find a job or trapped at work — disliking your job is not a reason in itself to set up in business. You need to have the right attitude and personal qualities, as well as a good business idea.

- There's clearly gap in the market, or something you think should be done … Unless this is something you're really passionate about, give it a miss — you may long for a hairdresser or fairtrade grocer to open up at the end of your road, but is that really the business you want to devote your day-to-day life to?

> *You may long for a hairdresser or fairtrade grocer to open up at the end of your road, but is that really the business you want to devote your day-to-day life to?*

- An escape from it all — you still have to work hard and engage with the world, all the more so because you will have to persuade them to be your customers…

- You want security — setting up a business entails much higher risk than hiding behind the skirts of a big organisation, so if you need the security of a predictable salary and benefits, stay where you are.

- You want to have more fun — setting up a business can be fun, but it's a lonely process at the outset, with long hours and a lot to learn, and you will have to pay for your own office party.

WHAT TYPE OF WOMAN RUNS A BUSINESS?

The 'true businesswoman' is the media's best kept secret, as we are constantly bombarded with unrepresentative role models in film, TV and newspapers, which all thrive on the promotion of the stereotype. Business itself is stereotyped, with the rules of corporate life often related to laws of the jungle, the sports playing field and warfare – not environments which women identify with.

Stereotypes and role models?

We racked our brains to find businesswomen portrayed positively and accurately in the media. What we came up with didn't inspire us very much. In the movies, successful businesswomen are shown to be nasty/(breathlessly) nice (Sigourney Weaver/Melanie Griffiths in *Working Girl*); childless, lonely, power-dressing sexual predators (Demi Moore in *Disclosure*); alcoholic-workaholics (Stockard Channing in *The Business of Strangers*); frazzled versions of against-the-odds, superwomen (Diane Keaton in *Baby Boom*); or all want the same thing (according to *What Women Want*). The one role model we did like was Judi Dench as 'M' in the Bond films. In the papers, businesswomen are routinely described as 'blonde, mother-of-three' whereas you never hear businessmen described as 'grey-haired, father-of-two'!

So both men and women are left with the impression that women can't be successful and decent human beings, or successful and mothers.

At any gathering of businesswomen you will encounter all types of people and personalities, from the flamboyant, outgoing party girl to the retiring mother of grown-up children. While we all have different personalities and outward appearances, we do also seem to share some personal characteristics and qualities that make us successful. The characteristics in Figure 1 are explored below one by one. Think about how each one applies to you.

Figure 1: Characteristics for success

Commitment

Once you set up your business, you not only work for yourself, but you have to do all the work yourself. You may genuinely enjoy what you do and love the idea of having your own business, but you won't like all aspects of running a business equally. The bad news is that even if you don't enjoy filing, database inputting or finding new customers, they all have to be done, and getting someone else to do it costs money. There is no external authority, no boss, parent or teacher that you are accountable to, and no ready-made assistant to do all the things you don't want to do – you are fully in charge. Commitment isn't just a case of putting the hours in (although that helps). It means self-discipline, prioritising effectively and doing things that are good for the business when you don't feel like doing them, consistently over days, weeks, months and years. What follows from commitment and self-discipline is healthy time management, and a balanced, growing business.

> *Once you set up your business, you not only work for yourself, but you have to do all the work yourself.*

Resilience

There will be plenty of things that distract you from the big vision when you start up a business. Self-employment stretches your perseverance to the limit: just when you've dealt with the inevitable rejections (amazingly not everyone wants to be your customer) along comes another setback to test you just that little bit more. On the home front, relationships with friends, family and colleagues may need a little tweaking as you take on board the inevitable personal changes that result from your new venture ... not always without a little pain. If you can pick yourself up and dust yourself off, and laugh at your mistakes rather than let them paralyse you, you will have a better chance at business (and life).

> *Lucy: After three years in business, I had just got to the stage where things were ticking over nicely, having found professionals to deal with my two nightmares: accounts and IT. Suddenly, in the same week, my accountant disappeared just before my tax return was due and my computer crashed. Meanwhile, business was busier than ever, and the children were on school holiday. I gained a few grey hairs that week (nothing my hairdresser can't put right...) but got through it. Running a business means that you're ultimately the only person responsible, and you have no choice but to deal with things when they happen. Over the years this resilience grows and grows. On some days I feel pretty invincible.*

Self-awareness

How well do you know yourself? How accurately could you describe your strengths and your stumbling blocks? Can you do that without falling into the trap of thinking there is something wrong with you? Can you accept the less pleasing parts of yourself with grace and good humour? It's a tall order to do that all of the time, but you do need to know yourself well, and accept yourself as you are, while also being willing to grow and learn. As employees and students, we receive regular feedback from our managers, teachers or peers, and if we need to develop new skills, we may get support such as training or coaching. As a self-employee, we have to find that feedback and support ourselves. Self-awareness is one of the prerequisites for setting up a business, but increased self-awareness is one of the rewards.

> *Self-awareness is one of the prerequisites for setting up a business, but increased self-awareness is one of the rewards.*

Decision-making

If you are someone who prefers to follow another person's direction rather than make decisions, then setting up a business on your own may not be for you. Women who set up their own businesses are generally those who want to influence and shape things, be in control, and do things their way. While these are not always seen as assets when you work for an employer, they are definitely assets when you work for yourself. Your clients need you to be in control. You in return need to accept full responsibility for the ways in which you and your business act. You decide … and the buck stops with you.

Self-belief

Believing in yourself and your service or product is a prerequisite for selling it to someone else – if you don't believe in it, why should someone else? You have to provide focus, stability and energy to any business, particularly a new one, and that comes from believing in what you do, and believing in your ability to provide it. This is not to say that you shouldn't listen to other people, but that you as the founder need to believe deeply (and after careful thought and research) that it will work. Small businesses are different from large ones in that they are first and foremost about the people that run them – the business fits the person and not the other way around. Self-belief will be fundamental in your relationships with clients and in building your business. Even if many of us start off with symptoms of the 'impostor syndrome' (see Introduction), with experience and effort we can grow the seeds of self-belief that exist somewhere deep down.

Communication skills

Good communication is key to developing good relationships with clients, suppliers and your wider network – whether through conversations or in writing (articles, brochures, press releases, website and email) or via your website and email. Depending on your business, you may need to attend networking events, give interviews, talk in public and give demonstrations. The key to good communications is to be natural and professional, to speak/write from the heart but not to use over-emotional language, and to treat your audience as equals. In the early days, particularly, you will need to ask lots of people for lots of things, and having good communication skills will help greatly. We write about communication skills in more detail in Chapter 6.

Assertiveness

Being assertive is something that a lot of women find challenging, not surprisingly, given that we're brought up to 'behave nicely' – which often is code for putting other peoples' needs before our own. Being assertive means first of all knowing what our needs are; secondly stating them clearly and directly; and finally being open to whatever response we get from the other person. Like good communication skills, assertive behaviour means talking to others as equals: not behaving passively (as if others are superior to us) or aggressively (as if others are inferior). Assertive behaviour signals strength, confidence, sensitivity and respect for others: all qualities you will need to have (and be seen to have) in business. See Chapter 6 for more information about assertiveness.

Flexibility

However much planning and research you do before setting up in business, you are bound to be surprised by the twists and turns that your path will take. Your business plans, priorities and products will need to adapt to your clients' situation and market conditions. You will need to revise your expectations as you encounter the reality of, say, a longer lead time than you thought, or more or fewer customers than you had expected. Keeping focused on your end goal throughout (not just at the outset) will help you deal with the ups, the downs, and the unexpected.

Values

Large companies sometimes list their values on the final page of their brochure, but not all their employees may agree with, or embody these values. In a small business, however, integrity is not a case of good marketing or public relations; what we believe in and what is important to us come across in everything we do. Behaving ethically isn't an optional extra or a way of getting more business – there is no other option. (And yes, you will get more business.) The problem, again, is that we don't have many role models around us operating authentically. So what does it mean, to operate your business with integrity?

> *Behaving ethically isn't an optional extra or a way of getting more business – there is no other option. (And yes, you will get more business.)*

- Be honest with yourself from the start about what you can personally offer and achieve.

- Be honest about what your business offers, and about how you believe what you do is unique to you.

- Keep learning – go to trade events, go on professional and personal development courses, read books, magazines, write, speak.

- Keep accurate records, including financial records and customer information, keeping abreast of all legal developments in the area and adhering to any statutory requirements that apply to your business.

- Believe in your product or service.

- Your clients, suppliers and employees are people first and foremost; treat them as you would like to be treated yourself.

- Be flexible – if you feel uncomfortable with the way things are going at any point, revisit and review (and pay attention to any warning bells, however faint).

This list of personal qualities may seem like a tall order. It also may seem at odds with the predominantly male examples of leadership that you see around you, but don't imagine you're not qualified for the job. The headmistress of one London girls' school told us: 'A man will apply for a job when he can only do one of the things on the list of requirements. A woman will *not* apply for it if she can do all of the things except one!'

But be aware that there is a shadow side to all great qualities. Over-assertiveness can become bossiness, too much resilience and self-belief can make you insensitive, too much flexibility can lead you to over-commit yourself. Don't let the balance tip too far towards this darker side of who you can be.

> **One of the big rewards of setting up a business is the huge personal growth that is an inevitable consequence of running your own business.**

Personality is not all it takes – knowledge of your subject area, knowing the right people, having a way in to prospective customers and a bit of luck all help. You need to be sure you have the stamina and energy levels that setting up a business entails and that you are willing to take appropriate risks. One of the big rewards of setting up a business is the huge personal growth that is an inevitable consequence of running your own business. Even if you don't have the full shopping list of qualities to begin with, you will be well on the way by the time you're up and running.

WHAT'S STOPPING YOU? ('I'D REALLY LIKE TO BUT...')

If you are still hesitant about the idea of entrepreneurship, it may be for one of the following reasons, and we have suggested some solutions that may help you overcome these hurdles.

'I need to keep the money coming in'

Keeping the money coming in is one of the biggest hurdles you will face when starting up a business. Moving from a regular income to the situation where you may or may not get paid by clients in three months' time requires a lot of practical reorganisation. If you are giving up an income to pursue a business, you want to keep costs as low as possible, so think about how you can reduce your outgoings and find other sources of cash. Look into taking a lodger, doing a part-time job alongside the business for a while, taking a career break (to try out your idea with the safety-net of a job offer if you need it), or working evenings and weekends while you get started.

Setting up a business will inevitably cost you money. You can either fund the business yourself, or raise finance elsewhere (see Chapter 2). If you borrow money you will need to cover all your living expenses as well as the costs of setting up the business, so you'll need to build a salary into your calculations. If you have a mortgage, you might also be able to take a payment holiday for the first few months of the new business.

'I don't want to use my home as security'

You may not have to, and you certainly shouldn't unless you are comfortable with that. Decide how much money you need to borrow, research what is available and find out what security other than your home might be acceptable. Talk to lots of people – not only your bank manager and business advisor but also potential investors and people who are running businesses already. There are plenty of businesses out there which didn't rely on a loan secured on a home to set up. See the next point and the section on finance and business plans in Chapter 2.

'I don't have a house to use as security/I am claiming benefits'

If you are claiming benefits, then you potentially have a lot to gain by setting up a business – not only financially, but also in terms of getting back into the job market – on your terms.

There are many grants and awards available to female entrepreneurs (see Resources in the Appendix). Our advice here would be also to do your own research – the policy in this area is confusing and official agents don't always have the best information themselves, but there is lots of free advice and support out there. If you are renting, need investors, and don't have a house to use as security, you are still in a position to set up a business. Use a personal guarantor or apply for grants, awards and loans targeted for those without a property. See Chapter 2 for more information about finance.

'I think I'd like to but I'm not sure it will take off'

Do as much research as you can. As well as researching yourself (see 'What type of person runs a business' above) and researching your market (see Chapter 5) do as much as you can to test the idea. If you have a product, can you set up a stall at the local market and get feedback from customers? If you plan to offer a service, can you try it out on friends? At some point there will be no alternative but to take the leap, and the only sure way to fail is not to try.

From the founders of Innocent – drink-makers

In the summer of 1998 when we had developed our first smoothie recipes but were still nervous about giving up our proper jobs, we bought £500 worth of fruit, turned it into smoothies and sold them from a stall at a little music festival in London. We put up a big sign saying 'Do you think we should give up our jobs to make these smoothies?' and put out a bin saying 'Yes' and a bin saying 'No' and asked people to put the empty bottle in the right bin. At the end of the weekend the 'Yes' bin was full so we went in the next day and resigned.

'I'm worried about the impact it will have on my career'

This *is* your career! Are you thinking you'll be looking for a job soon because you expect to fail, or is it genuinely a safety-net? If it's the former, then are you sure you're ready? If it's the latter, then remember that any recruiter will look favourably on your career choices providing you can tell a coherent story about why you did what you did and what you learnt.

'I don't think I know enough about business'

Read the rest of this book before you decide. There are many examples here and elsewhere of women with no formal qualifications or business experience before self-employment, like **Chey Garland** of Garlands Call Centres, who won the Veuve Clicquot Business Woman of the Year Award in 2005, and **Liz Jackson**, who employs over a hundred people at Great Guns Marketing, and left school with 'a handful of C-grade GCSEs'. If you do need to get some training, then it may be available free in your local area or through evening classes. If lack of confidence is getting in the way, a mentor or coach will help. Learning the basics of running a business is really not too difficult, and there is no better place to learn than on the job.

> *Learning the basics of running a business is really not too difficult, and there is no better place to learn than on the job.*

'What will other people think?'

Some will be supportive, some will be critical, and some will be somewhere in between. What matters more is what you think and what you would say to yourself if you were your best friend and biggest supporter (which you will need to be). If you think your desire to set up a business will conflict with the needs of other people in your life, it is worth exploring this at an early stage. If there are some valid and real objections from people close to you, you may have to adjust your plans … or not. The judgement of other people is something you are going to have to find a way of dealing with, perhaps like Eliza Dolittle in *My Fair Lady*: 'She'll listen very nicely then go out and do precisely what she wants'.

'I think it will be lonely working on my own'

An element of loneliness is inevitable when you are setting up on your own. Even if you spend the whole day on the phone to clients or in meetings with suppliers, you may miss being able to drop your professional role and talk about what's on your mind. This is just the flip side of having no one to tell you what to do, so don't forget the freedom that you are getting in return for occasional loneliness, and find practical ways to support your need to see other people. You may find a networking group provides that 'staffroom' feel that you require (see the Appendix), or you may think about going into business with a friend or colleague.

'Who am I to set up a business?'
We can't say it any better than Marianne Williamson:[ii]

Our deepest fears
Our deepest fear is not that we are inadequate. Our deepest fear is that we are powerful beyond measure. It is our light, not our darkness, that most frightens us. We ask ourselves, 'Who am I to be brilliant, gorgeous, talented, fabulous?' Actually, who are you *not* to be? You are a child of God. Your playing small does not serve the world. There is nothing enlightened about shrinking so that other people won't feel insecure around you. We are all meant to shine, as children do. We were born to manifest the glory of God that is within us. It is not just in some of us; it is in everyone. And as we let our own light shine, we unconsciously give other people permission to do the same. As we are liberated from our own fear, our presence automatically liberates others.

'I wouldn't be able to be a good mother if I had a business too'
We think this is such a big issue for working mothers that it deserves it's very own section, coming next.

WORKING MOTHERS, OTHER CARING RESPONSIBILITIES – AND GUILT
If you have children or other dependents, setting up a business means that you will have more demands to consider and more arrangements to make than if you're free of responsibility (although you're probably used to that by now).

Today's parents do have much more freedom of choice than previous generations did, but still things aren't always easy and there is as much stereotyping, criticism and lack of support out there for working mothers as there is of non-working mothers.

Whether to work or not, and whether to set up a business, are all part of the larger question that you face of how to care for yourself, your family and your home. What is important is that your choices are, at least, acceptable to you and your family, and, at best, that they are wholeheartedly supported by those close to you. Not everyone will agree with your choices, or support your desire to set up a business. The trick is to listen enough to people you trust to make an informed and sensible decision, but not to let them make the decision for you.

The effect on your children of setting up your own business (and on you if you don't)

All mothers want their children to grow up happy, healthy and successful. Most of us wonder (and often worry about) how our circumstances, actions and choices will affect our children's futures. We are constantly bombarded with reports telling us what is 'best' for our children, from cutting out E-numbers, to the latest must-have educational toy. In the midst of this constant pressure and focus on isolated facts and commercial products, it sometimes helps to remind ourselves that the traditional values of love, care, time, trust and respect are really what children need. They thrive on these essential elements and are pretty resilient (and unpredictable) as far as the rest of it is concerned. The best you can do is to lead by example – to bring up balanced children, you need to maintain a balance that works for you in your own life. You can create that balance by ensuring that no one thing in your life, whether it is your business ambitions, your partner or your children themselves, is the focus of all your attention.

Your children should never be an excuse for not achieving your ambitions. You can set them a good example by following your own interests and having a good family life. In practice it's impossible to meet everybody's needs perfectly, whether we have a business or not, no matter how hard we work or how clever we are. That impossible state of harmony would only last a second anyway, until someone changed their mind. It's a bit like doing the housework — it is never done, but we need to do what we can to keep chaos at bay, while living our lives in the meantime. Balance and openness of communication, not perfection, should be the end goal.

Your children should never be an excuse for not achieving your ambitions.

Children have different needs from parents and rely on their parents to meet those needs, so you do need to think carefully about how setting up a business will affect them. Some children will find their mother's business a source of interest, security and inspiration (and maybe a summer job); for others it will be something that they have no interest in, or see as a rival for your attention.

A child's reaction will depend on many factors: their age, personality, health, genes, where they live, their friends and neighbours (and yours), their relationship with you, and so on. Even though you can't control how your children react to your business, you do have a say in:

- what they are doing, with whom, while you are working on your business

- how they hear about what you do from you and your partner

- the hours that you work

- what you bring to your time with them — stories, games, money, energy, moods, inspiration, interest, support, etc.

Rather than worrying about the views of the in-laws, or mothers at the school gate, it makes more sense to make decisions about the factors you do control, and observe and talk to your children to see how what you do influences them.

Ultimately, with our partners as much as with our children, if something is right for us and we do it with respect for our relationship with them, then at some level it will probably be right for them too.

> *Bella: My mother went back to work when I was very young, which was fairly unusual for that time and where we lived. I don't really remember much at all about her doing it, it was just what she did. I do remember challenging her about it in my difficult teenage years, but even then I knew I was being unfair. Now, and even then, I was proud of her, and grateful for the example that she set me and my sisters.*

> *Lucy: When I've had a good day at work, my children definitely share the benefit of that with me. I am physically and mentally recharged, much more attentive and enthusiastic and enjoy my time with them more. They bring me stories of what they've been doing at school and nursery, and I bring my renewed energy to their lives.*

When I've had a good day at work, my children definitely share the benefit of that with me.

The guilt

> *Mother guilt. It comes with the birth, is brought forth from us with the placenta, grows like the piles of laundry, and stays with us forever like we believe the child will.[iii]*

According to best-selling author, Susan Jeffers,[iv] motherhood guilt is a relatively new phenomenon created by a society that has 'gone slightly mad when it comes to the raising of its children'. There are countless myths and theories about how children should be brought up and – no matter how ridiculous or unproven – they add to the general battle-cry of 'Blame the mother!' A common reaction to the oceans of blame is to feel pervasive and non-specific guilt about whatever choices we make, from whether we listen to whale music during pregnancy to whether we choose to use childcare. It seems easier, and more acceptable somehow, to feel guilty than it does to laugh – or feel angry – at the impossible expectations placed upon us.

Some of the guilt-peddlers: people and places that send us messages of guilt

- Society in general
- Media
- Other women
- Children's teachers
- Strangers
- Family, friends and neighbours
- Our children themselves
- Work colleagues/managers
- Doctors and other health professionals
- Therapists
- Our inner 'chatterbox'
- Childcare experts

> *Women judge themselves when they wake up in the morning, then spend the day finding more things at which to fail.*

However, we have to ask why we are so susceptible to being judged. Author **Stephanie Calman,** who founded The Bad Mothers Club, says 'Offer a man a home-made biscuit and he'll say, "Yum". Offer one to a woman and she gasps "Oh no! You've made biscuits. I haven't." Women judge themselves when they wake up in the morning, then spend the day finding more things at which to fail.' Stephanie concludes that the problem is that we are not setting our own goals, but allowing others (see box above) to set them for us, and then 'failing'.

She adds:

> *If you want to open the floodgates to serious guilt, just use childcare. Having your mother mind your kids is fine, even if she's a borderline*

psychopath who drinks sherry while they wander into the road. Paying someone is different. The newspapers love to cite research that shows nurseries make children aggressive, or turn them into shoplifters, or are the root of all society's ills. When I read that stuff — with the evidence to the contrary playing happily beside me — I feel bad about it all over again. It's as if the guilt is never expiated but merely dormant, able to be reactivated at any time. 'You want instant guilt? Just add one tabloid!'

If we want to work, for financial or other reasons, that is a great incentive to conquer the 'guilt that serves no purpose'.

Dr Liz Nelson (OBE), founder of market research company Taylor Nelson Sofrès plc, which now employs 14,000 people, told us: 'Women feel guilty whatever they do. They feel guilty if they have children and don't work, they feel guilty if they have children and work part-time, they feel guilty if they have children and work full-time! So they might just as well go for it!'

We provide practical guidance for childcare in Chapter 2.

Make it work

To make running a business work with having a family, you have to treat yourself and them with fairness and consideration, be reasonable about what you can do, and trust your parenting instincts. Often we make family decisions as a result of what our parents did or didn't do for us. That may not be a bad start, but try to consider the broader context of who you are, what you believe and the society that you live in before making any decisions about how best to accommodate your children's needs.

Advice for making it work
- Set your own goals — don't allow others to do that for you (this sets a great example for your children too.)

- Ignore the guilt-peddlers. Be clear that you are choosing your own life direction, with the best information you have about your family's needs, and with everybody's best interests at heart.

- Honour all the roles you have in your life – but ensure there is give and take. You can't go to networking events every night of the week. On the other hand you may be able to enjoy an impromptu day out with your family.

- Draw out the boundaries between work and family and stick to them. Block out the children's sports day in the diary, and also make sure you're not disturbed unnecessarily on your work days. (And only have one diary!)

- If you have a partner, make sure the partnership is working well. Women generally feel that they're doing not enough of the household/childcare when they're 'only' doing half.

- Put as much effort as it takes into finding childcare that you are happy with, and your children are happy with. Once you've made a choice, give it some time to work, but revisit it from time to time to make sure you are all happy.

- Be good to yourself too and provide some breathing space in whatever way you need it – don't allow yourself to be run ragged by all the roles in your life.

- Don't overcompensate your children by buying them lots of toys and presents because you feel guilty.

- Don't even begin to feel guilty about having your own career and life goals!

DECISION TIME

While we were writing this book, a lot of people told us of a bestselling product or service they once designed in their head … but were too busy to look into; or that they had considered going freelance … but hadn't got round to it. It's understandable how this step – decision time – sometimes doesn't happen (with predictable results).

It is so easy to find reasons not to make a decision, from 'my boss/children need me at work/home', to 'when I have more space in my life, I'll think about it'. Sometimes these reasons are genuine, and the 'maybe later' decision is the right one, but it could be that what is driving the lack of decision (rather than a 'maybe later' decision) is fear: fear of what other people will think, fear of failure, fear of all the effort/changes that will be necessary, fear of not doing it right. This fear is an inevitable part of making any changes in your life. If you look back at the choices you've made in your life, there will have been plenty that you initially felt fearful of, but did anyway, with positive results and a step-change in your confidence.

> *If you look back at the choices you've made in your life, there will have been plenty that you initially felt fearful of, but did anyway, with positive results and a step-change in your confidence.*

How do you make decisions?

Most of us have a pattern of decision-making which applies to us as much when making life-changing decisions as it does to buying a holiday. When you're planning a holiday do you:

- Research all the deals and options available in advance … or turn up at the airport with your passport and toothbrush?

- Ask family/friends/co-travellers/strangers for ideas … or decide on your own?

- Keep travel articles neatly filed in a box throughout the year … or decide based on that week's special offers in the travel agent's window?

- Go to a different continent each time ... or try to get the same apartment for the same week as last year?

- Use a travel consultant ... or book everything independently on the Internet?

- Take out a loan, save up in advance, or spend from your current account?

- Stay at home because you can't decide what to do?

Scan through the exercise above to reflect on how you generally make decisions and prepare for change. You might want to plot your findings on the following scales:

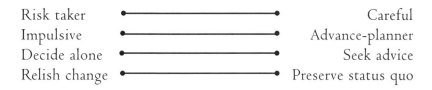

Risk taker	Careful
Impulsive	Advance-planner
Decide alone	Seek advice
Relish change	Preserve status quo

Begin to understand more about yourself: how much information you tend to need, how much help and external advice you want, what timescale you need, how certain you need to be. Reflect on the positive decisions you've made in your life, and how you made them. When you're ready, use the following steps to lead you through the process. You do need to do some research during the decision-making process, and may need to come back to look at this again and again. If you are a 'doer', all this reflection may sit a bit uncomfortably with you, and feel like a waste of time, but try doing a light version of it just picking up the salient points before you whizz on with your plans.

1. Decide to make the decision!

Articulate in your own mind the decision you are facing, and commit to a timescale for making it. For example, say to yourself, 'I am deciding whether or not to set up a Chinese restaurant in the High Street, and I am going to decide Yes, No or Maybe later by the end of the month.' Make your decision 'question' as specific as possible, and make your deadline a comfortable one. This could be days, weeks or months – you know what you need.

2. Create some quiet time and be your confident self

Give your 'question' the respect and time it deserves to be fully considered, by creating some quiet time for yourself. This may mean blocking some time out in the diary, visiting a favourite quiet place, meditating, or whatever you do to create space in your life. Many people find that a journal is a good way to create a reflective space and this is useful whether you set up a business or not. Start off this quiet time by reflecting on successes in your life. Ask people in your life for feedback or reminders of your positive qualities if this will help you. The feeling of confidence that this will build in you is the antidote to the fear that was standing in your way.

3. Do some research, and start your business plan

The amount of time you spend on this phase is up to you, and to some extent will depend on your decision-making style, your idea and your circumstances. Market research and writing a business plan are covered in detail in the next chapters and form a part of this decision-making stage. Starting your business plan at this early stage is a good way of structuring your thoughts, and ensuring you've considered all aspects of setting up a business. At this stage your business plan may be just a few pages of scribble in a notebook, or a picture or diagram setting out where you want to be and how you want to get there.

4. Road-test your idea, but keep it safe...

At this stage, your business idea is still forming, but it needs some rattling and shaking to see if it is sound. Speak to people selectively about your idea to gauge their reaction. Spread the net as wide as possible – wider than your 'inner circle' of colleagues, friends and family, and deliberately seek out people who tend to take a different view to you. Look for relevant discussion groups on the Internet or look for events, networks or associations you may be able to link up with. Be brave about contacting people you may not know well but who may be able to advise you (it's good practice for running a business). If you are enthusiastic (and you should be), then let your enthusiasm show and see if others become 'infected'. Don't forget to ask yourself honestly what you think of your idea.

Be brave about contacting people you may not know well but who may be able to advise you (it's good practice for running a business).

Throughout this stage don't forget to protect your idea like a fragile egg, and don't let the 'dream-killers' get at it. If you don't have one already, then this is an ideal stage to get a coach or mentor involved or take your idea to a business advisor.

5. The decision

As your deadline for decision-making approaches, you will have started to become clearer about what your decision is likely to be. If not, then it may be you need some more quiet time or some more research. In the end it will be one of the following outcomes:

- **'Yes'** – you are ready to go ahead with the business idea. Your circumstances may not be ideal but they are certainly workable. You are willing to take the plunge wholeheartedly, the sacrifices and risks are manageable, and/or you have put in place the appropriate safety nets. You are not being pressured to set up a business against your will; this is completely your decision and your responsibility. It helps to articulate why you want to do this – there will probably be a variety of push and pull factors.

- **'No'** – having learnt what a business involves, found out more about the market, or found out more about yourself, you have decided not to go ahead. You have ruled out setting up a business, having learnt something new about your environment, business ownership, and about yourself.

- **'Maybe later'** – you are still interested in setting up a business, but something needs to change in the market or in your life before that happens. For this option to apply to you, you need to articulate fully what conditions may need to be met for you to reconsider the decision at a later date. For example, 'I will reconsider setting up my restaurant once I have learnt more about how I might get a loan' or 'I will reconsider opening my training company once I have saved up a financial cushion for me to fall back on'.

Think of the worst thing that could happen

Part of making the decision is accepting the very worst thing that could happen to you as a result of running your business. If you are thinking of setting up a plumbing business, the worst thing you think of might be flooding someone's multi-million-pound house. Professional indemnity insurance can provide some comfort, but some 'worsts' are beyond insurance. **Brenda Burling** had the idea of setting up a nursery and thought about it long and hard. She knew that the worst possible outcome would be the death of a child in her care. Realising that this was a possibility, however remote, and knowing that she would put in place everything that she could think of to avoid it, she still decided to go ahead. The Cheshire Day Nursery Group is now a thriving and successful business.

6. And finally, 'Get out of your own way!'

You're the one who is going to set up this business and make a success of it – no one else. The business is you, and you are the business, and success depends on you being clear and confident about what you can achieve. You are the biggest obstacle that stands in your way. Self-doubt demons can creep in when you're not looking, whispering how you might fail, and how much easier it would be if we just kept things as they are. Move your focus of attention away from these demons, and go back to your self-belief. The demons will disappear if you don't pay them any attention.

Visualise a future in which you have a successful business.

Once you've made the decision to go ahead, go back into your quiet time and visualise a future in which you have a successful business. Practice speaking and acting as if it is already successful, and do this aloud to a coach, friend or in front of a mirror. Start thinking of yourself as a business owner having taken the decision and made the changes necessary in your life to set up a business. Notice what feelings or objections come up in you, address them or ignore them as you feel appropriate, and go back to your place of quiet confidence.

DEFINING THE SHAPE AND FEEL OF THE BUSINESS – GET INSPIRED!

Defining the shape and feel of your business, now that you are committed to doing it, is a very exciting stage. No doubt you already have some good ideas about the big picture of the business but now is time to bring it all together and paint some of the main detail onto the canvas.

Get in touch with whatever inspires you to be creative and look at things with fresh eyes. Remember how different things look when you come back from holiday? Publishing consultant and creativity coach **Julia McCutchen** says: [v] 'Whatever the source of your inspiration, and it can be a mixture of different things at different times, the essential factor is that you discover what works for you, and then make sure that you give priority to regular immersion of yourself in your chosen activity. Try it – it works'. Julia suggests some of the things in the following list for getting inspired:

- Attending a conference on a subject of interest
- A trip to the theatre or cinema
- Listening to the inspiring ideas of others
- Attending a music concert or festival
- Making or sculpting a model in clay
- Playing a musical instrument
- Reading a book for pleasure

- Attending a literary festival
- Cooking a creative and colourful meal
- Gardening
- Visiting an art gallery
- Walking in nature
- Painting or sketching a picture

Bella gets her inspiration from quiet reflection in a room overlooking her garden, and from her local transport system:

A year into my business, I needed to reshape and redefine what I did. As well as doing a traditional business plan I used a series of visualisations to 'dream' my new company into existence. From one particularly powerful vision, I came up with my spiral logo. The spiral also appears as a stone motif in my front garden, so I see it every time I go out. That works for me with 'big vision' planning, but I use different activities to inspire me in different tasks — when I need to write or review something, I can often be found on the number 200 bus! It travels on a loop from my house to a rather nice coffee shop and then back to my house. At first I found myself resisting doing this (or telling anyone what I was doing), as it seems so ridiculous, but then I thought I should just do whatever worked for me. There's something about being an observer of the world going by, safe inside the bus, that makes my thoughts flow. I've spent a lot of time on the number 200 while writing this book, much to the amusement of the bus drivers, one of who asked me if I'd ever finish my homework.

> **There's something about being an observer of the world going by, that makes my thoughts flow.**

From this place of inspiration, completely on your own to start with, develop a clear picture of what you intend to do — your 'shape and feel' statement. Keep revisiting it until it truly represents the core of what you want your business to be and to mean to you. It doesn't matter if the picture is 'right' or not, or even if it is actually what you end up doing. This is all part of the process of getting there (wherever 'there' is).

Include any of the following elements, or anything else that is important to you in your statement:

Your Shape and Feel statement
- What do you do?
- What are you called?
- Who are your clients?
- How do they find you?
- Why do they use you?
- What hours do you work?
- Where do you work from?
- Do you travel?
- Do you have staff?
- How does that fit with your commitments to family?
- What type of a business person are you?
- What do you expect to gain from running a business?
- What is the most important thing about your business?
- What happens in the future?

SO, HAVE YOU MADE A DECISION?

This chapter has taken you through the background to setting up a business, and led you towards a decision. Check that you have:

☐ Considered your circumstances and drivers for setting up a business

☐ Recognised in yourself the personal qualities you need for business ownership

☐ Addressed personal factors that might be holding you back

☐ Made a yes/no/maybe later decision about whether business ownership is for you

☐ Defined and refined your business idea

CHAPTER

2

GETTING STARTED

At the end of Chapter 1, you made the exciting decision to go ahead with your business and defined in broad terms how it will take shape. It can be tempting to start trading as soon as you have your brilliant idea, but in the midst of the initial excitement, there are a series of steps that need to be undertaken calmly and logically before the business is actually up and running. The stages listed below are not chronological – the reality of this stage is that there is a lot going on at the same time. The important thing is to address all the issues that are relevant to your business before you start trading. Trying to retrace your steps later on can be expensive and complicated.

Lucy: I have always been impulsive and setting up in business was almost an overnight decision. I had the idea and bought the domain name for Gina's Nannies within the space of an hour while my husband was out playing golf. I began trading the next day. Looking back, I can see that more preparatory work would have saved me time, energy and money at a later stage, and I would advise anyone to take a deep breath and count to ten before leaping into the unknown.

If I ever set up a business again, I would give myself plenty of time and space to get the basics in place, because these steps take longer than you think they will.

Bella: It was a much slower process for me. I set up my business when I got an offer to do some freelance work that I couldn't refuse. I found a firm of accountants on the internet, they guided me through setting up the company and

I started the contract. It was only when it finished a year later that I had to tackle many of the steps we talk about in this chapter. I was lucky in that I got the right advice from the start and I had money coming in from day one. If I ever set up a business again, I would give myself plenty of time and space to get the basics in place, because these steps take longer than you think they will.

GETTING OTHER PEOPLE INVOLVED – YOUR 'DREAM TEAM'

When setting up your business and beyond, you will often need quick solutions, expert advice, and general encouragement. If you can set up your 'dream team' in advance you will be better prepared when the need arises.

Talk to anybody and everybody you know about your plans, and be open to offers of help, general advice and specific contacts. Follow up all contacts, even the ones you think may not lead to anything – you will be surprised where help comes from and this is the time to cast the net wide.

When it comes to paying for advice, it's understandable that you want to keep costs to a minimum, and 'professional services' charges (for legal advice, design, accountancy, IT, coaching) can seem expensive uses of limited time and money. But at this stage of your business, good advice and planning are worth their weight in gold. Some businesswomen do choose to do their own accounts, build their own website, etc., but unless you already have skills in this area, it is generally safer to use a professional.

CASE STUDY

Debi Harris and **Jo Dew** of Porous Designs interior designers found that investment in graphic design early on really paid off:

As a creative service-based company, first impressions are of utmost importance. We therefore decided very early on in the business that we would invest time and money in developing an identity that reflected the ethos of our company, i.e. timeless, sophisticated design solutions. The company name is debossed (not embossed) on our letterhead, compliments slip and business card, which was the graphic designer's solution to representing our attention to detail and uniqueness of approach. The reverse of our business card lists our services by activity, i.e. 'meet, talk, design, measure…' all the way through to 'inspire', which was again the idea of the graphic designer. All this has been a great source of conversation and a very good ice-breaker with new clients. We discussed having a pictorial logo, but decided against it as we wanted the company name to become our branding tool. The colour was chosen from many shades of green for just the right tone, and our graphic designer gave us invaluable guidance on paper/card/envelope weights and the shade of white to use. There is no doubt that when we present our business card, the first impression of the business is one of professionalism, quality and considered design … the rest is up to us.

Below is a list of the people you will need to consider including on your 'dream team'.

Accountant

To start with, you may find you are able to complete accounts yourself. Basically this involves listing each item of income and expenditure and keeping all invoices and receipts. General accountancy advice is widely available in books and on the Internet, but sooner or later you are likely to have a question relating to your particular circumstances that you need specialist help with. You may also decide that the effort you spend doing your accounts – which is almost invariably greater than you think – is better off being spent elsewhere on your business. There are accountants who specialise in helping small businesses, providing start-up packs (e.g. pro-forma spreadsheets, invoices, basic guides) and reminders of the many deadlines during the financial year.

Bank manager

When you set up a business, whether or not you are applying to borrow money from a bank, you need to open a business bank account. You may be able to set up a business account at your existing bank, but not all banks provide the facility and many will refer you elsewhere. In any event, you will meet with an advisor, possibly the branch manager, who will talk you through the terms of business and explain the fee structure. Generally you should be looking for free banking for at least a year. Otherwise choosing a business bank account is the same as choosing a personal one – choose based on interest rates, branch access, internet facilities, overdraft facilities, bank charges and the personal service they provide. Ask if they have a women's business unit and what, if any, services they provide specifically to women-run businesses While many banks do also provide business guidance, you need to be aware that they will have the bank's best interests at heart, and may not be your best source of impartial general advice. For further information see our section on finance later in this chapter.

Technology expert

All businesses need an email address and some kind of presence on the internet, whether it's a simple one-page website or a full online shopping site. There is a section on websites in Chapter 5. An IT professional can help you set up your work computer, or network, and provide you with IT support, and you could consider setting up a standing arrangement. At least keep the number of an on-call, preferably mobile, technology expert close at hand. It's Murphy's Law that your computer will fail just when you need it most. Depending on your business, you may also need specialist assistance and support with cash tills, swipe card readers, phone systems, etc.

Lawyer

Most business owners need legal advice at some point. If you are setting up a partnership, employing people, or simply trading with the public, you may need to consult a solicitor to ensure you comply with the law and understand your obligations and responsibilities. Even if setting up your business seems straightforward to you in legal terms, it is important to undertake a professional review of your standard contracts and terms and conditions – something that many small businesses just don't do.

Business advisor

General business advice is available from many sources, including government agencies, your local Chamber of Commerce and other bodies. Specialist advice for your business area may be available from trade organisations or local business support initiatives, both of which offer help to start-ups as well as networking opportunities. If you are using free or low-cost advice at any point, be aware that the quality of advisor and information varies greatly and you might find that you get what you pay for.

A mentor or coach

Coaching can help you set off in the right direction, and provides you with a supporter, teacher and sounding board during what can otherwise be a lonely, uphill ride. The questions that a coach can raise with you may reveal some important blind spots in your thinking, or may lead you to challenge your vision to suit your circumstances and personality. Ideally this includes encouragement to aim high while ensuring that your goals suit you … and that you don't sabotage your own success. It may be tempting to use your friends and family members in this role, but they will have their own perspective on your business. You may find yourself shaping the business to meet their wishes and desires rather than your own.

A mentor is someone who is a few years ahead of you in experience of your field, and is willing to guide you through your issues using their relationship skills and their breadth of experience. A coach is someone who will help you to enhance your performance in your individual and business goals. A good coach or mentor will take a holistic view of your goals to ensure they sit comfortably with your skills, personality and your wider situation, and will provide the encouragement and insight to help you remove barriers (real or imaginary). What matters most with a coach or mentor is that you have a personal rapport with them and you can see that they can help you achieve your goals as you want to.

> *A good coach or mentor will take a holistic view of your goals to ensure they sit comfortably with your skills.*

> **Emma Reid** *of Grey Sells said, 'I was lucky enough to have two great mentors. Hearing about their experiences and how they dealt with problems similar to mine was very helpful — especially where money worries are concerned.'*

Mentoring is likely to be an informal arrangement where you can pick up the phone as you would to a friend. Coaching is a more structured arrangement, with regular times to meet. Both have their benefits — coaching gives you valuable space and time to think about what is important and to address issues and problems, and mentoring gives you quick access to someone else's experience.

> **Bella***: I meet my coach in person once a month for an hour and a half, and we may have telephone or email sessions in between our meetings. I generally go along to my sessions having prepared a list of issues I want to talk about. Over the years, we have covered everything from personal issues affecting my work to practical questions such as 'how should I deal with this tricky client situation?' As well as giving me practical help and support, having a coach has kept me focused and on track when things aren't going smoothly. Over the years, I have learnt about myself, and this has enhanced not only my business, but also my personal life, and the balance between the two. When I was looking for a coach, I contacted trusted colleagues for personal recommendations, chose someone to call and went along to meet her. It was important for me that I liked and respected her, that she lived nearby and that she had her own coaching practice so she could be a coach and a mentor to me.*

Tips for recruiting your dream team

- Try to get a personal recommendation from someone you respect.
- Wherever possible, meet a potential supplier face to face to decide how compatible you are on an interpersonal level.
- If you don't like someone after the initial meeting, don't use them.
- Ask for client testimonials and take up references personally.
- Tell him/her what you want to achieve and discuss how you might achieve that with their help. Let them know your expectations.
- Ask questions until you are satisfied, but also rely on your intuition – do you have a rapport with this person?
- Find out if their values, beliefs and ethics are compatible with yours.
- Find out what experience, training and professional affiliations they have.
- Decide what practical arrangements work for you – location, cost, times of meeting, frequency, face-to-face, telephone or email contact.
- Read any contract you are asked to sign in full and get independent legal advice on significant contracts.
- If you have any reservations about someone's approach, try raising this with them (don't ignore it).
- Don't think cheap is necessarily cheerful.

WORKING WITH BUSINESS PARTNERS

Another way of finding the skills you need to run the business is to find a business partner, or even more than one. Working together offers you a way to share the load and the success, and the legal framework is usually simple to set up (see Chapter 3).

Even if you originally had the idea on your own and don't have a business partner in mind, you should still consider whether you would ideally prefer to work with someone, as there are always ways of finding partners through networking, advertising and direct approaches. Equally, even if you have already discussed the idea with someone you know, you should give serious consideration to whether this person is the right partner for you and your business, or whether you do, actually, want to go it alone. Here are some things to think about.

On the one hand, if you work with someone:

- you always have someone to talk to
- you both invest time and money in the business
- there are more ideas, input and energy
- you don't have to do everything yourself, and your partner may love doing things you don't
- you could develop a very strong relationship
- you share the risks
- the business could be more successful than if you work alone
- there's always a shoulder to cry on, or someone to have fun with
- you are less likely to take out any frustration on your family if you have a business partner to offload to.

But on the other hand:

- you share control
- you share the profits
- you share the decision-making
- there will be things you disagree about
- you may test a good relationship beyond its limits.

Working with someone you have a close relationship with – a family member, friend or partner – has obvious risks, but also the advantage that you know each other well, and, crucially, have ways of communicating when things go wrong. If you are considering working with a man, then these same considerations apply, but we would add an extra one: beware the risk of taking on the role of 'chief supporter and champion' to his 'dynamic business hero'!

There is a big difference between getting on with someone and running a business together. Here are some questions to ask yourself about your business partner(s):

- Do you share the same or similar goals? For example:
    - the type of business you want
    - the location you want to work from
    - the amount of money you want to earn
    - the number of hours you want to work
    - the standard and quality of your work
    - how flexible you are
    - how driven you are
    - your level of commitment
    - your willingness to invest money
    - your short-, medium- and long-term vision for the business.
- Are there any unresolved disputes?
- Do you find it easy to communicate, which often follows from similar outlook, interests, backgrounds, values, and standards?
- Do you have similar circumstances at home, e.g. both single, or have children the same age?
- Do you have complementary skills, which don't completely overlap, and can you agree your respective roles in the business?
- Do you trust and respect each other?
- Do you know each other on personal level, and like each other?
- Do you both feel equally powerful?
- Do your instincts say that you could work together?

> *Beware the risk of taking on the role of 'chief supporter and champion' to his 'dynamic business hero'!*

The important thing with any business relationship is to have shared goals and a mutual desire to make it work.

Tips for working together

- Before taking the leap, do your research independently. Write down separately your expectations and reasons for setting up a business, and for working together. Be bold and honest.
- Talk through some possible scenarios together to see if you have the same ideas.
- Get a contract agreed and signed and make sure you understand your legal responsibilities and your commitments to each other.
- Assign tasks and roles to suit your skills, circumstances and personalities, but share the leadership role.
- If you disagree, listen carefully to your partner, and understand his/her point of view before stating your own.
- Discuss what decisions you can take independently, and what needs to be agreed by both of you.
- Always discuss irritations and problems, and always clear the air.
- Be flexible, and create an atmosphere of 'give and take'.
- Make time for the personal side – keep checking that you and your business partner are happy with the way that things are going, and don't forget to find out what is going on in each other's personal lives.
- Use a coach or facilitator who has your shared goals and interests in mind.

CASE STUDY

Diana Colquhoun and Julia Linford met through their daughters, and became friends first and then business partners. They share a love of gardening and working outdoors, and set up a gardening company FlowerPower. Julia told us:

We both loved gardening and chatted about that, among many other things, most days while waiting at the school gates. Diana then studied for a diploma course in garden design, and set up

FlowerPower as her own garden design business. She subsequently asked me if I wanted to join her, and I said yes, I think it works for us because of our friendship and, if anything, has enhanced our friendship. Our backgrounds are similar, and there is an implicit understanding that the business fits around our families — we don't usually work during school holidays. We love working outdoors, and do most of the physical work ourselves, although for a large job, we may use subcontractors. Recently we worked flat-out on a display garden for the Hampton Court Flower Show, and were delighted to be part of a medal-winning team.

CHOOSING YOUR LOCATION – WHERE WILL YOU WORK?

Are you going to be working from home, from an office or shop or from more than one location? Are you going to be working from your car or van? This may be dictated largely by your business type, or you may be able to choose from the outset, but there are practical and personal aspects to consider before making the decision. Cost will be a major factor. Mobile working, travelling where your clients need you, may be a good angle for your business.

CASE STUDY

Aromatherapist **Abi Davies** decided to set up on her own after years of working for beauty salons and sports centres. She invested in a high-quality, portable massage table, and organised a large bag with her essential oils, towels and blankets. She says:

I love being able to give my clients a massage in their own home. They are more relaxed there, and don't need to get dressed and go outside after a massage. It also means that I can massage mothers and fathers in the evening while their children are asleep upstairs. I do end up carrying lots of stuff around with me, and working in the evenings, but I've got myself organised now and I've got used to it. That, and the massage, keeps me strong!

Whether or not the business plan allows for expenditure on premises, there are a number of considerations to bear in mind when choosing and designing your work space.

What affects clients?

Your business image will come across in everything, from your address to the pictures on your walls.

Where you choose to work may have practical implications for your clients and customers as well as influencing their perception of your business. Your business image will come across in everything, from your address to the pictures on your walls. The questions below will give you some indication of how to keep their interests in mind:

Client needs

- What is the impact of your business address on your headed paper? Do you need an impressive office building to maintain your business image?
- Are cachet and class crucial to your business image?
- How much do you rely on passing trade?
- Is there good transport and parking?
- Are you going to be affected by noise?
- What other businesses are operating around you?
- Do you prefer the idea of anonymity? Consider using a PO box.
- Are clients and customers going to be visiting you at your place of work? If so, you will need to consider carefully your choice of surroundings, furnishings and decor to ensure you are giving the right message.

If you want to work from home, but give the appearance of something grander, consider giving your home a name. 'Acme Services, Acme House, High Street' sounds more impressive than 'Acme Services, 15 High Street'. Changing a house name involves a few official hurdles. Contact your local authority in the first instance, who will liaise with the Royal Mail to ensure the name doesn't clash with any property nearby. To be really thorough, also tell the Land Registry and Ordnance Survey.

Sarah Holland runs lifestyle management and concierge service Life Support from her home, but rents a reception facility at a prestigious London address.

Perception is everything. Having a South Kensington business address sounds much more professional than 'The Dingley Dell'. I know from my literature and from my address that people have been reassured and impressed by the fact that the whole thing sounds like a professional, established organisation. The only problem is when people keep asking to do presentations at my office! Given my line of work, it has proved invaluable to have a mailing address where packages can be received during the day when I'm out and about.

What affects you?

You will find that you share some of the requirements that your customers have but what else do you need from your work space? Here are some ideas.

Your needs

- How do you feel about the existing decor and furnishings? Do they need changing and, if so, what is your budget?
- Can you adapt the space to suit you?
- How can you maximise the positive effect on your energy and mood?
- Is there sufficient ventilation, natural light, heating, etc?
- If you are working from home, is your work space separate from your living space?
- Can you match and blend these requirements with those of your clients and customers?

Working from home – the pros and cons

Working from home is what many people dream of – that house you have spent all your money on but only seem to sleep in, that garden that you never get a chance to see in daylight. There are plenty of advantages but not all homes are suitable and not all businesses can be run from home. Clients of a virtual PA may be pleased to know she works from home (they will not be paying for a fancy office), whereas if you run a manufacturing business or legal practice, you will almost certainly need to move straight into offices or workshops. If working from home is a possibility for you, consider the following lists of pros and cons, each of which is dealt with in more detail below.

Reasons to work from home
- Cheap (free)
- Available now
- Flexible
- Convenient
- No commuting required
- Tax advantages
- It's home!

Reasons not to work from home
- Business image to consider
- Family and friends perception
- Distractions
- Planning permission
- Children disturb you
- Lack of focus
- Work can spill over into home life, and vice versa

Bella: Working from home works well for me: it puts clients at ease to meet in a comfortable and private home environment. Originally I had a room for meeting clients that doubled as my office but it became tedious to have to clear away my books, papers and computers several times a week. So we divided up our bedroom and converted the smaller room into an office, leaving the client room calm and uncluttered. Sometimes I work at clients' premises, which I enjoy for a change of scene, and I'm considering renting a room to enable me to expand my business. On a daily basis, I have to be quite disciplined when I need to plan, write or think and I do find it a challenge not to get diverted by the household chores, and because the office is so tiny I need to keep it well organised.

Lucy: I have learnt a lot about myself and about self-discipline since I started working from home four years ago. My first problem was credibility with family members. After all, I was a mum at home before, and I was still a mum at home, wasn't I? Their perception of me made it difficult for me to take myself completely seriously, and in the early days I found it easy to slip back into a housewife role, tidying up and sorting out washing while the business phone rang unanswered. I found I grew into my businesswoman role over time, and after a lot of saying 'no' to persistent invitations to coffee, I managed to convince everyone around me that I really was running a nanny agency. As I felt released from their perception of me, so I also felt 'entitled' to act like an entrepreneur. I am clearer about separating my roles as mother, wife and business owner, so the washing is likely to fester in the basket all day until I am 'home' again in the evening. My advice is – don't mess about, be clear with everyone (including yourself) from the start about your intentions. Tell them it's not a hobby, it's your new job.

> **Tell them it's not a hobby, it's your new job.**

And don't forget that it's their home too. Be conscious that they may feel a bit cross about having to keep quiet, avoid your clients, or having you on the phone all the time. Recognise the impact on them of sharing their home with a business (your business). Make sure they don't feel like second-class citizens in their own home – much easier if you have their support to start with, and are prepared to recognise and make up for any inconvenience to them with an occasional treat.

Our verdict is that working from home demands self-discipline, and the psychological separation of work from life, if you are to reap the many rewards and benefits available to you.

Working from home – practical steps

If you do decide to work from home, be realistic from the outset, and think ahead. The fact is that as a business grows, so does the physical space it takes up. In terms of practical arrangements, you may need to consider putting some if not all of the following in place:

- If you have to work in a bedroom, put up a screen or create a division so that you cannot see the main room from your desk or vice versa.

- If you are going to work in a communal living area, ensure that the other occupants of the house are happy with this.

- Train your family – starting with these new rules:
    - Don't shout at me from downstairs – I might be on the phone to an important client.
    - Don't answer the business phone – it's mine!
    - Don't expect dinner on the table every night (children excepted).

- Make rules for yourself about your working hours, and inform your family accordingly.

- Make a clear distinction in your mind between work and non-work time – one of the most common problems faced by home-workers is the inability to create the separation necessary between work, chores and relaxation – don't be lured into changing beds when you should be drafting reports!

- If the majority of your home is going to be used for a business and you are going to be employing people at your home, you may have to apply to your local authority for planning permission for change of use.

- Speak to your accountant about the tax benefits of working from home. You may be able to set off against your income some of the costs of running your home (cleaning, electricity, spending on redecoration and furnishings). Keep all your receipts from now on and give them to your accountant who will decide which costs are tax-deductible.

- If you are going to be keeping confidential client records in your office, you will need somewhere secure to store them.

Commercial premises: shop, restaurant, office, workshop, warehouse

If you are going to be opening a shop, restaurant or factory and employing staff, using specialist equipment or storing goods, you will need to find suitable premises. Your first step will be to undertake detailed research into the location, facilities, availability and cost, and decide whether to buy or rent space. It's very much like buying or renting somewhere to live, so don't be put off by any unfamiliar jargon, and use your solicitor and business advisor to help you with any specific questions. There is a lot of information about finding, buying and renting property on the internet, and also in our Resources section (see the Appendix).

Unless you can afford to buy your business premises outright, the price you pay for premises is likely to be the major upfront and ongoing cost to your business, so it's worth spending a lot of time and effort getting it right.

CASE STUDY

*Interior designer **Annie Stevens**, of Annie Stevens Design Ltd, moved her business into rented premises, and then out again. Despite years of high growth and soaring demand for her services, the financial strain of running a shop drove her back to home-working again: 'the rent was £12,000 a year in itself, someone had to be there to man the shop, and on top of that there are all the hidden extras — business rates, parking, a raft of phone lines, etc. It also meant that half my money was tied up in stock, which didn't make financial sense.'*

If you do decide to rent premises, you may wish to use a commercial agent as well as scanning the local press and asking around.

Buying property – buy outright or mortgage?

If you buy your business premises — either outright or with a commercial mortgage — you don't have to worry about complying with a lease, and the building is a business asset straight away. On the other hand, you will be much more committed if you own the property, and you will have extra costs and responsibilities, e.g. for maintenance, safety and security, not to mention the costs associated with purchase, such as removals and stamp duty.

Many an inheritance or redundancy payoff has been frittered away on commercial property that turns out to be a bad investment.

Finding a commercial mortgage is much the same as finding a residential mortgage. The rates of interest are usually slightly higher, but you still have to shop around for the best deal based on deposit, fees, repayment choice, overdraft, etc. If you are lucky enough to be able to buy the property outright without a mortgage, this will considerably reduce your monthly outgoings, but you will be investing a lot of capital in the business, which is then exposed to the property market. Do beware when buying property – many an inheritance or redundancy payoff has been frittered away on commercial property that turns out to be a bad investment.

Renting property – lease or licence?

Most premises, from a whole building to a single room, can be rented under either a lease or a licence arrangement. Leases tend to be more rigid, formal arrangements than licences, measured in years rather than months, whereas licences are more informal and shorter term. Leases offer greater continuity and security, but you can find yourself tied into something unsuitable if you don't do your research or if things don't go according to plan. Licences are less onerous, and can be more appealing to start-ups but the extra flexibility costs more. Be aware that there is sometimes a premium to pay – a one-off payment to secure the property that you want. The same principles apply to this as to the rent – research and negotiate.

When renting or buying commercial premises

- Make sure you use a solicitor to check all agreements and advise you of your obligations and commitments.
- Make sure you understand your lease – e.g. what access

rights are there to common parts? What are your maintenance and security responsibilities? How long are you committed for? Can you sublet? What conditions are attached to subletting?

- What guarantee is required – is someone willing to act as a guarantor? Is your home required as security, and if so, is that acceptable to you?
- Consider the impact of your environment, location and premises on you and clients (see above).
- Consider taking space alongside people who will lead to useful work contacts, provide company or inspire you, as artists do in artists' studios.
- Do as much research as you can – look at lots of different properties in different areas, and speak to agents, owners landlords and tenants.
- Always negotiate the price – discounts of 25 per cent are not unheard of, but your research will be your best guide.
- Understand what insurance you need/want – for building, office equipment, contents, public liability.
- Find out what the local business rates are – these are payable based on the square footage.
- Find out the cost of utilities such as electricity, gas and the cost of local authority charges such as rubbish collection and parking.
- Ensure you comply with Disability legislation.*
- Ensure you comply with Health and Safety legislation.*
- It can be exciting looking for property, but don't get carried away, and don't take the first thing that comes along.

* The Health and Safety and Disability obligations relating to premises are quite onerous but this is an area where you just need to grit your teeth and get on with it. See Resources for more information.

Vital considerations when opening a shop or a restaurant

The factors that make a shop or restaurant a success are many, varied and unpredictable, but what you sell – product – and where from – location – are key. Finding the right location for your shop or restaurant involves not only plenty of research, but a good 'eye' for what will work. There are some specialist aspects of running a shop or restaurant, such as security, stock, pricing and cooking, which we don't consider here. Whole books are written about choosing the location of your shop, and maximising the effectiveness of your window but briefly, these are some things to consider:

- **High street vs 'up the road'** – high-street properties are a lot more expensive than those off the main street, but you are paying for 'footfall' (see below). It's unrealistic to expect your customers to walk off the beaten track to a shop or restaurant (do you?) no matter how wonderful it is.

- **Terrace vs corner** – corner might mean you're at the far end of the street, and will get less footfall than in the middle of the street, but it also means you have two display windows. Footfall and display windows are both factors that affect the rent.

- **Footfall** – this is the term for the number of customers entering your shop or restaurant (the retail equivalent of the showbiz 'bums on seats'). You can buy statistics from marketing companies for many locations, ask other owners/tenants, or just stand outside a shop at different times of the day and week and count people. Footfall includes browsers as well as customers.

- **Shop size** – work out what size you want and then look for your property. You pay rent and rates for every square foot, so make sure you use it all.

- **Rates** – these are set by the council. Rates are high for the first few feet from your window, and decrease as you go further back. A wide shop with all shopfront windows but not much depth will have higher rates than the same size shop at right angles with only a small window at the front.

- **Shopfit** – what will you need to do to get the shop or restaurant ready for your business – furniture, displays, signs etc? This can be a huge outlay of time and money.

- **Shopfront** – the shop window and lighting are critical. You can do a certain amount with clever lighting, but the weather has a big part to play. In the daytime, a south-facing shop can suffer from a stuffy interior, fading stock and fainting staff (unless you have air conditioning). The windows of a north-facing shop quickly become mirrors on a sunny day. Good use of lights can attract evening customers to a restaurant, or catch the attention of window shoppers who return the next day.

- **Neighbours** – Who are your neighbours? A discount store? That's fine if you offering discount products yourself. A pub? Ideal if it's a pub that attracts families after their weekend lunch to the children's clothes shop you're setting up next door; but not so ideal if it's a rough pub and your doorway gets used as a hotel or toilet late at night.

- **Competition** – is there already a business like yours around? If so, the grouping could be good (estate agents, jewellers and restaurants often cluster together to attract browsers) or it could be too much competition. Don't give yourself the added task of taking on an established business for your first shop or restaurant.

- **Social profile** – is it an affluent area? Is it an up and coming area (the estate agent will usually tell you it is, but rely on your own research)? Is your business appropriate to the area? There is little point in setting up a designer furniture store in a run-down part of time.

There is naturally more choice available when the economic

situation is depressed, and less when it is buoyant – the premises you want may not exist at the price you can afford, so know what you are prepared to compromise on, and what you're not. Talk to your local Chamber of Commerce, get facts, figures and details first hand wherever possible, and talk to the people who have lived and traded in the area for years.

CASE STUDY

Helen Furze and Paula Rogers set up their specialist recruitment agency, Furze Rogers Associates, after many years working for high-street recruiters. Their business offers quality, openness and a personal service, and they wanted their office to reflect that. Helen told us:

> We wanted to move away from the shabby image of many recruiters – handwritten adverts on cards in the window, messy offices, and sales targets on the wall, visible to clients. We decided what was important to our clients was that we were less than two minutes from a station, and that we had professional-looking meeting rooms. We narrowed our search down to one street, and used one estate agent. We didn't want a display window – we rely on advertising and word of mouth. That meant that we could look at property above shops, but the problem was that most properties on that street are Edwardian, built for accommodation, rather than offices, and we didn't want to spend much money on refurbishment. We looked for six months, and probably saw four or five properties in that time. Eventually we saw an office that was already owned by a recruitment agency who were moving to bigger offices – that was a really good sign, and it didn't need any work at all. Paula negotiated the lease, as she had done it before, and knew what to look out for. Within eight months of starting to look, we were in! We made a big effort to get it looking exactly right – redecorated, and added nice furniture and plants. Now our clients give us good feedback about our offices, our office reflects our business image, and it's a nice place for both of us to work every day.

We wanted to move away from the shabby image of recruiters – handwritten cards in the window, and sales targets on the wall, visible to clients.

Extra considerations when taking office space

If you are renting office space, you have the additional option of using serviced offices, sometimes also called suites. Serviced offices are fully functioning offices, and include furniture, heating and lighting and basic facilities (parking, reception, broadband access, telephones, fax and photocopiers). Other facilities, such as telephone answering services, meeting rooms, videoconferencing, mail receipt and clerical support, are usually available at an extra cost. Serviced offices are let under a licence arrangement, and are available for a day, week, or by the month. They can be useful for flexibility – expansion or a quick start early on – although the cost of licensing a serviced office is higher than leasing an office space.

Business equipment and stationery (and backups)

You can do a lot with just a PC and a telephone, and your filing and information systems do not necessarily need to be sophisticated at the outset. One system you do need to put in place if you are using a computer (and you probably will be) is a way of backing up the information that you need to run your business. As well as your files and emails, you should also back up your contact lists, financial information, and any spreadsheets or databases you use to store information. Ideally this should be done every day, or at least weekly – ask your technology advisor to design something easy to run that copies everything you need onto an external disc. It always seems like a pain to do, but it's much less than the pain of losing your business because of the indiscriminate computer gremlins.

Office essentials

- Office space, desk, chair, filing cabinets, drawers and storage.
- Mobile phone – shop around for the latest deals and consider investing in a sophisticated mobile or Blackberry if you need to get your emails on the move.
- Landline – some businesses operate only by mobile.
- Computer – some businesses, e.g. design-based industries,

work better from a Mac but generally documents travel better by PC.
- Printer, fax machine, photocopier, scanner (these often come as a package).
- Email address.
- Business cards – shop around for a good deal but get the best you can afford.
- Basic stationery – see separate list below.
- Shredder.
- Specialist equipment if relevant.

Stationery list – large retail outlets should be your first port of call
- Copier paper (80 gsm).
- Quality letter paper (100 gsm) for documents sent out to clients.
- Letterhead, compliments slips, business cards with logo.
- Envelopes.
- Files and box files, file dividers.
- Pens, pencils, stapler, staples, paper clips, hole punch, sticky notes.
- Diary for appointments and wall planner for quick reference.
- Journal to record phone calls and messages.
- Set of index cards for hard copy customer records.
- Punched plastic wallets for storing documents in files.
- CDs for backup.
- Spare printer cartridges.
- Index cards and card box.
- Accounts ledger.
- Calculator.
- Filing trays.

ORGANISING CHILDCARE

As part of developing the vision for your business, you will have considered how much time you are prepared to spend on it, and if you have children, you may have already investigated the cost and availability of childcare.

There are a number of childcare options available to you. If you have children at school, you will be aware of the after-school clubs, breakfast clubs and holiday clubs on offer. However if you have preschool children and (as for most of us) there are no willing and youthful grandparents or neighbours to step in, your basic options are employing a nanny or childminder or using a private day nursery.

Nurseries vary widely in cost and in their standards of care but are generally an inexpensive and effective option if you have one child and are near a town or city. Good nurseries can be booked up for months in advance so you need to plan ahead – we know of some where you need to register your baby in as soon as you find out you're pregnant. To find a nursery you can ask your local council for a list, and ask other parents in your area. Have a good look around the nursery before committing yourself and ask lots of questions – how much outdoor play is there? Are the children fed freshly cooked food? Are the staff all non-smokers (you will find that answer a definite 'no'!) What is the staff/child ratio? What is the staff turnover like? (If the staff don't like working there, is it good enough for your children?) If you have a baby, look at the sleeping arrangements provided. One word of warning for parents of young babies: you will be asked to keep your child at home for at least two days if he/she is on antibiotics, which can end up being quite frequently, with the rate infections are passed around.

Nannies are a more expensive option but usually more economical than putting two children in a nursery, and extremely convenient: a nanny will look after a sick child, and you can expect to find your children bathed and in pyjamas when you get home. If you work from home and your nanny looks after your children there, you will have to find creative solutions to the problem of your children, or the nanny, interrupting you at bad times. Despite the nanny registration scheme offering tax incentives to parents using qualified nannies, the nanny industry is still largely unregulated, and there is no legal requirement for a nanny to have training, or to be police-checked. Sharing a nanny with another family can be a cheaper alternative, but make sure you can agree on what you want, as nanny sharing can result in disagreements between the closest of friends. To find a nanny, first ask other parents for a recommendation of a good local agency. Then check the *Yellow Pages* and internet to compare it to others. The chances are most nannies will register with several agencies, and you can pay vastly different fees for the same person. Nannies quote their salaries net, so if you employ a nanny you will need to make provision for the extra cost of paying her tax and national insurance. Finally, it is essential that you take up nanny references personally and thoroughly, or ask for confirmation from the agency of exactly which referees have been contacted and with what result. Don't rely on written references alone.

Childminders are usually the most economical option of all, available throughout the country. They are regulated by the local authority and charge either a daily rate or hourly rate per child. Your child will be looked after in the childminder's home, which is inspected regularly by Ofsted. The services offered by each childminder will vary according to a number of factors – how many children they are looking after at the time, the ages of the children, which schools the children attend and whether the childminder has children of her own – so you may have to shop around to find a childminder whose circumstances fit best with your own. Some may require you to provide food for your child, some may ask for paid holiday, so make sure you are aware of what you are committing to. To find a childminder, contact your local council and ask for a list of registered childminders in your area.

General tips for your childcare search

- Your council usually has a list of childcare options available.
- Your local library may have a noticeboard where childcarers advertise and where you might be able to place an advert.

- There are plenty of internet sites where you can place adverts for childcare vacancies either for free or for a fee (see the Appendix).
- Tell lots of people you are looking for childcare. Women are instinctively good at helping each other out.
- If you know any nannies, ask them if they can help you find someone. The nanny grapevine is very effective.
- Once you've found childcare you are happy with, make sure you take up references personally for childminders and nannies and talk to other parents who have children at the nursery you are looking at.
- Trust your instincts.

Louise Cooper of Gingham Hearts, bespoke party planners, says her main difficulty is lack of childcare. Living on a shoestring herself, she felt that the cost of childcare was prohibitive, given the meagre profit she was making at the outset. She found she was doing most of her baking and making when the children were asleep 'It's like the Elves and the Shoemaker … after each cake or gift sold I was able to buy more materials and equipment … but no elf came to help me in the night!' Louise eventually employed various teenagers to assemble party packs, while she concentrated on more specialist tasks, and found that some young people were capable of blowing up balloons while keeping an eye on her children at the same time – Bingo!.

MANAGING YOUR TIME

Being self-employed means you do have a measure of control over when, where and how you work, and how rigidly or flexibly you schedule your time. In addition, because it's your business, the time you spend on it feels like time well spent. **Susanna Riviere** changed career after 26 years as a lawyer to become a leader and meditation teacher, and told us, 'I may have a busy day, but it's MY busy day! Even a packed day isn't stressful, in the way it used to be in a busy office.'

> *I may have a busy day, but it's MY busy day!*

However, all first-time business owners underestimate the time that they will need to get the business fully up and running, and the work diary can easily end up clashing with home life, childcare arrangements, hobbies, social or other priority commitments. In all the enthusiasm you feel about your new business, it is easy to devalue your existing responsibilities or forget they exist. So give some thought to how you will fit all your commitments into the time available. You could do this either by listing everything you do and how long it takes (bottom-up) or by estimating how major chunks of your day are spent (top-down), and check that it all fits into a 24 hour day! Figure 2 shows a top-down example.

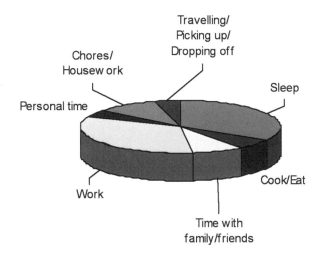

Figure 2: Breakdown of daily commitments

Now check that you have considered the following – how much time per day do you spend:

• sorting out washing and ironing
• tidying up
• going through the post, filing, household administration
• stacking the dishwasher
• arranging your social life
• gardening and mowing the lawn
• chatting on the phone to friends
• going out in the evenings?

And if you are a mother, remember you need time to:

- make up baby food
- make packed lunches
- arrange babysitters
- deal with children's social life and extracurricular activities
- spend time talking and just 'being with' your children
- help with children's homework and reading
- pick up and drop off your children
- take children to hairdressers/dental appointments/ doctor/shoe shops.

Top tips for time management

- Make time to list what you do with your time. Include everything, and list the people you spend your time with. A detailed list/pie chart might be useful here – see Figure 2.
- Notice how you think about time, and how you respond to time pressures – for example, do deadlines motivate or intimidate you? When do you do your most productive work? Do you set aside separate time for responding to people, or are you constantly reacting to emails and phone calls? Do you say yes when you want to say no? How do you prioritise and plan? Do lists help or hinder? Do you procrastinate?
- Do you have a daily or weekly routine? Or does flexibility work best for you? Do you work/play late in the week and catch up on sleep at the weekends (or wish you could)? If whatever you are doing now doesn't quite work, then try something else for a week – keep the same hours at weekends, go to bed an hour earlier, or work in the evening when you normally watch TV.
- Notice how your energy levels vary with the things that you are doing. Notice the 'sinkers' – the tasks that seem to suck energy out of you, and the 'lifters' – things that make you feel energised and uplifted. Do the same for the people in your list.
- Does washing pile up at home, or does your post remain unanswered for weeks? A good rule of thumb is that if a task is going to take less than two minutes, do it now.

Plan for your business

- Get a work diary and make sure there is only one diary in the house.
- List the things that you will need to do to get your business off the ground, and everything you expect to be doing when you're up and running. Add 25 per cent to the time you think it will take (or speak to people who have done it to improve your estimate).
- How do you think your business will impact on your current work–life balance? Does it take you closer to how you want to spend your time, or further away? What is the impact short-term and long-term?
- Talk about how you manage your time with a friend, partner or coach. Talk or write about what happens to you when your life is in balance, and what happens when it gets out of step. Get into the habit of having a business review every week or so, and plan for it as if it was a business meeting. If you have a coach, this is an ideal thing to do together.
- Schedule some breaks into your diary – actively block time out for you to catch up or recharge, and guard it fiercely.
- Think of your energy like money in your bank account– you can only take out what you put in.

Setting up a business requires you to be responsive and flexible, which in practice means you have to work when you don't feel like it (and crises and deadlines come all at once). For someone motivated enough to set up their own business, working hard and juggling commitments is not usually the problem – the issues are usually either that we are not working productively and staying focused, or that we are not spending enough time on ourselves or our businesses.

Time in a coffee shop can be work, if you take along a pen and paper. A walk in the park, with a problem in mind, can let the solution bubble to the surface.

Working for yourself can be much more flexible and less stressful than working in an office – you never have to pretend to work, you can choose your hours, and you don't have to do it at a desk. Time in a coffee shop can be work, if you take along a pen and paper. A walk in the park, with a problem in mind, can let the solution bubble to the surface.

Being realistic about your time commitment and then putting the whole thing into practice does demand some discipline. If you have a business partner it is an area that you both need to look into carefully as it will affect your relationship if you resent your business's intrusion on your personal life, or if she wants you to put more hours in. It can be very difficult to run a business with a partner who is looking for a different work–life balance from you.

We need to be compassionate with our need for space to recharge and relax. There are not many good role models in our business culture for doing this, as lunches get shorter, days get longer and things appear increasingly urgent. Changing the pace of our lives requires effort, and when you're setting up your business you're likely to be going at full speed and won't want to slow down. Something business-related but different from your normal day, for example going on short courses, or reading newspapers can be a good way to recharge and expand your thinking, with positive results for you and your business.

CASE STUDY

Justine Dalby is *co-founder and director of Premium Sourcing, a company that imports and sells promotional merchandise which is given away free on the covers of magazines. Although Justine doesn't have children, she has other responsibilities outside work and in particular spends a lot of time with a friend who suffers from MS. As well as growing her business to its multi-million turnover, Justine makes sure she gets time out to recharge, riding her horse and supporting Arsenal FC. 'I do have a great feeling of freedom and control, but it's hard work and it has always eaten into my personal life.'*

Scheduling downtime in your day and sticking to it will help you keep you work–life balance on target – just a few minutes a day will make a difference. Most of us know what we need to do to feel recharged, whether it is reading, seeing people, exercise, gardening, or listening to music. Downtime should not be yet another time-management factor to beat yourself up about. Just keep an eye on it – if you have the energy, go for it, if not, recharge.

> **Lucy**: *Time management continues to be a challenge. I am the sort of person who finds it hard to say no to new commitments, and find myself so booked up with tennis lessons, school responsibilities and book clubs that my business can suffer. I think the problem is that if you are the type of person who can set up a successful business, you are likely to be an active, enthusiastic person who takes things on and looks for new challenges. My advice is to only go to choir practice if you have done your filing first!*

> **Bella**: *At first I struggled with the inflexible routine that a new baby brought to my working life. I had been used to working, sleeping and going out when I felt like it. That was suddenly no longer possible. In time, I got used to the change, and became much happier with a set pattern – every work day became like that day before you go on holiday – you know, where everything gets done, just because it has to. I really don't think that the quality of work or preparation time has suffered, it's just that I procrastinate less, and am much more focused. I wish I'd learnt this earlier!*

SAY IT IN A SENTENCE

In Chapter 1, we talked about defining the shape and feel of your business. Once you have decided to go ahead and start the business, your idea needs to be developed further and crystallised so that you can communicate it simply and effectively to others. So how can you achieve that? Using your 'shape and feel statement' from earlier, summarise the essence of your business in one sentence. This is what Lucy came up with for her business:

Gina's Nannies is an agency that helps busy parents to find the perfect childcare solution, and offers a personal, professional service from a mother of three and qualified solicitor who has personally interviewed every candidate.

It describes exactly what Gina's Nannies does, and gives a strong impression of a personal and top-quality service that parents would want to use.

Bella's sentence is:

Enspiral provides coaching, facilitation and training workshops to enable men, women and organisations to make work a healthy and rewarding part of life.

If you were to strike up conversation with a stranger in a lift, and inevitably the 'so, what do you do?' question arose, you would have that little sentence ready in reply. This is what the American business manuals call your 'elevator pitch' – what you would say to a potential client if you briefly found yourself travelling in the same lift. You probably wouldn't say it exactly as it is written, although you could use elements of it. Depending on the environment, Bella says something like 'I help people to become self-employed' or 'I help people to move from unhappy employment to happier employment'. Lucy might say 'I run a nanny agency providing excellent nannies and great customer service'. These more informal openings are much more appropriate to real conversation than delivering of a prepared sentence, and tend to spark interest and further questions, when stuck in that mythical elevator.

As part of that statement, remember to give an idea of the qualities that distinguish your service or product from others on the market. These qualities are your unique selling points (USPs), and you can read more about those in Chapter 5. You need to be convinced

> You need to be convinced of your own USP before you can convince someone else, so take some time to ensure that the USP is realistic and achievable.

of your own USP before you can convince someone else, so take some time to ensure that the USP is realistic and achievable. Your USP statement should form the basis and reason for launching the business. Learn it, live it, breathe it.

DETECTIVE WORK

Detective work, otherwise known as market research, is a vital procedure you need to go through before you set up your business. The point of this exercise is twofold:

* to look at what other comparable businesses (if any) are up to
* to position yourself in the market accordingly.

The results of your market research will need to be summarised in your business plan, because anyone considering getting involved in your business will want to know that your idea has 'got legs'. It doesn't stop after the launch either – throughout the life of your business you will need to have your eye on the ball constantly to make sure you are keeping up with the market.

Look at the market

Summarise what you know about the market that your business belongs in. You need to assess the state of the market generally – are there businesses like yours in existence already? How many? Where are they located and why? Where are they advertising and how? What is the market they are appealing to? Are they succeeding? Is the market growing or shrinking?

Where will you fit in?

Once you have understood what is out there already, imagine your business being established within that environment. How will you fill the gap in the market? What geographical area will you cover? Is your USP enough to make you stand out in the market? What is the likely profile of your average customer? What will your share of the market be, and how will you retain and increase that share?

Look at the competition

The easiest and most obvious place to assess the competition is the internet. Most decent-sized businesses have a website, and a Google search should give you a good starting point. Use a few different search terms to ensure that you have done a thorough job, and save the sites that you find to your Favourites folder. Make notes of pricing structures, branding and the general look and feel of the site. Can you register online? How time-consuming is that? Note what you like and what you don't, so that when the time comes you can learn from the successes and mistakes of other people. Check the Yellow Pages and local directories for other competing businesses and visit their websites if they have one.

Mystery shopping

This means contacting businesses directly as if you were a potential customer. You will get lots of valuable information about the competition, and will experience what it's like to be a customer. If it gives you an ethical dilemma to pretend, you could always consider sharing the results of your research with the business you're investigating. If you are ordering a product or brochure, make a note of the time between your phone call and receiving the information. Note their manner on the phone; how much information did they ask for; was there a follow-up call after the pack was sent out? Look at the way they present their hard copy information – in a brochure or leaflet? What size? In what state did it arrive? What impact did it make on you? All this information will help you make decisions about what kind of service you want to offer and will give you an idea of what promotional material works.

CASE STUDY

Kelly Chandler of the Bespoke Wedding Company told us that market research and mystery shopping was the key to their success:

We contacted a lot of the potential competition in different ways. We did a fair bit of mystery shopping (pretending to be brides), which got some responses, allowed us to test customer service and work out mainly how we wouldn't do things. We also tried the honest route of just seeking advice from well-established companies and telling them that we were starting up. We expected to get knock-backs but actually most people are nice and accept that good competition is part of business, so were happy to help. In particular, if you are looking to do things a bit differently from the competition (and you are not an exact carbon copy), they will happily share information. We got lots of advice from companies in the USA where our industry is more established. You have to be bold and pick up the phone, though. People are busy and often avoid emails and letters, as we do now! However, as our industry is in its infancy, we were very disappointed that we could not easily find official reports and figures which pertained to our potential market. We were concerned about this at one stage but the simple fact is that, in new and relatively untested markets, there will be no figures, so you just have to be brave and start making them. Be careful of assuming that your peers (friends/family) are necessarily your clients; in our case, generally speaking, they are not and perhaps we listened to them a little too much. One vital thing we missed out in our research was to get feedback on our pricing. We massively undercharged to start with (although we gained heaps of experience). Finally, market research with a theoretical business only got us so far. The biggest part of our market research has been undertaken since starting the business two years ago and working with real live clients. We offered our services for free to our first set of clients, which enabled us to really use them for full market research and business building. We continue to ask our now paying clients questions about their motivations, why they hired us, where they work, live, what they read, all to help us with future marketing and understanding our future clients' needs.

> **Be careful of assuming that your peers (friends/family) are necessarily your clients; in our case, generally speaking, they are not and perhaps we listened to them a little too much.**

CASE STUDY

Leila Wilcox of Halos 'n' Horns said:

We did loads of market research, and I think that's why we've been so successful. To begin with, I asked friends, all of whom said yeah, it was a good idea, good luck, go for it ... but not much more on the detail. The best input came from going out with a clipboard to talk

> *to strangers — accosting mums with children in the street. The products out there at that time were either so-called organic products in dull packaging costing a fortune, or they were bright, funky and full of additives. The mums I talked to told me that they wanted additive-free products that were scented, colourful, but also affordable, and that's what we created.*

FINANCE AND BUSINESS PLAN

It helps to have some experience of managing your personal finances before you consider running a business, and your own financial situation should be well organised. That doesn't mean you can't have debts before starting a business, but just that you are good at setting spending limits, sticking to them, and are capable of shopping around for financial products. Most importantly, you need to be able to face your finances head-on, without fear or panic. We talk about your relationship with money in Chapter 4.

Setting up a business invariably costs money. Exactly how much money may be partly up to you and partly dictated by your business. For example, if you are setting up a small business from home, and don't require any specialist equipment, premises or staff, your start-up costs can be very low, and you are likely to finance the business yourself. If you want to open a smart shop, or employ people straight away, you may need to find some money from an outside source (capital).

You are likely to measure the success of your business (at least partly) in terms of income generated; to make more money the business has to grow, and to grow the business you are likely to need money to invest in people, premises, whatever. So we can safely conclude that you need money to make money. Many women tend to imagine at the outset that they are not in business primarily for financial gain, but faced with the alternative of a larger or smaller market share, most of us would not need much time to think about it, would we?

Options for funding your business

Your options are:

- pay for the business with money you already have (self-finance)

- borrow from friends or family (debt)

- take out a loan or use an overdraft facility (debt)

- apply for a grant

- issue shares (equity) in return for investment.

Set limits at the start as to how much you are going to 'borrow' from yourself to invest in the business, and monitor that closely.

Self-finance

If you fund the business yourself, make sure you keep clear records showing what money is yours and what belongs to the business. You should still open a business bank account and follow proper accounting procedures. Set limits at the start as to how much you are going to 'borrow' from yourself to invest in the business, and monitor that closely. Plan in advance when and how you are going to repay yourself.

Debt

If you borrow from friends or family, always draw up a contract – no matter how much you think nothing can go wrong. If nothing else, it's good practice for drawing up contracts with your future customers and investors. All the arrangements may seem clear and mutually understood now, but you'll have lots to think about in the months ahead, and things will change. Your benefactor may want a straight repayment of the capital with no interest, repayment with interest, or may want an element of control over the business or a share in the profits in return for their investment. Record details of all discussions including the timing and amount of repayment, interest rates and other expectations and ensure both parties sign a copy.

If you take out a business loan, this will usually be from a bank, and it works very much like a mortgage for a home, with fixed arrangements for interest rate, loan period and repayment amounts. You will usually be asked to provide some form of security for your loan, such as business premises or equipment, or possibly (and more commonly) your house. What this means is that if you fail to repay the debt, the creditor (the bank in this case) can force a sale of your house in order to pay itself off. An alternative to taking security is taking a guarantee – another person or business can guarantee repayments on your loan, so that if you fail to repay, the bank can turn to your guarantor instead.

There are a number of alternative credit facilities available apart from the standard bank loan. Most business bank accounts come with an automatic overdraft facility which you can use as well as or instead of a loan. This is more flexible in that you only use it if you need to, and you only pay interest on what you borrow, but the fees and interest rates are higher, and the overdraft can be withdrawn by the bank at any time. Some women finance their business by extending their home mortgage, or taking out a personal loan, supposedly for the 'new bathroom', but be warned that if your bank finds out you are doing this for business purposes, they might understandably impose tighter restrictions and look for extra security or guarantees. Where start-up costs are low it might be tempting to fund a new business with a credit card (statistics show that a lot of women do this to avoid putting their homes up as security), but the repayment charges are extortionate in comparison with what is on offer elsewhere, so that is definitely a route to be avoided. Other institutions such as the Prince's Trust or local enterprise initiatives offer loans at better rates than the banks, and many of these actively encourage women to apply. See the Resources section in the Appendix for further information.

Grants

There are a number of grants available for small businesses – usually one-off payments of a few thousand pounds given by local, national or European government bodies to influence aspects of business practice. The Prince's Trust is well known for funding start-up businesses, especially for young people, and they also offer mentoring and other support. Grants are worth looking out for because this is effectively free funding for your business, but you usually have to meet some criteria specified by the awarding body. Some funds select by age or gender, and others specify business type (e.g. manufacturing business) or region (e.g. North East).

CASE STUDY

Liz Jackson founded her telemarketing company, Great Guns Marketing, at the age of 25 with £5,000 from the Prince's Trust. She set up her business from the lounge of her rented flat. Liz's business now has a turnover of more than two million pounds. She told us: 'I was very determined to set up a successful business – this was my third attempt, and I was delighted to get help from the Prince's Trust – part loan and part grant – but I also got some good advice and a leg up.'

Equity

Equity finance means giving someone a share of your business (and therefore a share in the future profits) and control over the direction of your business in return for an immediate injection of cash ('capital'). The more money you want to raise, the greater the shareholding and control the investor will want to take off you. If you want to raise a large amount of money (in the millions) your first port of call should be a venture capitalist or investment fund, but if you want to borrow less than that, a 'business angel' is your best bet. They all do the same thing, but venture capitalists and investment funds are large companies, and business angels are usually private individuals with money to invest. A business angel is likely to be an experienced business person with a head for facts and figures, so don't be fooled by the soft name. Business angels and venture capitalists will want a say in your business, an exit strategy in place and a return on their investment, which may not be what you want, or at least not on their timescale.

Make sure you are happy with the degree of control you give up to an investor. Look at their other investments to check that they are compatible with yours – you may not want your ethical fair-trade paradise turned into a profits-over-people money machine. This is one of the dangers you are exposed to if your shares are ever traded publicly on the stock exchange. Always use a solicitor to draw up and check the shareholders' agreement. See the Resources section for details of women-focused investment opportunities.

> **Make sure you are happy with the degree of control you give up to an investor.**

CASE STUDY

Leila Wilcox founded Halos 'n' Horns with a £15,000 personal investment and £30,000 from a business partner. She said, 'I borrowed part of the money I needed from my nan and grandad, and more from other members of my family. That made it very personal and meant that I just knew even more that I had to make this work. I wasn't going to let them down, and I am pleased to say I haven't.'

CASE STUDY

Eileen McKay, or Leemac, as she is known, had an ambitious plan to raise £15 million to build her dream in the Scottish Highlands, The Leemac Clinic, coupling the best of conventional medicine with the best of complementary medicine. She obtained a proportion of the funding from Trapezia, the investment fund operated by Stargate Capital dedicated to women-focused businesses, and looked to investors elsewhere for the rest. She has found that a lot of the men she talked to about her project simply didn't believe the size of her vision 'to be globally pre-eminent in a groundbreaking paradigm shift in health care' and give her a 'yes dear' pat-on-the-head treatment. But she believes that her dogged perseverance and determination to fulfil her dream really paid off, and reluctantly acknowledges the vital part that the business plan has to play in securing funding.

The purpose and contents of a business plan

The term 'business plan' can mean anything from a few rough notes and headings to a full set of glossy presentations and charts. It has various purposes:

- to help you make the go/no go decision (see Chapter 1)

- to record the concepts and financial plans for the business

- to shape the business and plan for its launch

- to communicate your plans to friends and family

- to communicate your plans to colleagues, business partners and banks

- to raise funding.

Even if you don't need to raise money at the outset, a business plan will keep you focused on your financial goals and will act as a standard by which you measure your material success. The principle behind it is simple: any prospective investor or lender will need to know as much as possible about the business and will be looking to see that you fully understand the financial implications of what you are doing before they make the decision to invest. Most banks now provide business plan forms which are easy to complete, ask for information in plain English, and don't assume your title is Mister. The quality of the standard forms and business literature you get from a bank can also give you an indication of how user-friendly they are.

Whether you consult one of the hundreds of books devoted to the art of writing a business plan, use a form provided by your bank, or follow guidance from the internet, you should include the following information, as well as the information from your shape and feel statement in Chapter 1.

What to include in your business plan

- details of business, contact numbers, details of activities, status
- your business USP
- date trading begins
- objectives (short, medium and long term)
- details of key people in the business
- how your business is structured
- your relevant qualifications and past career history
- details of business premises/equipment and anticipated future needs
- details of products and services provided, pricing, customers and competition
- the state of the market, your comparative strengths and weaknesses
- an assessment of cost, profit and risk
- financial situation, projections and requirements

The form your business plan takes will be partly dictated by the purposes for which you need it. If you are borrowing money from a bank, then focusing on facts and figures, and using their standard format, is highly advisable. If you are going to see an investment bank in the City, then a highly polished presentation will be expected. If you and your business partner are setting up without external investment, then a few pages of A4 will do, as long as it covers all the bases.

CLOSING SKILLS GAPS

You may already know enough to set up your business, or there may be some gaps in your knowledge that you need to fill. You will need to have a basic understanding of business, as well as any specialist knowledge and skills particular to your business area. In either case, there is bound to be a course, book or internet site that can help you.

It is worth choosing at least one course to go on before you start up your business. As well as teaching you something new,

It is worth choosing at least one course to go on before you start up your business.

going on courses gives you confidence, new insights and puts you in touch with other people in the same boat as you. Some professional bodies require you to attend one of their courses before you can join them, and for certain business types, there may be a legal requirement for training (e.g. to obtain a food hygiene certificate if you are setting up a catering business).

Essential skills for businesswomen include:

• basic IT skills (typing skills are vital)
• basic financial awareness
• an understanding of the mechanics of the business world (the depth of understanding required will depend on your business sector and type).

Useful skills and other training may include:

• basic book-keeping to reduce your own costs and to maintain control of cash flow
• specialist/vocational training
• updating yourself with things that may have changed since you were last at work
• voice coaching, presentation skills training
• negotiation skills training
• assertiveness training
• employment law, health and safety legislation training
• specific IT training relating to setting up and managing databases, backing up your system, troubleshooting, etc.

Whatever you need to do in terms of closing these skills gaps, a lot of it can be learnt on the job, either during working hours or by taking an evening class to obtain a relevant qualification. There are a lot of free or low-cost training courses available, and you can also find lots of information in books such as this one, in trade journals or on the internet. Don't be put off if you have always wanted to be a florist but know nothing about it.

Jane Geldart of Daisy Jane Flowers started training for her floristry business by taking two days off per week from her job in an advertising agency:

> *I had known for a while that I wanted to start my own 'flowers for events' company. I was trying to work out how I could learn about flowers and the event floristry industry while still having a regular income. I knew that I had a good relationship with my employer so we came to an arrangement (pardon the pun!) whereby I could fulfil my role as Group Account Director on an agency's important account on a part-time basis. This meant that I could attend the courses I needed to at the Jane Packer School of Floristry and still pay my mortgage. During the wedding season I worked every weekend (for little or no money) with a florist. This gave me not only hands-on experience but also the confidence to know that my new skills and my commercial experience were enough to start up my business. I kept working part-time at the agency until I had worked with a few clients and, when I felt the time was right, I took the plunge.*

SO, ARE YOU READY TO GET STARTED?

This chapter has taken you through all the preparatory steps leading to the launch of your business. Check the list below to make sure you have:

☐ Established where you are going to work and why
☐ Completed your market research
☐ Refined and clarified your USP
☐ Worked through your finances and business plan
☐ Looked into how you will manage your time and childcare
☐ Established whether there are any gaps in your knowledge or training which need filling

In the next chapter we deal with the legal and technical aspects of setting up a business, and help you to turn your plans into reality.

3
BUSINESS BASICS

If you come from a business, accountancy or legal background, you will have a good general idea about the practical and 'left-brain' issues of setting up in business. If you don't, this may be the section that has put you off in other business manuals

Tell the world it's not just an idea – you really mean it.

– quite understandably! When you are feeling excited by the prospect of business ownership and all the challenges and possibilities in store, the thought of filing forms and registering with the Inland Revenue can put a bit of a dampener on things. But it needn't do. This stage is where you put the final touches to your project, and tell the world it's not just an idea – you really mean it. Think of it as taking your driving test – you may be very competent behind the wheel, but you need to pass the test and get your full licence before you can go out on your own.

In this chapter we cover the information you really need to know about the legal and practical aspects of running a business. For further information on any subject covered here see the Resources section in the Appendix.

BUSINESS TYPES AND STRUCTURES

You have probably noticed the words 'company', 'business' and 'firm' being used indiscriminately in the media and common conversation. There is a general lack of awareness about what these words really mean, and the more they are mis-used, the more confusion this creates. So let's clear up the terminology first. The word 'business' is a generic term for anyone trading, i.e. selling a product or service. Microsoft is a business, and so is Gina's Nannies. There are three main types of business: a company, a firm (which is the same as a partnership) and a sole trader business.

This section explains how to choose between the different business models. Your decision should be made with the advice of an accountant or business advisor who is familiar with all the tax and legal issues affecting each type of business vehicle.

The business model that will best suit you will depend (among other things) on what your business is going to do, whether you are going into business with someone else, and factors relating to you and your personal situation. The structure you choose need not be set in stone at this stage. For example, you may start off as a sole trader and become a company or partnership at a later stage.

Sole trader

This is the simplest, fastest and cheapest way to start up a business, and is the method favoured by a lot of women who feel disinclined to jump through the administrative hoops that a company or partnership involves. A sole trader runs the business herself (but can employ other people). Once the business is making a profit, it is straightforward to withdraw money for your personal use.

If you are setting up in business as a sole trader, you need to come up with a business name, set up a business bank account and register as a sole trader with the Inland Revenue. Your only administrative commitment is the production of annual accounts for the purposes of your tax return. You will be taxed on profits earned during the year.

As a sole trader, you are personally responsible for all the debts and obligations of your business. So if you owe money or are sued by a client, your possessions, even your house, may be on the line. If, however, your business is by its very nature low-risk, and you are unlikely to be sued for millions by a client for negligence or breach of contract (or the risk is insurable), then this option is well worth considering.

Reasons to set up as a sole trader

- You are setting up on your own and the business is low-risk.
- You want to give it a go on a trial basis, without the financial and administrative commitment that other structures involve.
- You want to carry on an activity that you are doing anyway, but on a commercial footing, and without a complex legal structure.
- You do not benefit from the 'ltd' after your name – it will not affect your market status or image.
- You want easy access to the funds in your business bank account.
- Tax and other reasons specific to your business sector (consult your business advisor).

Private limited company

The word 'company' should only be used to describe a business which takes the form of either a private limited company owned by private individual shareholders or a public limited company. There is a common belief that a public company (plc) means publicly owned but this is in fact not always the case. If a public company's shares are traded on the stock exchange it is said to be 'listed', but there are public companies which are not listed (see below). The name 'company' does not apply to any other form of business, although now you know this you will notice the word used much more widely than it should be.

The people involved in a limited company are:
- shareholders – (the owners)
- company secretary
- director(s) who make the key decisions
- staff – who do the rest of the work.

In your start-up company, you are likely to be a shareholder, a director and a staff member. Some limited companies, generally the larger ones, also have non-executive directors. These are directors who are not involved in the day-to-day running of the company, but who sit on the board and receive a salary. They give the directors an independent view from which to seek advice and they also keep an eye on what the directors are doing to make sure nothing untoward is going on. Being a non-executive director is like being a school governor or member of the parish council, with a salary.

A limited company is owned by shareholders but has a separate existence from them and does business independently from them. This means that if you, as a director, sign contracts on behalf of your company, it is the company itself, not you, which is a party to that contract. The company pays you as a director and/or a member of staff for the services you provide, so ironically you are now an employee again.

You will be able to access profits in your company for your personal use in the form of your salary (as employee and/or director), and through dividends (as shareholder). Dividends are paid out of company profits on a regular basis to shareholders.

You may have heard the term 'share capital' – this is effectively the kitty that you contribute to when you set up the company and pay for your shares. The kitty is the pot of money that the company uses to buy equipment and premises and pay salaries – all the things a sole trader simply pays out of her business account. Your share capital can be as little as £1. The proportion of the kitty (together with any other assets) that you put into the company when you set it up (or 'incorporate') will be reflected in the proportion of the total shares that you own. If you are contributing all the money and/or assets, it is likely that you will own all of the shares, unless you are giving someone else shares in the company in return for services they are going to provide. If your share capital exceeds £50,000 you can call yourself a public limited company (plc) even though your shares are not traded on the stock exchange. This could be seen as slightly misleading to the general public but does make your company look big and important, which can put you at an advantage. It's a bit reminiscent of the system (no longer in operation thankfully) whereby Oxbridge graduates could 'upgrade' their degree from a Bachelor of Arts, by buying a Master of Arts degree for £10.

You can either buy a company off the shelf (a 'shelf company') or you can set one up yourself from scratch with the help of an accountant or business advisor.

There are a number of legal requirements to comply with in setting up and running a company, including the production of accounts, annual returns, and the registration and filing of documents with Companies House. Most of these tasks should be performed by your company secretary and, although numerous, are relatively straightforward. The company secretary may be a trusted friend, someone within the business, or your accountant may be happy to do it. All the information about your company that you file with Companies House is available for public inspection. This means that, for a small fee paid to Companies House, anyone can find out what your profits are or any other basic company information.

The main legal documents required to form a company are the Memorandum of Association and the Articles of Association, both of which you register at Companies House. The Memorandum tells the outside world what sort of company it is, whereas the Articles are the internal (but public) rulebook, setting out how the company will operate. You may also want all the shareholders in your company to sign up to a shareholders' agreement, which is a private document governing aspects of the business which are not in the public domain – arrangements for profit sharing, rights to acquire each other's shares, who has a right to appoint directors, and other rights and obligations. You can change a shareholders' agreement relatively easily, whereas any amendment to the formation documents needs to go through a formal process of approval by shareholders and the amendment filed with Companies House.

A limited company is responsible for its own debts, and your financial risk as a shareholder in the company is limited to the amount you have invested in it (that's what the 'limited' means). You will not be personally liable beyond that.

In theory, setting up a private limited company is the low-risk option, as your liability is limited and the company acts independently from you. In reality, however, liability is rarely completely limited because if you are going to be borrowing money or taking a lease, most banks and landlords will require shareholders and/or directors to put up personal guarantees, so if your company goes bust, they can pursue you personally for repayment. The set-up costs and running costs for companies can be higher than if you are a sole trader, as you are likely to be employing the services of an accountant or business advisor to assist with your filing and registration duties. However, such outside involvement can constitute a welcome independent assessment of your business, and at least some of these costs are costs that a sole trader may incur in any event.

CASE STUDY

There are 'aesthetic' reasons to go for the limited company as a choice of business vehicle. **Mary Tyler**, director of IT executive search and business performance company, Davidson Hall Limited, believes that being a company rather than a sole trader conveys a different image to clients, and gives her added status in their eyes:

My accountant recommended that I go limited rather than sole trader (which I had been before) for a number of reasons, although not many of them to do with tax. The tax loophole that made it more attractive for me to be a sole trader was closed around 2003/2004 but the overriding reason to be limited was that my clients, who are mainly corporate entities, feel much more comfortable dealing with a limited company than a sole trader. The word 'limited' also allows me to appear larger than I am, which is important in my field.

Reasons to set up a company
- There are more than one of you.
- You are on your own but insuring your business is too expensive or impractical.
- The appearance of being more professional/a larger business
- Tax reasons.

Partnerships and limited liability partnerships ('firms')
If you hear the word 'firm', think 'partnership', and it will come as no surprise to you that this business model is made up of partners, rather than shareholders. There are two types of partnership, the ordinary partnership and the more recently introduced 'limited liability partnership' ('LLP'), which is – guess what – a partnership with limited liability.

You need to consider a partnership set-up only when you are going into business with another person (or more than one person) as an equal (or quasi-equal), not as employer and employee. Your partner will be involved in the running of your business, will own a share of the business and take out a share of the profits (although the percentage share need not be equal).

The key characteristics of an ordinary partnership are that you and your partners are self-employed and you will be individually personally responsible for all the business debts and liabilities. This means that if one of your business partners is sued, for example, for negligence, your home and other assets could be at risk. So it is absolutely essential that you go into partnership with people you trust, preferably someone you have worked with before. A limited liability partnership offers a solution to this, by limiting your liability to the amount you have invested. You will still have unlimited liability for your own negligent acts, but not those of your partners. So for all the benefits of limited liability (if that is a priority) without the headache of quite so many filing requirements, consider the LLP option. But bear in mind that this option may cost you more in accountancy fees.

Ordinary partnerships are not registerable. LLPs are registered at Companies House for a small fee. The partnership deed or partnership agreement works like a shareholders' agreement, governing the relationship between the partners, their voting rights, holiday entitlement, benefits and obligations, and what happens if the business fails, or if one partner wants to leave, or is thrown out.

Val Howard and Mary Fitzhenry set up their babysitter training business, Safesitters, as an ordinary partnership. They decided they wanted to avoid the expense and administrative complexity of setting up a company, and found the registration requirements for LLPs similarly offputting and expensive.

> *In a matter of months we had signed a partnership agreement, business had doubled and the vision was reality.*

Lucy: Although I set up Gina's Nannies as a sole trader, when the business grew I decided to take someone on to share the work. I went into partnership, rather than down the employment route, mainly because I wanted whoever it was to be highly incentivised to bring in business. I had a vision of someone I was on an equal par with, a sort of clone of myself. I needed to be able to talk through decisions and the direction of the business. My husband was a good listener and advisor but I needed to take the pressure off him a bit, too. Cash-flow issues meant I couldn't take on the risk of an employee, who would have to be paid come rain or shine. I was talking to a former lawyer colleague and friend about the situation when she offered to come in and help me out. In a matter of months we had signed a partnership agreement, business had doubled and the vision was reality.

Reasons to go into partnership

- You are setting up a law or accountancy firm (by law these must be partnerships).
- You are setting up with one other person and looking to avoid the complexity of company registration and administration.
- You are setting up with another person and equality of status is an important factor to you.
- On the specific recommendation of your business advisor.

ALTERNATIVES TO A 'TRADITIONAL' BUSINESS
Buying a franchise

You may wish to consider buying a franchise if you have not come up with your own business idea and/or there is an existing business you want to replicate and be a part of. Coffee Republic and McDonald's are franchises, as is the image consultancy Color Me Beautiful and other 'party plan' businesses like Virgin Vie, where you can operate as a self-employed consultant representing a larger organisation. You will normally be buying the rights to a particular geographical area, and benefiting from the advertising, marketing and support that the main business has put in place. Buying a franchise allows the franchisee to take advantage of all the goodwill and expert advice of an existing business which is already making money.

You will be bound by a franchise agreement, and depending on its complexity may need to consult a lawyer to protect your rights and ensure you fully understand your obligations.

Check the restrictive covenants in your contract. These are the clauses which attempt to restrict you from setting up in competition or taking confidential information after you leave the business, and represent a significant tie-in if things don't work out in the longer term. They are not always enforceable, but consult a lawyer rather than relying on your own judgement.

You can research franchise opportunities on the internet, through franchise associations and franchise magazines. Franchises for sale are also occasionally advertised in local and national papers, as well as at the actual franchise premises.

CASE STUDY

Helen Fell has bought and run two different franchises – a cleaning agency and a leafleting company.

Having taken voluntary redundancy from the civil service I had a sum of money to invest in a business, and I chose the franchise route mainly because it offered me a great opportunity to effectively run my own business right away. If you find the right franchise, the support and education you receive gives you all the tools you need to be in business. Things like monitoring the results of your marketing activity are vital in business and lots of businesses fail because entrepreneurs don't know the basic rules. It has been a great place to learn. You also meet people from all over the country, and the loneliness of working for yourself is more than made up for by the support network you build up through conferences and so on. It's a misconception that all franchisees are limited in what they can do marketing-wise. I am completely in control of my advertising spend, and learn from other franchisees what works and what doesn't. Being part of a franchise, you are not a small company working alone. You have the advantages of being part of a large organisation, which in turn has large buying power. This can result in its franchisees being able to acquire very useful discounts for things like printing and directory and Internet marketing. Depending on how ambitious you are, you could find a franchise rather restrictive later on

> **Either way, franchising is a great way to learn how to run a business without taking on many of the risks involved in traditional start-ups.**

when you become more experienced in business — your wings will be somewhat clipped. But for some it will be a business for life. Either way, franchising is a great way to learn how to run a business without taking on many of the risks involved in traditional start-ups. Also, since we are all limited by our geographical boundaries there is no competition involved — none of us is secretly planning nationwide domination (I don't think...).

Reasons to buy a franchise

- Cashing in on the success and goodwill of an established brand.
- Tried-and-tested, documented processes and support systems.
- A proven business model with facts and figures to support plans.
- A ready-made professional network with other franchisees.
- Someone else has done all the hard work before you arrived.
- Training and other support.
- You choose how you market yourself.
- You can get going (and get earning) quickly.
- You have the money to invest or are willing and able to borrow it.

Disadvantages of buying a franchise

- The cost of buying the franchise and getting independent legal advice can be high.
- It requires a long-term commitment from the outset.
- There can be a lack of control over the overall business direction, marketing and branding.
- You may not have much creative input; you could feel like an employee again.
- Some franchisors advocate unethical business practices — check that what you are being asked to do is legal and acceptable to you.
- The personality, plans and ambitions of your franchisor will greatly affect your franchise business.

Franchising an existing business

An alternative to buying a franchise is of course setting one up yourself. This is a good model for growing a business without taking on employees, and while spreading the risk among other entrepreneurial individuals.

Sue Botterill's priorities when setting up Mymag were to make money while working from home with young children, and she rightly assumed that these would be the priorities of a lot of other women, who for either financial or 'brain drain' reasons didn't want to be full-time mothers. She launched her franchise (although she doesn't like to call it a franchise) Mymag very soon after setting up her own magazine in Solihull. She sold the idea (which is a complete package with built-in support for launching local magazines) to franchisees by concentrating on a number of benefits: demand for the product, low maintenance, no stock, no employees required, low cost and low risk. From the success of the venture it would seem she was right – she has 800 franchisees in place and demand is still high. Not surprisingly, given the phenomenal success of Mymag, a number of attempts have been made to copy the system and Sue is taking legal action against the people in question, most of whom are ex-franchisees jumping on the bandwagon.

CASE STUDY

Freya Bletsoe and her husband Steven started Homefinder UK Ltd to help people find and buy property, initially in south Wales, and now in Yorkshire. They knew they wanted to grow their company and that their business model was perfect for franchising. They have spent a lot of time and money researching how to go about it.

There's lots of information out there for franchisees, but not so much for franchisors. Franchising consultants charge an absolute fortune, largely for the time they need to research and learn about your business – very galling for us, having done so much work on our model already. We found that setting up the franchise, even though it is a franchise of our existing

Setting up the franchise is equivalent to running a whole new business.

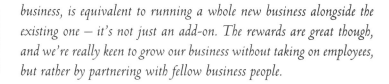

business, is equivalent to running a whole new business alongside the existing one – it's not just an add-on. The rewards are great though, and we're really keen to grow our business without taking on employees, but rather by partnering with fellow business people.

Top tips for franchising your business

- Run the business first yourself so that you are speaking from experience and have more credibility.
- Design a 'business-in-a-box' product which is all that your franchisees will need to run their own business.
- Make sure you have the time (now for setting up and later providing support to franchisees). Setting up a franchise, even of your existing business, is like running a whole new business and requires equivalent research, time, effort and energy.
- Expect to be able to answer any detailed question that your franchisee may have about finance, sales, processes, etc.
- Develop your systems – bespoke IT systems are an essential tool for any franchisee and will provide a huge incentive to go with you rather than go it alone, so make them good.
- Carefully document all the processes that the business performs, design systems and procedures to support them, and back everything up with examples.
- Consolidate your business knowledge and experience – you will need to educate your franchisees in basic business skills, including marketing, PR, book-keeping and IT. Think about how you are going to do that (without plagiarising, of course). You will also need to train franchisees in the specific processes and key skills required for running that particular business.
- Business support – most franchises are sold on the basis that the franchisor will provide ongoing support to franchisees.
- Make it irresistible and unique – remember other people may be offering or thinking of offering a similar franchise on the market. How are you going to be different and better?

- Offer flexibility – franchisees are usually looking for an element of control, as you are.
- Show you understand their position – think about your target franchisee and make the package appealing to them.
- Show how much money they can make – they will want to know the bottom line.
- Be approachable and likeable – serial franchisees always say they have a much better experience if their franchisor is easy to get on with.
- Create communities – buying a franchise can seem like a lonely idea – by creating links and communities among your franchisees you will satisfy that need for the 'staffroom' atmosphere.
- Get legal advice – particularly on restrictive covenants – to ensure you are not robbed of your investment by 'me-too' businesses. Drawing attention to these clauses at the time of signing contracts may save you time and money defending lawsuits at a later date.

Launching a social enterprise or co-operative

Social enterprises are business with a social purpose. They compete in the marketplace like any other business, but with explicit social aims. Profits largely go back into supporting these aims, rather than to the owners and managers for personal gain, although of course, they do get paid. Well-known social enterprises include Café Direct and Jamie Oliver's restaurant, Fifteen. The sector is very diverse and the business models for social enterprises range from limited companies to co-operatives and trusts. Social enterprises are managed differently from traditional businesses, often having a 'triple bottom line' to measure not only the financial amounts involved but also the social and environmental impact that they have.

Social enterprise, the Day Chocolate Company, buys its cocoa from a visionary Ghanaian farmers' co-operative, Kuapa Kokoo. The chocolate company guarantees its suppliers a fair trade price, and also pays a 'social premium' which goes into a farmers' trust fund for social projects including fresh-water wells and medical training. A third of Day's shares are owned by Kuapa Kokoo, which is another way that profits are shared, trade is fair and relationships are enhanced. MD **Sophi Tranchell** said, 'The UK chocolate market is incredibly mature and dominated by Mars, Cadbury and Nestle. To come in as a little player was kind of cheeky'. Cheeky or not, it has worked – the company now supplies chocolate bars to, among others, Tesco, Waitrose, Sainsbury's and Starbucks.

Co-operatives are just one form that a social enterprise may take. They are businesses that are democratically owned by and driven by their members. The most famous UK co-operative, the Co-operative Group (comprising the Co-op supermarket, the Co-operative Bank, etc.), has more shops than any other retailer in Britain. Co-operatives are associated with member-driven ethical trading. The Co-operative Group has been a pioneer in the field of fair trading and environmental awareness and, as you will be aware if you have ever been to a Co-op, your customer dividend card gives you a share in the profits.

There are a number of different structures that co-operatives take:

- Worker co-operatives are owned and controlled by their employees. Either all employee members are directors, or some of them are elected by their colleagues as directors to manage the business – and are accountable to their fellow employee members. They should not be confused with partnerships like John Lewis, which has a similar staff-involvement policy.

- User co-operatives are owned and controlled by the users – for example, in a childcare co-operative the parents of the children being cared for are the owners of the business and accountable to their fellow members.

- Co-operative consortia are owned and run by a group of businesses. For example, a group of organic farmers might form a co-operative for selling their crops. This is also a popular structure for social care co-operatives.

- Multi-stakeholder co-operatives involve community representatives and other stakeholders as part of their membership.

Buying a going concern

Another alternative to setting up a new business is to buy a going concern – that is an existing business, perhaps with premises, employees, contracts and customers already in place.

Another alternative to setting up a new business is to buy a going concern.

Businesses come up for sale all the time, and there are a number of situations in which it would make sense to go down this route:

- If you see a business up for sale, which is just the business you wanted to run, in just the right location.

- If your ambitions are to run a nationwide or international business and you don't want to wait the long time it takes to build up a chain.

- If you have a considerable sum of money to invest, and want to fast-track the set-up period and get trading quickly.

Buying an existing business can be a long and complicated procedure. You are taking on responsibility for premises, assets, employees, debts, reputation and the business's future.

So where do you start with buying an existing business? If you have found a business that you want to buy, then you are halfway there. If on the other hand you are just beginning to consider this as an option, you will need to do some research. The best place to find businesses for sale is on the internet, in local or trade press magazines like *Dalton's Business* or through business transfer agents who operate in a similar way to estate agents (and should be members of the National Association of Estate Agents). Ask around your business and personal contacts as well, and try to attend conferences, seminars and exhibitions relating to your business area as these can be a good source of contacts and trade gossip.

There are many factors to consider when you are first looking for a business to buy. As well as the basic business questions, such as what does this business sell, where and how well, you will also need to assess whether the business will 'fit' with you personally – how well does it suit your ambitions, your personality, your know-how and your existing business, if you have one? The questions you need to answer before going ahead (for yourself, and for your business plan) include:

• Why is the business being sold?

• How has it been valued, and is it worth it?

• Are you prepared to take on everything it involves, from employees' pension rights to fixtures and fittings?

• Will a big cash outlay be required to bring the business to the level you want it?

• Can you afford all the other extra costs involved in a takeover, including legal fees and perhaps redundancy payments?

Find out exactly how the selling price has been arrived at. There is no single foolproof method for business valuation, even among the most experienced academics, accountants and business advisors. So this is one place where you really need your financial wits about you – don't just rely on the price that the agent or seller presents to you. You must research and understand the figures yourself, as the price you will pay for a going concern includes not just current assets but also future profits. You need to build, or at least follow, a financial forecasting model. At the end of the day, the business is only worth what someone (you?) are prepared to pay for it.

The process of finding out all that you can about the business you are interested in buying (and uncovering any skeletons) is called 'due diligence'. Due diligence involves looking at all the business and financial records kept by the business, asking a multitude of questions of the existing owner/agent, and obtaining professional reports from solicitors, accountants and surveyors.

At the end of the due diligence process you should know everything there is to know about the business, including:

- all about the employees' salaries (including taxes and national insurance), length of service, skills, ambitions, terms of employment, pensions and any outstanding claims – for example for discrimination

- all about the finances – accounts, profits, debts and liabilities, forecasts

- all about customers, contracts, suppliers, agents, marketing and research

- all about the assets that the business owns – products, premises, equipment, vehicles, intellectual property – what are they, how are they owned, what are they used for…?

- all about the compliance/regulatory requirements of that business

- All about litigation involving the business (past, pending and ongoing).

- All about the strategy, culture and character of the business – what has (or hasn't) made the business successful to date.

Buying a business is a complex process. But with the right advice and some good detective work, it can be a great way to hit the ground running.

If the process uncovers some surprises (and it inevitably will) but you are still broadly interested in going ahead, there may be scope to renegotiate, either on the price or on which assets and liabilities you take on. If this goes well, and you go on to exchange contracts on the purchase, there will still be a lot of work to do before the transaction is complete – transfer of leases, licences and contracts all take place between exchange and completion.

Buying a business is a complex process, and you need an element of crystal-ball gazing to complement the due diligence process. But with the right advice and some good detective work, it can be a great way to hit the ground running.

Here is a summary of the pros and cons of buying a going concern.

Advantages
- The groundwork and research behind the business have been done, the business direction is set and there are operational systems in place
- The premises, employees, suppliers and customers are all in place
- The business may have a reputation ('goodwill') that has been built up over years
- You won't need to start from scratch building a brand and marketing the business
- Borrowing money to buy the business may be straight-forward as it already has 'standing' and a proven track record

Disadvantages

- Cost: you will have to spend considerable sums of money not just on the purchase but also on associated expenses such as professional fees for accountants and lawyers
- Time: buying a business involves considerable investigative work ('due diligence') and this process, which is time-consuming and expensive, does not always lead to the deal going through
- Staff attitude to a takeover: you may have to deal with unhappy employees
- Risk: nasty surprises may lie in store and pop up at a future date, just when you think you're high and dry

Lynne Embleton's experience gives us all food for thought:

My chief bridesmaid and childhood friend Sue invited me in as a partner in a project to set up a day nursery in West Yorkshire, which was a very exciting proposition. There was definitely a lack of good nurseries around to cope with the increasing demand, as the town changed from a farming community to a commuter town. It looked like a real investment opportunity and I was keen to go with it. With four couples involved in the project — made up of teachers, lawyers and 'finance' people — the team seemed to be complete and highly qualified. But it wasn't as easy as it looked to find suitable premises. After a succession of battles over planning permission, financing and building regulations, we decided to try a different route and buy a going concern. Once we found a likely candidate, the first job was to look at the figures, which fell to me as I have an MBA and regularly deal with finance in my day job. The others had already successfully approached a bank for a loan, and then assumed that if the bank was willing to offer the money they were asking for, then the business must be worth it. When I had a detailed look at the figures I was not so convinced. I challenged them and suggested the business we were looking at was worth no more than £440,000 not the £525,000 they had provisionally agreed to. This was the last thing the others wanted to hear — they had totally set their hearts on it and, in my view, their emotional attachment was getting in the way of realistic business planning. Sue said she would 'dance naked down South Shields pier if they got it at £440,000' but I convinced the team to go in with a much lower offer on the basis of the factual evidence. In fact we finally agreed on £435,000, but there was no naked dancing – perhaps because of what happened next.

Very near to completion, the seller phoned to say that the wages were going up 10 per cent and was that OK? So I had another look at the figures, and it became obvious that we couldn't take that kind of hit or we would be making a loss. I also realised that the proposed figures I was looking at were 20 per cent higher than those we had already, not just 10 per cent. Then it dawned on me that the original wage figures didn't include tax and National Insurance. From being nearly there, after so long, the business was no longer viable, and the whole thing fell through. Houses had been remortgaged, money was sitting in the bank that couldn't be used to make the repayments without incurring huge penalties.

> **Looking back, I am still amazed at the 'real-world' financial naivety of our group, myself included, despite all the experience and qualifications we had between us.**

Sue and I had said from the start that the most important thing about going into business together was that it wouldn't adversely affect our friendship, and I'm pleased to say that has been the case. I've learnt some valuable lessons, though. Looking back, I am still amazed at the 'real-world' financial naivety of our group, myself included, despite all the experience and qualifications we had between us. I hated feeling like the bad guy for bringing the financial inconsistencies to light and tackling them head-on, despite the fact that they would have ruined us and the business had we proceeded. I am amazed that the bank gave us such bad advice (it's clear that the bank isn't really taking the risk – that mainly falls to those of us putting in the equity), and at the lack of knowledge there appears to be in general about valuing businesses. I also learned that you need to be careful about the content of the accounts – numbers are not always what they seem.

Selling at a market stall

Trading at a market stall, such as a craft fair or farmer's market, can be a great way to try out a new business idea. The way to get a stall varies from market to market, so the best thing to do is go along to a market and ask stallholders to put you in touch with the right people. Pick a friendly looking stallholder and you might get some useful tips too.

Genevieve Taylor launched the Home Gourmet Company so that she could spend more time at home with her 15-month-old son. She enrolled in a taxing but enjoyable month-long residential specialist cookery course to get trained in the art of jam and pickle-making. After just six months, Genevieve was making up to 300 jars of jams, marmalade, chutneys and pickles a week, and selling them at the Slow Food Market in Bristol – a market which was aligned to her own philosophy of using local, seasonal produce and minimising environmental impact. Genevieve said, 'The market has been a great place to meet like-minded suppliers as well as to reach customers directly. I've thoroughly enjoyed it, been amazed by my own success, and based on the popularity of the things I make, am inspired to take my business to the next level.' Genevieve has now taken on a business partner and is searching for commercial premises to allow her company to grow.

BECOMING AN EMPLOYER

Depending on your business, employing someone may be something you have to do from the outset, or something that you decide to do when you are expanding and taking on more work. Or it may be something you never do. Many small business owners, particularly women, find the prospect of becoming an employer a bit of a psychological hurdle, and some women we spoke to in our research had deliberately restricted the growth of their businesses in order to avoid the complication and administrative burden that employing people brings. The best way to approach this may be to take the long view – ask yourself where you want to be in five years' time – and what you want your daily life to be like. The

> *The chances are, you will want to be involved with the part of the business that you enjoy most, while employing someone else to take over the administration/ routine/secretarial work.*

chances are, you will want to be involved with the part of the business that you enjoy most, while employing someone else to take over the administration/routine/secretarial work. We deal with how to recruit, manage and build good relationships with your employees in Chapter 6, but below we cover the legal and practical aspects of being an employer.

Contractors and employees – know the difference

If you are taking on someone to work for your business, it is important to establish at the outset whether that person is an employee (with a contract of service) or a self-employed contractor (with a contract for services). Employees have rights that contractors do not, so it might be tempting to insist your worker is self-employed, but it is not enough simply to make that decision for your own convenience that your worker is a contractor rather than an employee. There are four key tests that will help determine a worker's employment status:

- control (do you control what she does, how and when she works?)

- integration (how integrated is she in the business?)

- mutuality of obligations (if you have mutual obligations towards each other, this implies she is an employee)

- economic reality (the bigger picture – is she in business on her own account or merely performing a role in your business?)

If, according to the four tests, you are sure you have an employee, you will need to consider your related obligations, the majority of which are set out below.

Payroll and PAYE

When you were an employee, your tax and national insurance contributions were paid by your employer to the government under the PAYE (Pay As You Earn) system. Now the tables have turned and you are responsible for paying not only your own tax and national insurance but also that of any employees you may have. If you don't have the time, skills or inclination to take on this task yourself, consider employing an accountant or a payroll company who will charge an annual fee in respect of each employee.

Contract of employment and statutory rights

Your employee is entitled by law to be provided with a statement of the terms of her employment, and it is in everybody's interests (although not obligatory) to have that contract signed before employment begins. It will give you something to refer to if things go wrong, and it focuses the mind on issues that might have been overlooked at the recruitment stage. The law requires certain clauses to be included in a contract including:

- names of employer and employee
- date of commencement
- place of employment
- hours of employment and overtime arrangements
- job title and duties
- notice period to terminate employment and any probation period
- salary – how much, how often, how paid
- holiday allowance and other leave entitlement
- sick pay
- grievance procedure
- disciplinary procedure
- pension arrangements clause (even if there isn't a pension you need to say so).

Ideally both parties to the contract should consult their own solicitor before signing the contract.

Unfair dismissal

It may seem a bit early to be thinking about this, but right at the beginning you need to think about what might happen if things don't work out. After a year's employment (at the time of writing), an employee is harder to dismiss, as she will have a potential claim for unfair dismissal which was not available up until that point. So effectively you have a year to 'try out' your employee before she is firmly entrenched.

Discrimination

As an employer you will be liable for any acts of discrimination towards your staff or potential staff, whether employees or consultants, including job applicants. There is legislation in place covering discrimination on grounds of race, gender, sexual orientation, religious belief, age and disability. Discrimination can be direct (you treat someone less favourably because of one of the protected reasons, e.g. because he is a man) or indirect (the imposition of conditions or practices which put one of the protected groups at a disadvantage compared to people not in that group). In most cases, you will be liable for the discriminatory acts of your employees.

Maternity and paternity rights, flexible working

Employees have a number of rights relating to parenthood. Expectant and new mothers have long had the right to maternity leave and statutory maternity pay, and government policy on this is changing (and becoming more generous to parents) all the time. All employees have the right to a period of 26 weeks of 'ordinary maternity leave'. A further 26 weeks of 'additional maternity leave' is now available to employees (with no qualifying period), but taking additional leave affects their right to return to the same job. Other rights already include paternity leave, parental leave, and the right to ask for flexible working hours.

Other obligations

If your employee is going to be working in your office, you will need to take the steps advised by the Health and Safety Executive on health and safety issues and you will also need to make sure you have an employer's liability insurance policy in place. See also the section below on Compliance.

COMPLIANCE – WHAT DO YOU NEED TO REGISTER AND WHERE?

Depending on your chosen business sector, there are potentially a range of regulations, compliance issues, licences, accreditations and trade bodies that may govern your activity. Good advice is available on the internet, covering businesses sector by sector, and showing you what you need to comply with and how. Here is an overview.

Licences

Check with your local authority whether your business needs a licence to trade. There are hundreds of business types that require licences, from casinos and pubs to childminders and gift shops.

Health and safety and the environment

Some of the activities that your business carries out may involve risks to you and your staff, your customers or the environment. You have a legal responsibility for the health and safety of your employees and the impact your business has on the environment. This may seem to be irrelevant – you are not likely to be setting up a nuclear power plant – but strict regulations apply to everyday businesses such as hairdressing, relating to the use of hazardous substances and day-to-day rubbish disposal.

Use of buildings

If you are using a new building or changing its use, altering the structure of a building or installing plant or machinery outside a building, contact your local authority to ensure you obtain the correct permissions.

Data protection

If your business holds information about other people, the data protection principles will apply to you. These principles state that personal information must be:

- fairly and lawfully processed for specific purposes

- adequate, accurate, relevant, and not kept for longer than is necessary

- kept secure and not transferred to countries without this type of legislation

The people about whom you hold data (who may be clients, employees, or candidates you place in employment) also have the right to see information that you hold and have it corrected if it's wrong. Beware of bogus agencies requesting payment for data protection registration or notification. For more on this, contact the Information Commissioner's Office.

Insurance

Some insurance policies are legally required. Other insurance decisions are a matter of personal choice. If you need to or choose to insure your business, the policies below are the most common and can be economically purchased as a package.

- Employer's liability insurance – a legal requirement if employing anyone even on a part-time or short-term basis/work experience.

- Public liability insurance – your legal liability to third parties for injury to others or damage to their property, arising in connection with your business.

- Product liability insurance – your legal liability to third parties for injury to others or damage to their property, arising out of goods sold or supplied in connection with your business.

- Business cover for business equipment, stock, goods in transit, money and documents.

- Legal expenses insurance – cover for business legal costs and expenses incurred in defending or pursuing a claim.

- Professional indemnity insurance to protect professional advisors against any legal liability resulting from a client suffering a loss due to unsatisfactory or inadequate advice given.

Consult an insurance broker (usually best found through personal recommendation) to help you find the right insurance policies for your business.

Trade associations for specific business sectors

There are a number of business sectors which are particularly popular with women – in particular, fashion and lifestyle, garden design, recruitment, childcare, life coaching, alternative therapies and interior design. These sectors are used to numbering women among their ranks, but women are also making inroads into traditional male sectors like building, construction and manual trades – they even have their own trade associations in some instances. You can find out about relevant associations on the internet. They are generally a very good place to meet people with similar skills, and often they offer subsidised training and support to their members.

ACCOUNTING

Accounting is all about keeping accurate records of your performance and using the information not only to get a picture of the financial state of your business but for strategic planning purposes. Although only companies need to file accounts in a prescribed format, it is good practice in every business to draw up a properly prepared set of accounts.

Once you start going to Harrods' sale with your business credit card, you may find it hard to match things up at the end of the year.

Where to start with accounting

Even if you haven't got an accountant on board yet, you need to keep accurate records right from the start.

- Use your business bank account for your business expenditure. Once you start using personal cheque books for business costs and going to Harrods' sale with your business credit card, you may find it hard to match things up at the end of the year.

- Keep copies of all bills and all your receipts, even before you have started trading. Even if you end up with an electronic book-keeping system, you should keep all your original paperwork.

- Buy a cash book from a stationers and record in it all your money in and out. Ideally these records should match your bank statement, if you have been good and not muddled up your money.

- If you are unsure as to whether spending on something is business related, check with your accountant.

Who's in charge of the books?

You can either leave your day-to-day book-keeping to an accountant (who may be one of your business partners, if you choose wisely), or if you are starting small you can learn the basics yourself and save some money. There are plenty of websites and textbooks which show you how to do this, and most banks now offer an electronic accounting system. See the Appendix for more information.

However, a good accountant can offer you a lot more than just book-keeping. They will ensure that your business is benefiting from current tax incentives and reliefs and can help you with your business plan, tax return, VAT return and Companies House filing requirements as well. They will deal with H M Revenue & Customs on your behalf and advise you on sourcing finance for your business.

Tips for finding a good accountant

Personal factors – As with all your dream team, you must be able to get on with your accountant. You may not necessarily meet him or her often or at all – some firms operate mainly by email – but it is essential that you can communicate effectively and that they understand your needs. If you prefer to deal with someone face to face, is this a possibility? Be equally careful at this point not to engage someone on the basis of whether you would befriend them normally – you are choosing a business advisor, not a soulmate.

Qualifications and experience – Anyone can call themselves an accountant or book-keeper. If your accountant is not qualified, then there should be a very good reason for you to use them. Qualified accountants (and solicitors) are required to complete continuing professional development courses to keep them up to speed with the changes in the current law. There are six recognised qualifying bodies in the UK but remember that qualifications are no indication of quality, and there are plenty of qualified professionals out there providing a very mediocre service. As well as qualifications, find out about the experience that the accountant has in your field of work. Can they really offer the services that your business requires? Do they have specialists at the firm? Always ask for evidence of their professional qualifications and their experience of your chosen field.

Fees – Find out how your fees will be structured and exactly what is included. Some firms will charge an hourly rate, some a rate for each piece of work undertaken; some are fixed costs, some variable. Some firms will offer a fixed monthly fee with no hidden extras, but read the small print.

Taxation for business

Tax is an unavoidable aspect of life, but it needn't be the headache it is made out to be. There are a number of different taxes you may be liable for: direct taxes on income and profits (income tax and corporation tax) taxes on capital (inheritance tax and capital gains tax) and indirect taxes (VAT and other duties). Below is a list of the main UK taxes and when they are payable.

(Note that different rules apply in Guernsey, Jersey and the Isle of Man.)

Income tax is payable by sole traders on profits and by partners on their share of profits (whether or not paid out), and on your salary if you are employed by your company. Income tax is also paid on dividends received.

Value Added Tax (VAT) is a tax on the sale of goods and services and is chargeable and payable by your business automatically if your earnings reach a certain threshold. You may not need to register for VAT at the outset, unless your profits either exceed the threshold or are likely to do so very quickly, or you are paying VAT on your business expenses. The annual thresholds for VAT are usually updated every year. Check the H M Revenue & Customs website for the current thresholds and the tests you need to do.

National Insurance (NI) is payable by sole traders and partners (class 2 for the self-employed) and may also be payable on profits (class 4). If you have employees, you will be liable for Employer's and Employees' national insurance (which should be a consideration built into your business plan) both on their salaries and also on any benefits in kind you may pay them.

Corporation tax is payable on company profits.

Capital Gains Tax (CGT) is charged when you sell something for more than you bought it for. When you or your business dispose of investments, land or other assets, there is a charge on the profit you have made on any amounts over the statutory threshold. When you sell your home, the main residence exemption usually applies so the tax does not arise, but if you use part of your home to run your business, and make deductions for tax purposes accordingly (i.e. deduct heating/cleaning bills from your profits before paying tax), you should be aware that CGT may become payable on a corresponding proportion of the sale price. You should consult an accountant on this.

If you take over a business as a going concern, part of the purchase price you pay may be for goodwill. You will need to keep a detail of this as it may feature as a deductible expense when you come to sell the business.

Inheritance tax (IHT) is payable on your estate when you die if the value of your estate exceeds the specified threshold. Remember that the value of your business forms part of your estate, although there may be specific relief available to reduce or exempt your business. You could transfer assets to younger relatives in later life but IHT is still payable if you die within seven years of the transfer, so go carefully during that time…

Below is a basic summary of your potential tax liabilities as sole trader, partnership or company.

Sole trader/partnership tax obligations

- Register with the Inland Revenue as self-employed.
- Complete a self-assessment tax return every year.
- Pay income tax on business profits, calculated on receipt of your tax return by H M Revenue & Customs if submitted to them by 30 September following the end of the tax year.
- Pay advance instalments of income tax based on previous year's profits (remember to allow funds for this).
- Pay income tax and NI on behalf of any employees.
- Pay class 2 and class 4 NI contributions.
- Submit a VAT return if necessary.
- Potential liability to CGT on disposal of assets.

Limited companies' tax obligations

- Company pays corporation tax on profits.
- You (if employed by your company) pay income tax on your salary.
- Potential liability to CGT on disposal of assets.
- Submit VAT return if necessary.
- Company pays income tax and NI on behalf of any employee.

Tax is an issue that requires expert input if you are going to make the most of your finances. Your accountant should be able to assist you with your tax return and will be able to advise you on how to make the most of tax incentives and reliefs applicable to small businesses.

BUSINESS NAMES

Women often think of a name for their baby before they even get pregnant (or reach secondary school), and similarly, they tend to focus on the name of their business before they have

Women often think of a name for their baby before they even get pregnant.

established exactly what the business will do. If this is you, release yourself from the name that is already sitting in the back of your mind so you can go through the decision-making process properly. The name of your business will have a strong impact on the customer's perception of you, and is not that easy to change once it's out there in the public domain. It's important to create the right impression, and not just to use your favourite word, or design an imprint of your own personality.

Your business name should reflect the nature and ethos of the business, while having the right 'ring' to it. It will become, like your own name, the label people will use for what you do and the words they say when they refer to you. Imagine them talking about you and using that business name. Is it easy to say? Is it easy for other people to spell? Does it convey what you want it to convey?

Lin Taylor spent four years living in Virginia, USA, and was infused with the American Pie ethos. 'While we were still living in the States, I was already planning the business of my dreams that I was going to set up on my return to the UK, selling handmade crafts with an American twist, conjuring up country charm and crackling fires at Christmas. I had the name in my head before we moved back here – Stars Stripes and Snowflakes. I like the way it just trips off the tongue. I have never looked back'.

Emma Reid set up her marketing consultancy specialising in marketing to the over 50s and finds that not only does the clever name, Grey Sells, get commented on all the time, it also 'does exactly what it says on the tin'. As does **Sally Robinson's** company Ample Bosom. Sally converted a barn building on her North Yorkshire farm to a place where she could make better-fitting bras and other clothing for large women.

You may be tempted to use your own name as the basis for your business. A lot of women business owners start out using their own initials as part of their business name. But don't forget that the customer doesn't know you, and will never know you as 'AB', but as 'Anna Benson'. If you want to be remembered by your name, use your name. Initials are bland and difficult to remember, whereas whole names have much more impact and exude confidence and self-belief. Women often don't have that self-belief and shrink from being so upfront, especially on start-up, and this is part of our gender-specific conditioning, but in business you need to get ready to stand up and be counted if you want to stand a chance of competing in the marketplace. At that point you may regret your inconspicuous name.

If you want to be remembered by your name, use your name.

Even if you have come up with a name for your business already, and are quite attached to it, do some research, listen to advice, and be aware of what other people associate with a chosen name. 'Pegasus', for example, may initially seem an attractive name, with its connotations of winged horses soaring to great heights, but there are hundreds of businesses with that name in the UK already (mostly taxi firms). When we considered setting up our women's business group with the name 'Women's Business', it was pointed out to us by a member who was a massage therapist that anything that can be misinterpreted, will be misinterpreted.

> **Anything that can be misinterpreted, will be misinterpreted.**

There are a few rules you need to bear in mind relating to name-choosing.

General guidelines

1. Choose a name that is easy to say, read and spell, and reflects an accurate and positive image of your business.
2. Bear in mind who you want to attract, and make the name appealing to those customers. Ask lots of people what they think.
3. If you have international aspirations or foreign customers, check the name doesn't mean something rude or otherwise unsuitable in other languages.
4. Don't choose a name for your business which is likely to be confused with another –
   - Using the name of a well-known brand to enhance your business is known as 'passing off'. Setting up a gift shop called McDonald's would not be considered to be passing off, but setting up a hamburger restaurant with that name will almost certainly land you in court.
   - Choosing a name that is the same as or similar to another local business or a national business will cause confusion.
   - Check with Companies House that your name hasn't already been registered.
   - Check with the Patent Office that your name hasn't been registered as a trade mark.
   - Look in the phone book, directories and on the web to check whether anyone else is using the name, or anything similar.

Some classic mistakes

- 'Rug's and Carpets' – if you are going to use an apostrophe in the wrong place, at least do it consistently. This sign, highly visible on one of the main roads in Cardiff, has thankfully now been changed.
- 'Pipe Dream Productions Wedding Videos' – would you really want to use a photographer whose name is associated with an 'unrealistic hope or fantasy' for your wedding?
- 'Excellant Builders' and 'On Suite Bathrooms' – the fact that they can't spell may not affect the quality of what they are offering but it appears unprofessional and it would put us off.

Specific rules for naming limited companies

If you set up as a company, you will need to register the name with Companies House. They can provide you with a full set of guidelines on name-choosing. The name must end with 'limited' (or plc if appropriate) and must not be the same or similar to any other company name. It must not contain any sensitive or offensive words or expressions. When the name (and the company) has been fully registered, you will receive a certificate of incorporation showing the company's registered name and number. There are special requirements relating to the displaying of company names; in particular, the name should be clearly shown outside every place of business, on every piece of correspondence (including emails) and on all business documents. You will also need to include your registered office address and company number on company documentation.

Specific rules for naming partnerships or sole traders

If you are a partnership or sole trader, you can either trade under your own name or a separate business name. The name you choose must not contain the words 'limited', 'plc' (so no pretending to be a company) or other designated sensitive words, or any offensive words. Your business name, your own name and your office address must be displayed on all correspondence and business documentation and at any location where you do business with customers.

PROTECTING INTELLECTUAL PROPERTY RIGHTS

All businesses have intellectual property. Intellectual property (IP) is a legal expression for the elements of your business which you have created personally through your ideas, and includes your business name, logo, literature and designs as well as patents and trade marks. Your IP adds value to your business and sets you apart from the rest. So whatever the extent of your IP, protecting it (stopping third parties from using or infringing it) is vital for the survival of your business.

Here is a list of the main intellectual property rights that exist, and how to protect them.

Copyright

Copyright is a right automatically granted to any creation that is put into material form. For example, there is no copyright in the idea you may have for a training programme, but as soon as you put it on paper you have automatic protection. If, on the other hand, you tell someone a business idea without writing it down, there is no copyright. There is no formal registration scheme for copyright, but it is considered desirable to include an indication on your work that copyright is reserved using the © sign, the date of the work and the author's name.

Patents

A patent is a set of exclusive rights granted by a government to an inventor for a limited amount of time (normally 20 years). If you have invented something new that you want to bring to the market, registering your patent early will protect you against others stealing and profiting from your idea while you work on the finer details. The first rule is 'Don't tell anyone your idea', or you may have trouble registering it. To be

The first rule is 'Don't tell anyone your idea', or you may have trouble registering it.

patentable your invention must be new, must involve an inventive step, must be capable of being used in some kind of industry, and must not be 'excluded'. The UK Patent Office provides detailed advice on what is and what is not patentable, and can put you in touch with recommended lawyers if you need one. However, the better and more ground-breaking your invention, the more likely other businesses are to copy you, and although they may be blatantly infringing your patent, it is up to you to take the infringer to court to have your rights upheld. Litigation can become a major part of an inventor's life. **Mandy Haberman** invented the Anyway Up Cup™ in 1990, only to find herself in constant court battles with infringers. Her website gives useful advice to inventors and is a voice for her campaign for a change in the law (see the Appendix).

Trade marks

A trade mark is a distinctive name, symbol, image or style used by a business to identify itself to consumers. If your business provides a service rather than a product, the mark is sometimes called a service mark. To protect your trade mark you need to register it with the Patent Office, but it has to pass a number of tests to be registerable:

- It must be specifically for the goods or services which it applies to.

- It must not be deceptive, or contrary to law or morality.

- It must not be similar or identical to any earlier marks for the same or similar goods or services.

In practice, many small businesses do not focus on IP issues at all – copyright does not require registration and if you aren't an inventor you are likely only to need to consider whether or not your logo or name should be registered as a trade mark. If you are considering registering intellectual property rights, speak to an intellectual property lawyer or trade mark/patent agent who will advise you on what is and isn't capable of registration. The UK Patent Office website is also very helpful.

SO, HAVE YOU GRASPED THE BASICS?

We have covered a lot of practical ground in this chapter. Check that you have:

- ☐ decided what type of a business to set up (and considered alternatives such as franchises, co-operatives or buying a going concern)
- ☐ learnt about employing people
- ☐ understood what compliance and insurance regulations apply to your business
- ☐ got started with accounting, book-keeping and taxes
- ☐ come up with a name for your business
- ☐ considered whether you have any intellectual property to protect

CHAPTER

4

PRICING, NEGOTIATION AND CONTRACTS

Pricing and contracts are the nitty-gritty of doing business, and will form the nitty-gritty of your business plan. How you price your product or service will play a major part in whether it will sell, and how you 'wheel and deal' will determine exactly how much money you will make in return for your hard work.

At a very basic level, the way to establish a price is simply to ask: What will people pay for what you give them? How much will they buy? Is it going to be worth it to you, after all the money and time you spend getting to the point of sale? If the sums don't add up, think how you could make it work for you – cutting costs, charging more…? By pricing correctly, negotiating confidently and getting clear contracts in place, you will be rewarded not only financially, but also by satisfied customers and a sense of personal freedom that results.

The financial targets in your business plan need to evolve into a clear 'menu' setting out the prices for what you offer, and alongside that you need to develop a confident 'patter' to let customers know what you charge without feeling apologetic or mercenary. If you decide that negotiation is an option, on price or any other aspect of service, you have to be clear what your bottom line is, and what you get in return for your compromise. Negotiation can seem intimidating – it's not something we do a lot in our culture – but it's a skill that can be learnt like any other.

Negotiation is – a skill that can be learnt like any other.

Out of the pricing and negotiation process comes the contract. Contracts form the basis of all trading. For example: 'I'll give you my car and you will give me £1,000'. But what if the car turns out to be useless? There are terms that are implied by law, in particular the Sale of Goods Act and the Supply of Goods and Services Act, which protect the customer in situations like this. If you are supplying goods or services to the public, you will need to be aware of these implied terms, and we deal with them later in this chapter.

PRICING

Having and spending money is a central part of our lives, and pricing is correspondingly fundamental to your business, yet it's something that we don't talk about very openly. Consequently there is a lot of unspoken anxiety and guilt surrounding the issue of money — not having enough, comparisons with others, or just worrying about it ... If you have just dismissed that idea while reading it, you could be one of the people most affected. Ostrich-like behaviour around the subject of money is one of the main symptoms of an unhealthy relationship with money. So, let's get our heads out of the sand and get real about money.

> *Ostrich-like behaviour around money is one of the main symptoms of an unhealthy relationship with money.*

Your relationship with money

We know that women are not generally motivated solely by money when they go into business ownership. Women are much more likely than men to list work–life balance as a primary reason for becoming self-employed, but remember that the more money you earn, the more living and the less working you will be able to do. So shall we let money take centre stage for the moment?

We asked you earlier about what type of business yours is going to be. What do you stand for? What do you want? How are you going to get it? What makes you special? Who are your clients? Part of your vision of the business is where in the market you want to place yourself. How you price yourself in relation to the competition will to a certain extent depend on your personality and your own relationship with money.

Lucy: I grew up with very mixed messages about money, with a mother who was excessively careful with it and a father who was the opposite, but in secret to avoid detection and punishment ... With these extreme role models in my past, it's not surprising that I feel worried about not having enough money, and yet when I have some I spend it straightaway – on holidays, clothes, home improvements, huge Christmas tip for the cleaner, a spell of 'I'll get this one' in the restaurant with friends. Something inside me says savings accounts, pensions, rainy day funds, are all boring. The aspects of my personality which make me want to be different, exciting, unusual, seem to stand in the way of financial prudence. Perhaps that's why I married a man who keeps me on the straight and narrow. It certainly helps that he hauls me back onto the beaten track with his finger pointing to our empty bank account.

Bella: The main message I got about money from my family is how important it is to be clear and accurate about it. My parents have always been generous with money but not reckless. My pocket money was mine to do with what I wanted, but if my mother gave me money to go to the shops, she would expect a breakdown of what I had spent and exact change. It didn't matter whether I had run an errand for her, or bought an ice cream for me and a friend – the accounts had to balance to the penny, and have receipts attached if possible. I worked for my father during school holidays and learnt how to submit an 'invoice' detailing the hours I worked, with dates, before I got my cash, even if it was written in felt-tips. Consequently I'm not frightened of being precise about money and learnt from an early age that what comes in has to match (and preferably exceed) what goes out.

Paradoxically, sometimes we fear having too much money. Does having lots of money mean that someone else doesn't have enough? Are we worth it? Money can bring power, but power can be misused. When money becomes the purpose of living, life loses its meaning. If you can learn to understand your beliefs about earning, saving and spending, your fear and anxiety will dissolve. Answering the questions below will help you to purge yourself of any finance-related stress that could be getting in the way of your pricing ideas.

What does money mean to you?

- What meaning did money have in your family when you were growing up? Was there enough money?
- How much do you talk about money, and who with?
- What do you fear about money?
- How important is having money to you? How much do you want? Why not more than that?
- What do you think of rich people? Poor people?
- How would having lots of money feel to you emotionally, e.g. peace, guilt, choices, superiority?
- Have you been/are you in debt or desperate for money? How does/did that feel?
- What would you do with your life if money was unlimited?
- Do you pretend that you have more/less money than you actually do?
- How much money do you need to live life as you want to? How much would you need set aside to feel secure?
- If you don't have enough money, what does that do to your sense of yourself?
- How do you motivate yourself to earn?
- Who do you know who has a healthy relationship with money – not just earning enough, but using it wisely?

The more you understand your own patterns, and the more honest you are about how you feel about money, the more able you will be to develop a healthy attitude towards money. Positive belief systems, wherever they come from, are helpful. One business woman we know of comes from a family of gamblers with a relaxed attitude to 'losing it all'. She has a thriving business and very little anxiety about money.

Do you identify with any of the following negative beliefs about money (and can you see then how limiting they are)?

Negative beliefs about money
- People who have lots of money have to work all week at something they don't enjoy and never see their family.
- It's always the rich people who are the stingiest.
- People will love you less if you have money – they will be jealous and judgemental.
- It is spiritually impure to have money ('blessed are the poor').
- There is not enough money to go around – if you have enough, that means someone else doesn't.
- We need to keep our wealth a secret.

Remember that dealing with money is just an ordinary part of life which many women do extremely well, whether it's household budgets or playing the stock market.

Can you identify with these positive beliefs about money, and add your own?

Positive beliefs about money
- Having money is fun.
- Having money gives you freedom and security.
- Earning money is a sign of our usefulness to our community.
- Being passionate about life does not depend on how much money we have.
- You can have money and keep your integrity and generosity.
- You can earn money from something you enjoy.
- Spending money can be a responsible thing to do.
- Having money can be a force for good.

Setting prices
So, now that all your money hang-ups have magically disappeared, and you are happy with the notion of getting

people to pay for what you do, how do you decide how much to charge? Charging a standard percentage on top of the cost price doesn't take into account one of the most important factors – what your customer is prepared to pay.

> *A lot of women go into business to do what they are good at.*

> *It comes so easily to them, they feel unhappy about charging much for their services.*

It's easy to underrate the need for what you are providing, and consequently what people will pay for it, especially if your business is all about your personal skills. A lot of women go into business to do what they are good at without appreciating how important what they do is to other people. It comes so easily to them, they feel unhappy about charging much for their services. Yes your price needs to be a reflection of you and what you offer, but it also needs to take into account your clients' needs, and the value to them, not you, of what you offer.

But alongside those market-driven factors, you also need to consider what costs your price needs to cover. These will include:

• all the costs of setting up your business

• all the costs of running your business – time, premises, supplies and expenses, staff costs, etc.

• all the costs of developing your business – marketing, training, coaching, networking, selling, advertising, etc.

• holiday, sick leave, maternity leave, etc.

• contingency for a rainy day, week or month

• making you a profit

• pension savings.

From 'reassuringly expensive' to 'bargain basement'

As part of your market research you will have investigated the pricing structures of your competitors, so you have an idea of the market you are in. You need to decide where you and your clients fit in:

1. **High prices – upmarket.** You will attract clients from a higher social group: high earners, corporate clients and those who aspire to being upmarket. The consequences of putting yourself in this price bracket are that you will be expected to provide a service or product of a very high standard, with accompanying standards of presentation, customer service, etc. You may have to increase your marketing/PR spend, as posters on church hall noticeboards may not be seen by your posh clientele, but glossy adverts in *Tatler* will. You will be dealing with a particular kind of customer – do you like these people? Will they like you? Are you a member (or aspiring member) of their group? Another consequence of being very upmarket is that you sell a little for a lot – think of a designer boutique versus a high-street outlet. Fewer customers paying more money will mean fewer overheads for you, but your customers will have correspondingly high expectations. Your investment of time and energy may be high for each sale, and so if a sale doesn't happen, you may feel that there was a lot of wasted effort.

2. **Low prices – downmarket.** You will attract clients looking for a budget solution, and are unlikely to attract the upmarket customers. The consequences of putting yourself in this price bracket are possibly a lower marketing spend than if you are upmarket, but the customers who come because you are cheap may leave as soon as you put your prices up. You may also find that cheap stock shifts fast, so you will need to ensure that you are equipped to deal with a fast business turnover – this may mean

> *The customers who come because you are cheap may leave as soon as you put your prices up.*

employing staff. It is very popular with brand new businesses to go in undercutting the competition, and it will get you attention, but think ahead and make sure your numbers really do add up.

3. **Middle prices – middle market.** You will attract all types of customers except the most upmarket ones and the most downmarket who are choosing on price alone. Being middle-market gives you a wide net and the opportunity to raise your prices later without losing half your customers. This is a popular option, but make sure you have sound business reasons for not moving up a grade. As your market is larger and more scattered, it can take a while to find the right place to reach your customers.

Pricing structures and refunds

If you are opening a shop or restaurant, then you generally price up your goods, with labels or a menu, and customers pay before they leave … or you call the police.

If yours is a services business, on the other hand, there are several charging options for you to consider:

- charging by the hour/day (lawyer, coach)

- charging a monthly retainer (IT support)

- charging for a service (web design, recruitment, plumber)

- paid by results (no fix no fee)

- a combination of the above (hopefully without calling the police)

Your choice of charging structure will depend to a great extent on how the indusry works, what you need to make the business plan work and what your customers will pay.

If you choose the hourly/daily rate, and you are not providing the service in the presence of your client, be prepared to provide detailed invoices showing what you have done and how long it took. If you choose the monthly retainer, then you need to be sure you are not going to be working flat-out for one client for a meagre fee. If you are charging a one-off fee for a service, you need to be very clear in your own mind that it takes into account the amount of time you may end up spending on the iterative process of making your customer happy. If you are paid by results, be sure that a) you can achieve them and b) your customer will agree and pay up.

In all cases, and whatever your terms of business say, you run the risk of the customer not paying up after you have done the work, which is why a lot of service businesses require customers to pay a deposit, and sometimes (especially in the building trade or other cashflow-sensitive services) make a series of regular payments. A well-written contract will go a long way to avoid disputes (see later). When you are drafting your terms of business, pay particular attention to specifying when deposits and interim payments are due, and check that this fits with your own cashflow obligations. Late-payment penalties are useful deterrents. You don't need to invoke your penalty clause as soon as an invoice goes unpaid by a day, but it is very useful if you end up in court over it. We talk more about cashflow in Chapter 6.

If you offer a refund, your terms of business should set out exactly what your policy is. Will the deposit for the website design be refunded if the client is horrified by your first draft? Will your recruitment firm reimburse the client if the temp walks out on day 3? A good starting point is 'what does the competition do?' but don't forget that the unique way you deal with a problem or complaint is more likely to get you talked about than all the uncontroversial good work you have done. If and when your business grows, or other people are

> *The unique way you deal with a problem or complaint is more likely to get you talked about than all the uncontroversial good work you have done.*

involved with customers on the front line, those people will need a clear policy in place that they can stick to, rather than a wishy-washy, sometimes-we-do-give-refunds-it-depends approach. Be firm, have a policy and start as you mean to go on. Similar advice applies to discounts, which we deal with in the section on negotiation below.

Raising prices

Prices are never right forever. They move – generally upwards – driven by inflation, market anomalies and, occasionally, you being skint despite working your socks off. Most businesses raise their prices at some time or other, and almost certainly in the first two years. When you establish your initial pricing structure, think about when you anticipate reviewing these prices. Are you going to offer a reduced price for the first three months to get yourself off the ground? If so, make it clear that your prices will be increased in month 4. Don't be afraid of turning people away with your prices. Do not feel obliged to reduce them to get a job.

Tips for raising prices

- Keep an eye on what the competition is doing, and keep up.

- Be clear and straightforward about when and by how much your prices are rising.

- Be bold – if you are going to do it, do it with conviction.

- Don't overdo it – bringing prices down again could be construed as an admission of defeat!

CASE STUDY

Emma Reid of Grey Sells finds that higher prices bring respect and imply top-quality service: 'I try to keep my prices reassuringly expensive and have been advised to put my prices up in the past. Feeling a wallet was a skill we learnt as consultants – the price is only what someone will pay you for your service.'

Top pricing tips

- If you offer a menu of goods and services, make sure that is clear, and consider discounting bulk purchases or developing packages or multiple items.
- If your prices aren't turning some customers away, they are probably too low.
- Undercutting is acceptable on start-up to bring in business, but limit the period or risk being labelled 'cheap'.
- Offer something extra included in your price to distinguish you from the competition and as an alternative to dropping your price.
- Constantly review your suppliers to make sure your overheads are reasonable.
- If your prices are getting you the right type and number of customers, and you are making a profit, they are probably about right.

> *If your prices aren't turning some customers away, they are probably too low.*

NEGOTIATION – GETTING TO 'YES'

Negotiation is what happens when two people or businesses, or a business and a customer want to come to an agreement, but have different expectations of the terms of that agreement. Most of us, whether or not we shop at the souk in Dubai, have at some point found ourselves in a situation where negotiation is required.

> A: 'I'll sell you this chair for £50'
> B: 'I'll buy it for £20'

They reach agreement by adjusting their offers until they meet. A goes down to £40, B comes up to £30, and they agree on £35. It's not always as straightforward as that of course. A may stick to her price and throw in a cushion. B may stick to her guns and they may agree at £25 or even £20, if she looks like she's about to walk away and the seller is desperate.

When to negotiate

In some countries, negotiating, or bargaining (not bartering – that is swapping) is part of the selling and buying process. In the UK it is not. Imagine arguing with the Tesco checkout staff about the price of their tomatoes.

In some situations, however, negotiating is acceptable and expected – usually when we buy big-ticket items like a house or a car, or when we buy goods from an individual rather than a business. In others, the option is open, but we don't always take it – it is pretty exhausting and time-consuming putting all that effort in to get 10p off your paperclips. So focus on negotiating where it will make the most difference to your business expenses. For example, if you are buying a going concern, buying one-off key services, especially at the cash-strapped start-up phase, e.g. advertising space, design, legal services; or buying vital ongoing services – such as rent and accountancy services.

Your clients will try to negotiate with you too and that may be welcome (they are interested) or not (you don't have much room to manoeuvre).

Negotiating, if you have not done it before, sounds rather intimidating and unnecessary. It would be so much easier to just pay the asking price rather than embarrass yourself by asking for a discount or a change in the contract. What if they say no? What if they laugh? What if they make you feel as if you have completely misunderstood what is going on here? Well, if that is the case they may be doing a good job of bluffing. If you give into a bluff, you are effectively taking money out of your pocket and putting it into theirs without getting anything for it. Wouldn't you rather hand over the cash to your children or a worthy cause? You don't need to think of it as a belligerent, macho activity – negotiating is fun, and women are really good at it. Don't assume big companies won't

> **You don't need to think of negotiating as a belligerent, macho activity – it's is fun, and women are really good at it.**

negotiate. The bigger a player they are, the more likely you are not going to be dealing with the owner, and the more likely you are to convince them with your confidence and bravado that your business is worth reducing their prices for.

> *Lucy: I negotiate all the time. I am the one who gets money off the bill in the hotel, gets an extra advert thrown in for free, I stick to my terms of business and when clients ask me for extra time to pay, which they often do, I don't give in. There is a fine line between good customer service and getting a reputation as a bit of a pushover, and although I am happy to negotiate my terms before I take a client on, I never agree to change the payment terms that a client has already signed up to. At the root of it is a determination not to be ripped off. I pay a fortune for lots of different products and services — holidays, membership of a gym, and in due course no doubt school fees, but I make sure that I am getting what I pay for. If the gym shuts down for two weeks, I want half my subscription back for that month.*

> *Bella: For me, negotiation, and pricing are inextricably linked with assertiveness and self-worth. I notice that as my confidence has grown, so has my attitude to doing deals. It is a bit of a chicken-and-egg situation to begin with, but partly because I know now that I have a lot to offer, I feel fine about saying no to negotiating on fees, and much less embarrassed than I used to be about bringing up the subject. There are some instances where I'll do low-cost work or even free work, but the client always knows what I would have charged. Someone I know, who does pro-bono work for a charity, still sends them an account of services for information rather than an invoice for payment, so they know the value of what they are getting.*

> **I notice that as my confidence has grown, so has my attitude to doing deals.**

As supplier, know when you are prepared to negotiate, and when you're not, what is up for grabs and what is set in stone in your terms and conditions. Develop a standard reply that is an alternative to saying no, e.g. 'the reason I don't negotiate is that I know from my market research that this is a fair price'. It's fine to explain to your client exactly why you are reluctant to reduce your fees, and what that might mean for the client, e.g. 'what I want to make sure is that I do good work for you at a price that is fair to me. I want to make sure I don't feel resentful about doing this work for you, and at that price, I think I would.' Decide how important the deal is to your business. Could it bring in more business as a result, or more referrals?

Choose a time when you're feeling confident – don't phone at 8.50 on a Monday morning expecting a relaxed and jovial haggle.

As client, choose a time when you're feeling confident, and the other person may have time – don't phone at 8.50 on a Monday morning expecting a relaxed and jovial haggle.

How to negotiate

Put yourself in the position of the other party. Is it a must-have or a nice-to-have? If the business is not essential to you, you are automatically in a better bargaining position, and if you can't get it for terms that are satisfactory, you can walk away. Walking away (physically or metaphorically) will show definitively that that is your last word, but it is difficult to come back from that, so be prepared to lose it. A valuable tool here is taking your time. Your seller won't know if you have given up or are still thinking about it. When the ball is in your court, you hold the power.

Negotiating isn't just haggling over price. Negotiations take place more commonly in a situation where two parties to a contract (e.g. a supplier and a buyer) meet to discuss and agree the terms of the contract. There needs to be give and take in order for both parties to feel satisfied, and it is that giving and taking process that forms the substance of the negotiation. You may want more time to deliver, a bigger order or another change in any terms of the contract. Negotiation is often undertaken by lawyers on behalf of their clients, particularly where there are large sums at stake.

Negotiation tips

- Enter negotiations confidently, reminding yourself of what you bring to the party. Be clear about how you benefit from a new deal.
- Be engaging, open about the negotiation process. It is a bit of a game, but don't play unnecessary games, e.g. pretending you have an eager customer round the corner when you don't.
- Have a 'negotiation structure' in your mind – 'I'll go in with this, and if they want to reduce here, then I'm not prepared to negotiate, but if they want to do something there, then I am'.
- Listen carefully to what the other party is saying. Step into their shoes, to see the situation from their point of view.
- If you need time to think, say so, and ask the audience or phone a friend or take whatever advice you feel you need to before you continue.
- Keep a notebook (and possibly a calculator) handy to record details as well as give you time to think.
- Don't appear too keen, or the other party will know they are in a better bargaining position, and don't make concessions too easily.
- As the supplier, remember the alternatives to reducing your price – add in extra services or guarantee speedy delivery, or encourage a bulk buy.
- As the supplier, don't give unnecessary discounts. Other customers may find out and become resentful and it makes you look inconsistent and flaky, not to mention losing you money, perhaps unnecessarily.
- Don't make last-minute concessions. If someone has agreed to buy/sell, don't throw in extras free out of guilt or a desire to console the 'loser'.
- Don't feel guilty about negotiating them down or sticking to your guns. Your guilt is their victory.
- At the end, summarise the decisions you have reached.

> *Remember the alternatives to reducing your price – add in extra services or guarantee speedy delivery, or encourage a bulk buy.*

- If appropriate, shake on it or clink glasses, to reinforce the agreement.
- Produce a written confirmation of the deal you have reached.

CONTRACTS – GET THE RIGHTS IN WRITING

Here we explain exactly what a contract is, why you need one, what to include, and most importantly the implied terms of contracts – what you are automatically agreeing to provide to your customer without even knowing it. A written contract is essential to any business relationship and, contrary to popular belief, quite easy to draft, so don't be put off.

A contract is an agreement, written or spoken, between two or more people or businesses, containing a promise and payment for that promise. A promises to pay B a sum of money in return for B agreeing to supply goods or services.

When is a contract not a contract?

Unless there is something passing from each party to the other, whether goods, services, money or equivalent (the legal term is 'consideration') then there is no contract. So if you say I'll give you my car for free, and then you don't, you are not in breach of contract because there was no payment involved.

One party has to accept the other's offer before the contract is made. If your neighbour offers to buy your bike for £50 and you don't agree, there is no contract, because you haven't accepted the offer.

The parties to the contract need to be intending to create what we call 'contractual relations'. So if you tell your mother you will sell her the chair for £20 and she doesn't pay you, you can't easily take her to court, because there is an assumption that there is no intention to create contractual relations within a family.

Drawing up a contract

When you are in business, you are going to need to get lots of agreements in writing – with your suppliers, clients, employees, associates, landlords and anyone else you do business with. We have set out some nightmare scenarios below which have really happened to people who didn't write it down, and could happen to you.

• Your employee walks out on you after three weeks with no notice at all.

• Your supplier sends you a bill for twice the amount you agreed on the phone.

• Your business partner spends the company's money on a laptop without your permission.

• You fall out with your best friend that you are in business with, because you each misunderstood what the other had meant by the '50:50' agreement made down the pub.

• Your client refuses to pay you for services already provided.

In each of those situations, a written contract would have given the wronged party a document to point to, setting out the disputed obligations. Drafting and negotiating a contract makes the parties to the contract focus on what might happen if things don't go according to plan (and often this upfront thinking means that things do go according to plan). Addressing these issues, and how each of you would react in that situation, goes a long way to stopping these things happening.

Here are some reasons why you should get all contracts in writing:

• It focuses the mind on what might happen.

- It overrides any previous conversations and removes ambiguities.

- It shows the world you are serious about business.

- If there is a legal dispute, you will have something to refer to and rely on.

- They are the accepted and expected ways of doing business.

- The contract is an expression and record of the relationship that you have set up.

There is a myriad of situations where you need a written contract. Some of them will not apply to you – if for example you are a sole trader running a small recruitment business from your home office, you will only need a contract with the clients you place candidates with. But the more complex the business, the more contracts/detail you will need.

Types of contract you may be entering into
- Supply contracts with your suppliers – their terms of business
- Supply contracts with your clients – your terms of business
- Employment contracts with your employees
- Shareholder agreements with your fellow shareholders
- Partnership agreements with your partners
- Services agreements for equipment or premises
- Lease agreements
- Agreements to purchase property
- Agreements relating to the transfer of shares/licences/leases

As a starting point for drawing up your own contract, try to have a look at your competitors' contracts and terms of business. Whether you are drafting a simple contract yourself, or whether the lawyers are involved, you will need to think about the following points. Not all of these will apply to every contract or set of terms of business, and the list is not exhaustive, but it is a good starting point.

Typical contract terms

- Define the parties, including their full names, business names and addresses.

- Define the product or service.

- Define any other terms which you use in the contract.

- Prices – cover everything, so you don't end up making prices up on the phone.

- Obligations, warranties and indemnities.

- Order and delivery procedure – method, cost, communications, timing.

- Payment procedure and penalties for late payment.

- Circumstances for refunds (including deposits).

- Insurance – who pays?

- Notices clause – agreements always refer to the parties' obligations to notify each other of one thing and another, so make sure that the notification procedure is reasonable and realistic and includes email.

- Whole agreement clause – make it clear that this is the final word on the subject for now and supersedes all previous discussions, agreements, representations, etc. Any future amendments to the contract must be in writing and signed by all parties.

- Governing law – for example, 'The Law of England and Wales'.

- Dispute resolution – how will you resolve any disputes that arise?

- Decision-making – business partners, shareholders, etc.

- Termination provisions – what is the exit strategy?

- Exclusions – what do you not want to be liable for?

Don't forget to sign and date the contract. If it is a partnership agreement or other agreement where there may be no consideration passing from one party to another, you will need to have it signed as a deed, which means getting it witnessed as well. Take legal advice to ensure that you are following the correct procedure here, otherwise the whole agreement may be invalid.

One unreasonable exclusion clause can invalidate the whole agreement.

Exclusion clauses (which aim to limit what you can be held responsible for) need to be fair and reasonable. If you are opening an ice rink and try to exclude your liability for all injuries to anyone however caused, or if you open a restaurant and exclude all liability for all your customers getting food-poisoning, then you will find yourself deemed 'unreasonable' by the court. One unreasonable exclusion clause can invalidate the whole agreement.

Your legal obligations and your customers' legal rights

You may have heard of the Sale of Goods Act and the Supply of Goods and Services Act. The purpose of these two pieces of legislation is to ensure that businesses sell products and services that meet minimum standards. As a consumer you will have probably relied on this legislation already – taking things back to the shop when they are faulty or holding back payment for shoddy service. The legislation implies terms into contracts, so even if nothing has been signed, the customer has something to rely on.

Supplying goods

If you are supplying goods to the public, you have the following obligations:

• The goods must be of satisfactory quality.

• The goods must be fit for their purpose.

• The goods must correspond with any description given.

This is basically saying that you must sell what you say you are selling, and it shouldn't fall apart. So when the hem on your new trousers comes down after two days, you are within your rights to take them back to the shop. When you are in business, of course, this means someone else bringing it back to your shop, so it's an extra incentive to have good quality control in place.

In law, it is the supplier, rather than the manufacturer of the goods, who is liable if the goods are faulty. A manufacturer's guarantee will ensure that the supplier gets a replacement or their money back, but take account of any cashflow issues that might arise here – as the supplier you may have to reimburse your customer before the manufacturer reimburses you and liability may greatly exceed the price being paid.

Supplying services

If you are supplying services, you have these corresponding obligations:

• All services you supply must be carried out with reasonable care and skill.

• All services you supply must be carried out within a reasonable time unless agreed otherwise with the customer.

• You must charge a reasonable fee, unless agreed otherwise with the customer.

> **Being a good businesswoman means providing a decent level of service, and most of us don't need the law to tell us that.**

Hopefully, this will come as no surprise to you – you would complain if you received shoddy or very slow service from a business you were using, or if the bill was too high. Being a good businesswoman means providing a decent level of service, and most of us don't need the law to tell us that.

If you fail to meet the requirements imposed by the law, you will effectively be in breach of contract and customers may well be entitled to compensation. In England and Wales, your responsibility to your customers can last for up to six years, depending on the nature of the goods or services (five years from discovery of the problem in Scotland).

But it's not just about bringing your trousers back to the shop. Anyone in business is forced to address the nightmare scenario – damage, injury or even death caused as a result of goods or services supplied by your business.

If anyone incurs damage to their property, of if they are injured or killed as a result of using goods or services provided by you, you may be liable under product liability or public liability law. Talk to a financial and insurance advisor about the policies your business will need to address this, and remember that it is illegal to exclude liability for death or injury caused by your negligence.

Distance selling

If you sell to consumers without seeing them face-to-face (via an Internet shop, for example) there are additional distance-selling rules that you must stick to. Most of them would be included in your terms of business in any event, but the law says that in your communications with customers, you must tell them:

- your business name

- your postal address for payment

- description of the goods or services

- prices and any VAT

- payment arrangements and any late payment penalties

- arrangements for delivery for goods or performance in the case of services

- the right to cancel during the 'cooling-off' period

- who is responsible for postage/delivery of returned goods

- how long prices are valid

- minimum duration of contracts.

Once an order has been placed you must send confirmation to the customer by post, email or fax. You must also make it clear if you intend to substitute unavailable goods with similar items.

You don't need to give the customer all this information upfront, but if you provide it after the service has started, the customer has the right to cancel an agreement for up to seven days after the information has been received. This is the 'cooling-off' period. The purpose of all of this is to protect the vulnerable consumer from the business vultures and sales bullies who put undue pressure on clients. Along the same lines as this, customers who enter contracts lasting more than a year must be given details of how the agreement can be terminated.

checklist

 have a standard contract or written terms of
ss?
 confirm in writing all verbal agreements or changes
ten terms?
 know who you are really making the agreement

 record the registered company number of the
ner or supplier on your agreements?
 always read your suppliers' terms of business,
ing the small, hard-to-read grey print on the back of
ivoices?
ir terms of business clear and unambiguous about
ou will do, when it will be done, how you will be
nd what will happen if there is a dispute?
 claim interest on late payment?
are buying or selling overseas, have you agreed
country's law applies?
ou taken legal advice?

contract

ick to our negotiation scenario right at the beginning
iapter, imagine that you and your friend agree a price
you will buy the chair. Once that is agreed (and even
 is written down), you have a contract, and if you
iat contract (i.e. you don't do what you say you'll do)
other person has a 'remedy' – if you don't give her the
n she gets her money back; if she doesn't pay you, you
hair back.

edies aren't always what the wronged party wants them
f you have paid for some IT support that doesn't
se, the court will not order them to jolly well do it –
ou will get your money back. Forcing a party to a
 to do what they say they were going to do is simply
ticable in some circumstances.

Contracts with other businesses

When you are selling your product business:

- Check who you are doing business v authorised? Do you know if you are organisation or a subsidiary?

- Record the registered number of the it's the only legal identification that

- Check business references – it's a qu precaution to take up testimonials.

- Exporters and importers, think about contract should state which country': dispute.

- If you use an agent or factor abroad w care; it is now more difficult to sack a Directives.

Legal advice

Some of the contracts you will be dealing

Use any legal contacts you may have – you may be surprised at how pleased they can be to have the opportunity to advise a 'real person'.

too complicated to do with (after all, you would be unlik or a house without consulting cases (apart from supply individual customers) the c contract may be getting their you would be wise to level t doing the same. Use any lega have as well as possible service from your Chamber of Comm

surprised at how pleased they can be to h, to advise a 'real person'.

Contract

- Do yc
  busin
- Do ye
  to wr
- Do y
  with
- Do y
  custe
- Do y
  inclu
  thei
- Are
  wha
  paid
- Do
- If yc
  whc
- Hav

Breacl

Goin,
of th
at wh
befor
breac
then
chair
get t

But
to b
mate
inst
con
not

If you are bringing a claim for financial loss resulting from a breach of contract (i.e. you haven't been paid for services or goods supplied, or have paid for them and they haven't been delivered), don't forget to include a claim for interest that has accrued on the sum owing. It's quite difficult to go back later and ask for it when the case is closed. Better still, deal with this eventuality in your contract.

SELLING – HOW TO GET THE CASH COMING IN

There is so much to do and think about when you are setting up your business, it is easy to lose sight of the fact that there is a bottom line. Whatever you tell yourself, and whatever your priorities, you have to bring in money. This is not to say that there aren't a million other reasons for doing it, but making money is an undeniable part of it. Good customer service is an essential part of selling, and we deal with that in Chapter 6.

Once you have a brand and marketing strategy in place, selling your product or service to customers should be like falling off a log.

Once you have a brand and marketing strategy in place, selling your product or service to customers should be like falling off a log. The actual selling process can seem a more frightening prospect than marketing, as the concept implies your personal active participation rather than sitting at home designing adverts and writing copy, but your passion for your business will carry you through. Don't be afraid of sales. You will be surprised at how easily you can talk about what you do and encourage people to buy from you – this could be because instead of feeling half-hearted about selling somebody else's product or service, this is something that you really believe in.

How you sell your product or service will depend to a certain extent on the nature of your business. Customers will inspect products in a shop and take them to a till or place an order; online customers and mail-order customers may make a purchase based on an image or picture; in a restaurant, they are buying something based on a description, but the decision to buy is often made before the menu is seen, when the customer comes through the door. In the service industry, services are mostly purchased by description, or via referrals. Customers may make a decision on the basis of your website, other marketing materials and hearsay, rather than meeting you in person.

What you are selling and where the sale takes place will dictate how much effort you put into the selling process. Your perfect displays in your shop and the evidence of desirable, quality products (together with excellent customer service) may do the selling for you if you are in retail, but a potential customer contacting you with a view to getting some legal advice, or looking into hiring a housekeeper, may listen very politely and then for no apparent reason go and take their business elsewhere. So if you are in the business of supplying a service rather than a product, you will need some special skills to maximise your chances of making a sale.

AIDA
This straightforward AIDA model lists four stages in the marketing and selling process which lead to a sale:

• get the customer's **A**ttention (show her a product, tell her about a product or service)

• stimulate her **I**nterest (show her or tell her about the benefits of the product or service, tell her about a discount or special offer)

• create the **D**esire to buy (show her or tell her why she needs this product or service and what it can do for her)

• explain the **A**ction to be taken ('just sign here…').

When you think about it, this is just a prescriptive form of a procedure you would probably go through quite naturally, starting with the general and moving to the specific, starting from a distance and moving more towards the personal. Imagine strolling into PC World, asking an assistant where the laptops are: he shows you them, tells you about any special offers, points out what will be most appropriate to you personally, and when you have chosen one, he guides you to the paypoint. That is AIDA in action.

Sales calls

When your customer has seen your advert or brochure and picks up the phone to call you, your selling job is more than half done. When you call a customer, on the other hand, you will have a harder job to do. For a start you won't know what you have interrupted, what kind of mood they are in, or whether they have someone with them and have put you on speakerphone, let alone whether your product is of interest to them. Try to follow the communication tips above, and incorporate the AIDA model:

- Enthuse about the service she is enquiring about/ the service you are calling her about –
    'We're offering our customers a fantastic new product'

- Ask open-ended questions to find out as much as you can about your client's needs –
    'So what kind of childcare have you considered so far?'

- Empathise with your customer's situation –
    'Gosh, it really sounds like you have enough on your plate without extra costs to worry about...'

- Tell her about any special offers or discounts –
    'We're offering a 20 per cent discount to the first twenty customers...'

- Tell her what benefits she will gain from it –
    'It will reduce your tax bill considerably'

- Tell her what will happen next/how to place an order –
  'What I'll do is I'll send you an order form…'

- If an agreement is reached, repeat what has been agreed –
  'So I'll send you the form now, and you can post it
  back with your cheque…'

- Make notes of your conversation and keep them with your
  client file, so that next time you make contact, you are
  reminded of your previous conversation –
  'So how was the skiing holiday?'

- Don't take a call if you are in the wrong place to talk – you may
  be wasting your one chance to impress a potential client –
  'Sorry, I've only got a few minutes before I need to be
  out of the door and I'd really like to be able to talk to
  you a bit more about this. Can I call you back
  tomorrow at 9am?'

Extra points when making a sales call

- Do your research, make sure you know who you need to
  speak to.

- Bear in mind that this may not be a good time for them to
  take that call, and be prepared to be brief and call back.

- Introduce yourself quickly, preferably with a common
  connection or interest.

- If it is a bad time, find out when would be a good time to call.

- Say why you're calling: 'I'm calling because I have a special
  offer and thought of you/thought what I do might be of
  interest to you in these ways…'.

- Be interesting – give them some information or share what you've been working on.

- If appropriate, find out as much as you can about what their big issues are by asking open questions, listen carefully to see if you could help.

- Even if it's a no, try to leave your prospective customer with something – whether that's a feeling of a good conversation or a promise to send them some information or call back in a few months (and do that).

Selling online

If you are opening a restaurant or setting up as a therapist or consultant, then online sales are not so relevant (although your website may attract customers to come to you) but for many other businesses, especially product sales and the travel and leisure industry, the internet opens up a multitude of selling channels and (provided you have the production and delivery facilities in place) can turn a cottage industry into an international success, or at least a bigger success than it would otherwise be. The internet auction site ebay provides an income to thousands of so-called 'ebay entrepreneurs' and ebay even has it's own Small Business Advisor. It is estimated that 70,000 people in the UK make a living by selling through ebay.

CASE STUDY

Denice Purdie used the ebay site to turn her hobby of making soap into a business in August after her husband was injured in a car crash and had to leave the Royal Navy. Purdie's Scottish Soap Company – based at her remote home in Colintraive on the west coast of Scotland – sells soaps, shampoos, bubble bath, and essential oils to customers all over Britain. 'My husband retired from the military after a car accident that broke two bones in his neck. We have four children and it would have been a nightmare to move, especially with everything else that was happening, but we had to think quickly, as we were running out of money fast,' she said. 'I was already making soap as a hobby and selling it at farmer's markets, and my husband had the idea that we could do that together – I could do the soap making and legwork and he could do the admin and paperwork.' Their company has greatly exceeded their expectations and now sells to ebay customers all over the world, as well as to 62 shops in the UK. Denice added: 'Even though we started it under difficult circumstances, it's been a great experience. I must say that running a company is a doddle compared to looking after four kids – you get perks and a tea break ... unlike most mothers!'

> *Running a company is a doddle compared to looking after four kids – you get perks and a tea break ... unlike most mothers!*

Setting up an online business from scratch, or as an add-on to an existing retail business, is not difficult – there are plenty of off-the-shelf products to help you do that, and most website designers will have done something similar for customers in the past.

Advantages of selling online
- Access to more customers 24 hours a day.
- Fewer overheads, no expensive premises, saving you money.
- FAQ pages can resolve any queries customers may have before they buy, saving you time.
- Customer orders and payments can be processed automatically and you don't have to work 'traditional' hours.

Selling in shops and to shops (retail)
If you are opening a shop, there are a number of techniques you can use to entice and retain customers including promotions, discounts and tactical layout. If on the other hand you want to get retailers to stock your product, you will need to do some preparation before you approach the shop owner. He or she will want to know how they will benefit from

stocking your product, how your product differs from what they already offer, how your product sells, what help you can offer with selling it (and therefore attracting customers into their shop), how it fits with their range, and how quickly you can help them restock.

Denice Purdie, who we met above as an Ebay entrepreneur, also sells her soaps to shops. She says:

There is no substitute for the personal approach. I visit likely-looking shops in person, taking along a free sample of soap and some literature about all of our products. Most shops are very friendly and interested, I think because I'm the very opposite of a pushy salesman. We have a policy of no minimum orders which has worked really well for us. We have a large and growing range, but recognise that not all products will sell in all shops, so I'm flexible about allowing free trials, and that open, helpful and honest approach seems to work very well.

IMPORTING GOODS INTO THE UK

There are two very good reasons why businesses import goods:

• to obtain materials or goods that aren't available in the UK

• to obtain goods or materials from another country where they cost less than in the UK.

As you can imagine, the process is more complicated than where both parties are in the same country, so there are a number of extra practicalities to consider as well as additional legal issues. When drawing up contracts with your overseas suppliers, you will need to pay special attention to payment methods, exchange rates, transport, timing, duty, storage and insurance. You'll also have to investigate whether you'll need a licence from the Department of Trade and Industry (DTI) to import goods.

The total cost of importation will include packing, transport, storage, insurance and customs duty. Bear in mind how much exchange rates fluctuate as this can have a huge impact on your forecasts, costs and profits. Also you need to consider which method of payment you're going to use – for instance, will your bank charge you for making a foreign currency payment? Do you have to arrange special credit facilities?

Importing directly for the first time can be daunting. So it's important that you devote time to finding exactly the right overseas supplier for your requirements.

One solution is to import indirectly, meaning that you use a third party to import the goods for you and you buy the goods from them. Although this may make things simpler in that you don't have to research the end supplier, you won't have total control of the process, which can be frustrating for some business owners.

If you're going to import directly, look for a supplier with a proven track record of supplying goods to the UK, who has knowledge of English and an understanding of the legal implications of dealing with a UK business. You may be able to find suppliers through your personal contacts – otherwise try your trade association, which could also help you with the contractual side of things, or go on your own fact-finding mission. Importing directly means that you have personal contact with the overseas suppliers. It's potentially more profitable but means that you are vulnerable to distance/language problems, exchange-rate fluctuations and the possibility of additional travel, costs and hassle.

CASE STUDY

Josu Shephard, founder of Jakabel, said:

> *As I passed through an airport in Malaysia on the way to Barbados on holiday, I bought a product that I had never seen before – a 'Swimsafe' floatsuit with a neck ring which stops children turning*

over in the water. I was so impressed with it (as was my daughter) that I did some research and approached the manufacturer. He agreed to give me sole distribution rights in the UK, and Jakabel (a combination of my children's names) was born.

Top tips for importing goods into the UK

- Make sure you know who your customer is, and that they really exist (if Aunty Margaret likes your Burmese handbag that's not enough – the shipping costs will cripple you if you haven't got thousands of hungry consumers ready to pay up).

> *Make sure you know who your customer is, if Aunty Margaret likes your Burmese handbag that's not enough.*

- Talk to traders who are already in the business – they're generally a friendly lot.
- Research the way business is done in your supplier's country. You can find a lot of useful information on the internet.
- Research the firms you intend to do business with by asking for trade references.
- Visit and inspect the companies you are importing from at least three times a year, and insist on tight quality and ethical control.

FROM PRICING TO SALE – ARE YOU READY?

In this chapter you have:

- ☐ Learnt about yourself and your relationship with money
- ☐ Decided where in the market will you price yourself and why
- ☐ Learnt when and how to negotiate
- ☐ Understood your contractual obligations to customers
- ☐ Developed draft contract terms and conditions
- ☐ Developed a sales strategy

5

BRANDING, MARKETING AND PR

It is easy to assume that as soon as you have opened your doors for business, customers will be falling over themselves to take advantage of all the wonderful things you have to offer. Even the most commercially minded entrepreneur can be guilty of indulging this fantasy. You may well feel that you deserve a medal (and a brief rest on your laurels) at this point after all the planning, not to mention getting through four whole chapters of this book. Getting business in is a fundamental yet consistently underestimated element of business ownership. Whole books are written about it. You can do a degree in it. It's called marketing and it's vital.

Any bank, investor or prospective business partner will want to know how you are planning to brand, publicise and market your business. Investors know from experience that these activities are central to the survival of small businesses. If you haven't come from a marketing background, you may have spent your working life under the impression it is a glamorous and rather airy-fairy pursuit, performed by double-barrelled debutantes before they get married. In fact, it's an art, a science, and a challenge which you now have to grasp with both hands. If, on the other hand, you have come from that background, then you'll know the basics, but you will find that marketing yourself and your own business rather than someone else's is an entirely different ball game.

> *You will find that marketing yourself and your own business rather than someone else's is an entirely different ball game.*

This chapter tells you what you need to know about branding, marketing and PR, and shows you how to apply the principles to your business.

WHAT IS BRANDING, MARKETING AND PR ALL ABOUT?

It's about making sure that your target customers hear great things about you. Constantly. You need to reach out to them, show them how passionate and capable you are and persuade them to buy from you. You may need to educate them first, about what you do, and why they need it.

If you are not a natural extrovert, the idea of going out and asking for business can be quite terrifying. What if they all run away at the sight of you coming? Remember the man from the satellite TV company accosting shoppers in the supermarket and brandishing clipboards and leaflets to get your attention. His insincerity and desperation, and your 'no thanks, I'm in a hurry', come to mind. Don't worry, there's more to it than that.

Think back to your experiences in employment situations. Were you the sort of person who thought the company website could be more easily navigable, whose ideas for attracting new customers were smiled at but never implemented, who secretly despaired at the unimaginative, uncommunicative brains at the heart of the business? Women are by their nature highly creative, communicative and imaginative.

And that is what branding, marketing and PR are all about:

- analysing the market (covered earlier in this book – market research)

- choosing, designing and communicating your unique business image

- letting your customers know about the great new things you are bringing to the market

• becoming and remaining your customers' first choice.

So forget the satellite TV salesman – this aspect of running a business is where women are at a real advantage. The fact that so many women work in the design and communications businesses just goes to show how look and feel and getting the message across are something we do instinctively well.

> *Look and feel and getting the message across are something we do instinctively well.*

BRANDING

'An inspiring belief backed by great capability breeds confidence – the sexiest thing a brand can have' (Helen Edwards and Derek Day in *Creating Passionbrands*[vi]).

Your brand as a small business relies heavily on who you are. More than just a logo or distinctive typeface, it is the sum total of what you are, what you stand for, what you look like, what you believe in, what you offer and how you do business. In their book *Creating Passionbrands*, Day and Edwards show how passion-driven brands, like Innocent and Google, inspire loyalty (and sales) for the product in customers and employees. You might feel disadvantaged in comparison to big multinationals with massive marketing budgets but actually what they would die for is the passion and personality that you as a small business have in bucketloads.

> *You might feel disadvantaged in comparison to big multinationals with massive marketing budgets, but actually what they would die for is the passion and personality that you as a small business have in bucketloads.*

It can be tempting to rush into business imagining that you are going to work on branding and marketing later 'when I've got time', but you can bet your bottom euro that as soon as your business is up and running, spare time is not something you will have much of. So it's worth focusing on the different elements that comprise your brand before you launch your business, to make sure that your passion and message get through to the outside world as effectively as possible. Every day we are faced with hundreds of marketing messages and now make choices and reject opportunities without even realising we are doing it. Can you explain why you buy Kelloggs Rice Krispies over the Sainsbury's equivalent? What is driving these decisions? The power of the brand.

The brand logo

In Chapter 2 you summarised in a sentence what your business was about, and focused on your unique selling points. When you don't have the opportunity to put this message across in person, you will be relying on something else to do it for you – your logo. Your logo communicates what your business is about, whether through the label on your product, the colour of your company notepaper or the design on your delivery van.

Defining the brand logo is an important process for every business owner, not least because it focuses your mind on what the business is all about, and makes you sum it up in an image, a colour, a word, a picture – a condensed symbol that will become the way you are recognised in the public domain.

You only need to look around your home or up and down the high street to see how far brands are entrenched in our minds – everything from the memorable lettering on a shop sign to a tiny emblem on a product. Examples of popular recognisable logos are the McDonald's golden arches, the Nike tick, the Mercedes three-pointed star and Captain Birds Eye's smiling bearded face.

Brands are desirable to those who value their symbolism – teenagers require the currently trendy trainers because the brand conveys a message – it says 'I'm in that gang'. Being part of a gang is an identity thing. It gives the member security and the feeling of support and belonging to a community. And, translating that into value, it gives the business the authority to charge more for membership.

How are you going to make your brand work like that? You may not be producing sportswear for teenagers, but the same principle applies. You want your clients to want to be associated with you, you want them to join your club, wear your badge. So make it a good badge.

> *You want your clients to want to be associated with you, you want them to join your club, wear your badge.*

How to choose and create a logo

A logo is not compulsory, but it is a useful tool in creating instant recognition around your brand. If you have a logo in mind, test it on your friends and listen to their advice – as with your choice of name, what works for you might not work for others, and it is crucial that any symbol will appeal to and be understood by your target customer. It's time to ask those questions again. Who are your target customers? What are their occupations, preoccupations, aspirations, lifestyles, shopping habits? Look around at how different brands, logos and straplines are clearly directed at different audiences. In what way will your logo attract your ideal customer?

There are a thousand different ways to produce a logo, and you may have a good idea already of how you want yours to look. Your may want to use your business name, produced in a way that is distinctive to your customers, or it may include a symbol and/or a strapline.

Bear in mind that a logo which is separate from your business name will take up more space on your business card and adverts. But if you are manufacturing a product and have a label to fill with your design, and the customer's eye to catch as they scan a whole shelf of competing items, you can go for something bigger and braver, as in Figure 3.

Figure 3: Innocent logo

Combining a logo with and making it part of your business name can be very effective, as in Figure 4.

announce it!

Figure 4: Announce it logo

If you are going to advertise in black and white (and most of us do at some point), having some solid colour (which will convert to solid grey) or white type on a coloured background will all help you stand out. Don't depend exclusively on any distinctive colours for your brand recognition early on, for this same reason.

> **Lucy**: I used to have my business name in pink and blue – useless in black-and-white adverts. Talking to a designer was the best thing I did. The new big 'G' is just as effective in black-and-white advertising (see Figure 5). When I took on a business partner, we agreed to change the background colour from pink to blue, but as long as the essence stays the same, I think you can get away with changes like that. I also have different forms of the logo to use in different media.

Figure 5: Gina's Nannies logo

> **Bella**: My logo is a 'grounded spiral' incorporating the word 'Enspiral', which captures the essence of what my business is about for me. The spiral represents how we revisit the same issues in our life from different angles, and is a calm and elegant shape, with a flourish in the tail. On my website it is a deep purple, but it also prints fine in black and white.

Figure 6: Enspiral logo

It sounds obvious, but do check that the logo is not being used elsewhere by someone else. You don't want to waste time and money on or worse still, go to market with a logo that someone else is already using. You may be sued for passing off or infringement of a trade mark.

When working on your logo and considering your audience and the practical aspects of design, don't forget who you are, what you stand for, what you believe in, and make sure that all that comes across. Your brand is your opportunity to revel in your uniqueness, to embrace the fact that you are different. It is a chance to show people what you do best, and leave them in no doubt that you are what they need.

> *Your brand is your opportunity to revel in your uniqueness, to embrace the fact that you are different.*

Top tips for your logo
- Keep it simple, clear and distinctive.
- Differentiate yourself from other businesses in your sector.
- Make it suitable for colour and black-and-white production.
- Make it suitable for production in different media (shop banner, advert in magazine, flyer, label).
- Make it suitable for different size adverts (too much detail will be lost on a small advert).

- Make sure it is consistent across all your fields of activity, and backed up by your appearance and values.
- Check it is not easily confused with any other logo.
- Make sure it is suitable for your target customers.
- Believe in it, and make sure your employees believe in it.
- Communicate it, using marketing techniques (see next section).
- Review it – rebranding can revitalise your business (but not too often).
- Put your logo everywhere, tattoo it onto your boyfriend's thighs (or your imaginary boyfriend if you are married).

Straplines and slogans

Your strapline is your chance to elaborate on your brand name and logo, using key words or a phrase or slogan that expresses your values and the essence of your business.

Your strapline should appear on your promotional material, adverts, business cards and stationery, and perhaps even your email signature. Seeing it, reading it, writing it, saying it, will all combine to help you believe in how you are making a difference, and what you have to offer.

Don't necessarily pick the first thing that comes into your head. It is tempting to just say what you do: 'portrait artist', 'childcare agency', 'organic food supplies', 'designer', but that can be a bit bland? If you can't think beyond that straight description, you may need to sit down with someone who believes in you and can come up with something more glowing and positive. You may need to do some of the visualisation we discussed in Chapter 1 – act 'as if': project yourself into your successful business self, and let your imagination run riot. Don't reject out of hand a strapline that appears to elevate you to a level you feel is undeserved, but remember that if you are going to make a promise, you need to deliver on it. You may find that delivering on it comes naturally, once you have had the bravery to come out and say it.

CASE STUDY

Antonia Rolls, portrait artist and painter from Sussex, attended a business strategy course and after some uncomfortable experimentation, came up with her strapline 'Artist Extraordinaire'.

I was encouraged to think out of a tiny narrow box by a fellow member of my business group (Cate Newnes Smith of Mountain Top). The first step, giving myself the permission to be Excellent, was utterly alien. Calling myself 'Artist Extraordinaire' meant that I escaped from the cramped and restrictive box called 'I can't do that'. The Artist Extraordinaire title means: a) I have made a statement of intent to myself, b) I had better live up to it, c) everyone automatically believes it and expects results. All of which, actually, is not difficult. It has been a release to set this standard. And no one has ever accused me of boasting; instead they are either amused and/or impressed. I believe the statement now, and so do they. Hooraaaay! And it is on absolutely all my business dealings. Shortly after rebranding myself, I began to get more and more commissions, I was travelling to America to see clients, getting featured in women's magazines, it was a roller coaster...

> **Giving myself the permission to be Excellent, was utterly alien.**

Examples of straplines and slogans

After the name
Tesco – Every little helps
Coke – The real thing
McDonald's – I'm lovin' it
Sainsbury's – Try something new today

Before the name
Your M&S
More reasons to shop at Morrisons (note the rhyme)
It's got to be Gordons
Beanz Meanz Heinz
The future's bright. The future's Orange

The words leading up to the brand name create a sense of anticipation and positive association

Around the name
No FT, no comment
It's a Skoda. Honest

Asking a question
Harmony: Does she or doesn't she?
The independent newspaper: It is. Are you?

Brave use of slogans
Virgin Atlantic: 'Hello Gorgeous'
Audi: Vorsprung Durch Technik
Remington: I liked it so much I bought the company
L'Oréal: Because I'm worth it (a shocking and naughty concept to the English)
Wonderbra: 'Hello boys'

Humour (usually in slogans relating to alcohol and tobacco)
Guinness Is good for you
Happiness is a cigar called Hamlet
Heineken refreshes the parts other beers cannot reach
Carlsberg. Probably the best lager in the world
I bet he drinks Carling Black Label
Gillette, the best a man can get

Call to action
Amex: Don't leave home without it.
Have a break, have a Kit Kat

Using an image
An image can be strongly associated with your product and combined with a call to action:

Give the dog a phone (Churchill Insurance)
Put a tiger in your tank (Esso)

Your appearance is part of your brand

From now on, you are on duty all the time. You are your business, and every impression you create reflects not only on you but also on your business. Many British women are so busy with their multiple responsibilities that they don't spend much time on their appearance and there can be a social taboo about being seen to care about what you look like. So at this point, we would like to give you permission to spend some time really thinking about what impression your appearance is creating.

Take a look at yourself in the mirror, exactly as you are now (yes really, you can) and give some thought to the questions below,

Appearance quiz
• How do you feel about the way you look?
• How do you think other people see you?
• What do you think your appearance says about you?
• Is that the message you want to give?
• If not, what changes would you like to make?
• Do you have any role models whose appearance and demeanour you admire?

What messages did you get in your past about how you looked, and how did you react? Most of us carry with us the messages we received as children or teenagers about the way we looked, and being aware of those is an important first step.

Looking good does not come easily or naturally to everyone. For a start, there are more important things in life than clothes, aren't there? If your skill set is website design or accountancy, you won't necessarily know what length of trousers is fashionable this year, nor may you care that much. But picture the following scene for a moment.

If your skill set is website design or accountancy, you won't necessarily know what length of trousers is fashionable this year, nor may you care that much.

There you are, dashing into the playground in your

tracksuit, pack-a-mac and unbrushed hair, just after the lesson bell, shouting at your three dishevelled children trailing miserably behind you. Stressed and embarrassed, you ignore smiles and glances from other parents, push your children inside the school gates and run home to take refuge in your office, your mobile clamped to your ear. What impression does this create: badly organised mother, possibly not implementing the ideal parenting skills, no concern for her appearance, rude and offhand, stressed, out of control…?

> *Lucy: Well, that was me not so long ago. I grew up with smart parents who despaired at my grunginess, and therefore unwittingly encouraged it. Even as an adult, I used to go round with no make-up, wearing jeans and baggy sweatshirts, hair tied up in a scrunchie. Only in the last year, as I became closer to 40 than 35, did I force myself to look in the mirror at not only my clothes and hair, but the overall impression I was creating – that I had no control, no time for anyone, not even my children or myself. I was the person who when told 'that top you're wearing is lovely' would say 'It only cost me £2 in Primark' instead of just saying 'thank you'. I had always had friends who enjoyed shopping for clothes and shoes and 'got their hair done' but for some reason I didn't feel that I deserved that. Deep down I felt that it was somehow morally irresponsible to spend hundreds of pounds on clothes when there were people starving in Africa. Meeting Stephanie Upton-Prowse through Wimbledon Women in Business changed my attitude to clothes. Now I think – you're going to buy clothes, so why not buy clothes that suit you?*

Stephanie Upton Prowse of Style Studio says:

> *I have always found it amazing the number of professional businesswomen I meet whose image does not convey their success. One of my clients is the HR director of a large company and it was hard to imagine her in that role. She was in colours that were too bright for her colouring, wore no make-up, her style was wrong for her shape and her clothes made her look much bigger than she actually was. I was so distracted by this that it took a lot of convincing that she was a high-flyer. How many other people had she failed to convince? I get my business clients to work through what their image needs to say about them.*

Stephanie's view is that make-up is essential for a professional image. Wearing no make-up can send out the signal that you are less capable than you are.

Stephanie told us how so many of her female clients thought that the 'black suit' was an essential (often only) part of their business wardrobe. Black has always been the rather dull uniform of corporate life, where blending in is expected, but when you're in business for yourself, blending in is the last thing you want to be doing.

You want your image to support your brand. You don't need to spend huge amounts on designer clothing – a well-selected bargain, a great pair of shoes or a good-looking handbag can transform your appearance. But pay attention to the details – your smart look can be totally ruined by bird's-nest hair and dirty nails. If you're at a meeting or giving a talk, you can be sure that your audience will check you out gradually from head to toe and notice details (albeit subtly or subconsciously) just as you do to them. Your clients will see your appearance as a reflection of the standards you bring to working with them.

> *Your smart look can be totally ruined by bird's-nest hair and dirty nails.*

It is worth consulting a style expert to guide you to put together a style that makes you feel comfortable and professional, expresses who you are, and makes you a strong part of your business' image. Style consultant **Carol Goodsman** of Alice Carroll works with women entrepreneurs and others to help give them the means and confidence to present their best possible image. Here are her top tips:

• The image you present will promote your brand most effectively if it shows the real you at your best. Consider the style of clothing and accessories with which you feel most comfortable: if you are at home in frills and floaty fabrics, a classic suit may be too severe for you; if you suit dressed-down styles and natural textures, don't feel you have to wear bold, dressy styles in order to make a statement. You will create the right impression if you work with your natural style, from your clothing right through to your accessories and hairstyle.

• Using colour to enhance your complexion will give you a younger, healthier look that will allow your confidence to shine. Look at colours against your skin and reject those that seem to overpower you or are too insipid for your colouring. Colour is also among the most effective ways of balancing your figure: if you carry weight on the top half of your body, for example, wear darker-coloured tops to play this down and create an overall impression of balance.

• It is important also to take into account the lines of your body. Look at your limbs in a mirror to decide whether they have a generally curved or straight look. This is dependent on your frame and not your weight. Reflect the curved or straight lines of your body in everything you wear to achieve the most flattering effect. Details are important and this rule should be followed from the general cut of your clothing to the shapes of jewellery and even the toes and heels of your shoes.

MARKETING

Marketing is all about getting your brand and your business into the public domain. When we say public domain we mean everything and everywhere that is not your own home. The more awareness there is about your business, the more likely you are to achieve sales. Through marketing you can:

• raise awareness of your business

• present your business in the best possible light, as you want it to be seen

• create a need and desire for your product or service.

The kind of marketing techniques that suit you will depend

very much on the kind of person you are. There aren't many women or men who possess the self-esteem to stand on a soapbox and sing their own praises. For most of us, the idea of putting ourselves in the spotlight is painful and unnatural, which means that the people who do it have learnt it and you can too.

How do you feel about promoting yourself?

- Are you frightened of being described as a 'show-off' or can't you wait?
- Did you feel proud or embarrassed if your work was displayed at school?
- In employment, did you ever have your ideas featured or promoted in the workplace – how did that make you feel?
- Did you feel a sense of satisfaction when praised or thanked by a boss or a client or customer and/or do you blush down to your toes?
- How does the idea of people talking about you make you feel?

Showing off is something most of us were consistently discouraged from in our schooldays. The British sense of reserve often applauds the acquiescent, diligent good girl over the more extrovert drama-queen. In business, showing off isn't showing off anymore, it's marketing. There are a whole host of different ways you can market your business without literally shouting from the rooftops.

> *In business, showing off isn't showing off anymore, it's marketing.*

Whatever tactics you employ, you can't get away from the fact that marketing is a continuous activity. Every time you go out, you will need to be looking and playing the part, carrying your business cards, ready to talk to any potential customer that you might end up standing next to at the bus stop. Your passion for your new business will drive this for you, and you won't even realise you're doing it.

Your marketing/PR shelf

To give marketing and PR the status they deserve, keep a shelf in your office devoted exclusively to them. On your marketing shelf you should keep:

- press cuttings relating to your business (useful for newsletters)

- publications relating to your business

- publications you have advertised in or had editorial published in

- a file of correspondence relating to marketing activities

- a file of contact numbers of newspaper and magazine editors, etc., who will be useful to your campaign

- a list of proposed marketing projects and new target markets.

Websites and email

A web presence is a vital tool in promoting your business. You can choose to create anything from one page to an all-singing-all-dancing website with online trading. A lot of women feel 'technologically challenged' and don't make the most of what's on offer. So how do you go about setting up a website?

Your first step is to register your domain name. Registering your domain name is like buying a permanent space in a car park. You are reserving a 'plot' on which you can build your website on at a later date. You will then park your named plot on a server belonging to the 'host' of your website. You can buy and register a name, build a site and have it hosted all by the same people, or you can shop around and have different organisations perform all those tasks separately.

Domain names

A domain name is a unique address that identifies your website, e.g. enspiral.co.uk. The ending of a domain name tells you something about the organisation that owns it, and these are the most common business-related endings:

- .co.uk is used for UK commercial enterprises (each country, except the US, has its own extension(.co.fr for France, .co.de for Germany, etc.)

- .com is usually an international or US website (as there is no .us extension in use)

- .org.uk or .org are used for non-commercial organisations

- .biz, .info, .tv and .me are available for commercial, information, broadcast and personal websites, respectively.

Domain names are sold through registration agents and prices and terms and conditions vary. Make sure you understand all the costs. Beware of any tie-ins – you may want your domain name to move with you to a different agent, if, for example you want to use another company's web hosting and web design services (see below). Sometimes, agents (like ticket touts) buy up names they think will be popular and sell them at a profit.

Bella: When I was looking to buy a domain name, my original idea, inspiral.co.uk, had already gone but 'enspiral' was still available and although it wasn't what I had originally planned, I liked it and bought the domain name enspiral.co.uk straightaway. The downside of the name is that it does get mixed up with inspiral.co.uk. Worse still, I found out recently that inspiral.com is a site selling female condoms! It looks like a temporary site, so who knows what it could be advertising next? If my business was heavily dependent on internet traffic, I would consider changing my name to avoid the confusion that arises, but it doesn't really affect me, so I'm keeping it.

Once you have your domain name, the next step is to find someone who can design and host your site for you.

Once you have your domain name, the next step is to find someone who can design and host your site for you.

Website design and hosting
One option is to buy a standard design site from a company that will provide you with the basic pages and background and allow you to add your own text, logos and pictures. Another usually more expensive option, is to have your site designed from scratch. Don't do it yourself unless you have done it before. It will take your precious time away from what you are good at. Beware of cutting corners at the outset and producing a disappointing site that will put potential customers off without you ever even knowing.

Top tips for choosing your website designer
- Find out what experience he/she has had of designing sites and look at previous work, including their own website.
- Find out what knowledge and experience he/she has of getting your site the highest search engine rating possible.
- Get a clear idea of their fee structure, e.g. how many updates will they do for free, is the email set up included, are there any charges if you want to move provider?
- Find out what happens if you don't like what they come up with.
- Can you make simple changes yourself?

Top tips for a good websites
- Make sure the look, feel and content reflect the brand and image that you want your business to portray.
- Keep it simple and easy to navigate and keep a 'Contact Us' link on every page.
- If you are selling online, make the route from home page to checkout as simple and straightforward as possible, and provide information (and reassurance for nervous buyers) along the way.
- Try to find a way of getting details from your visitors for future marketing (you can do this by asking for name and email address on the Contact Us page).

- Include client testimonials if you can (with permission).
- Consider paying for hits on Google and other search engines. Search the internet and see where you come up within the list of hits.

Email

You can set up one or more email addresses linked to your domain name, so as a small company you can appear bigger than you are by having info@newcompany.co.uk, sales@newcompany.co.uk, jane@newcompany.co.uk, etc., all of which can be combined to arrive at one email account on your business computer. One warning against having that catch-all email address is that it can make you more of a spam target. So if you find you are suddenly getting hundreds of spam emails, undoing your catch-all might be the key. As part of your email settings, you can also usually set up how your address appears to other people in their inbox, e.g. whether it displays your personal name, company name, position in company, and so on.

Ideas for promoting your business

Advertising

What do your clients read? Where does the competition advertise? Think about advertising in newspapers, magazines, national and local directories such as Yellow Pages and yell.com. Other possibilities are posters pinned to noticeboards where your customers work, play or study. You can also advertise your business on the web, not only on your own website but also on other websites commonly used by your customers. Internet advertising programmes like Google Adwords offer opportunities to move further up the pecking order, but you will need specialist advice on this if you want to make the most of it.

Tips for writing an advertisement

- Use an attention-grabbing headline – ask a question/offer a discount.

- Make it personal – think about what information your customer wants to hear.
- Make your design clear and uncluttered.
- Don't over-promise and risk disappointing the customer.
- Remember that businesses have a duty to ensure their advertisements are legal, decent, honest and truthful.
- Make sure your contact details are visible and accurate.

Email marketing

Keep a client database and email address list (but take into account Data Protection legislation); send out client newsletters regularly and you might find you actually get thanked for them, whereas all the time you are just trying to keep your business literally in their line of vision (although remember that once you start a newsletter you have to keep doing it). Offer recipients an easy way to come off your mailing list.

CASE STUDY

PR Consultant **Caroline Lashley** set up the Editor's Office, a virtual press office for solo entrepreneurs and small and medium-sized businesses. She has a wealth of media and journalism training and decided to put that to good use in her new business. She publishes two monthly e-zines, *Away From My Desk* and *Sister Business UK*, aimed at black and minority ethnic entrepreneurs. They are useful, lively and entertaining resources for small business owners to receive, and include useful information on forthcoming events, and interesting features, on business book reviews. She says, 'It does take time to set up an e-zine or newsletter, but once it's set up, keep it fresh and interesting – especially with good content. It keeps me highly visible in the eyes of my potential customers, and they get to trust me and call me for advice over time. It's some of the advice I'd give to clients, so yes, I'm taking some of my own medicine, and putting information out there to keep my phone ringing.'

Direct marketing

Consider direct mail and leaflet drops. Not all businesses are suited to leaflet drops – the more exclusive your clientele, the less likely you will be to be posting scraps of paper through their doors. If you decide to go down the direct mail route, you can buy customised mailing lists from legitimate organisations.

Promote new things on offer

Review your product/service regularly – what can you offer that is new and interesting/up to the minute/topical to show you are on the ball? You need to communicate all these things to your clients or they won't know about them, and regular communication will put your business back in their minds. Try to be the last person who offered them what you provide.

> **Review your product/service regularly – what can you offer that is new and interesting to show you are on the ball?**

Developing your personal contacts

Join a business network. Go to conferences and follow up on the contacts you make there. Tell all your friends what you are doing, as well as your doctor, dentist, builder and butcher, and you will be amazed at the business that generates – they will think of you first next time one of their clients mentions they need what you offer; join an association relevant to your profession and include their accreditation on your marketing material. There is more information about networking later on in this chapter.

Clever use of client testimonials

Ask all of your satisfied clients to produce a testimonial for you. Include these on your website and on your promotional material. Always obtain your customers' permission before using testimonials, and only use really good ones. A comment like 'It was a pleasure dealing with you' isn't really enough, but 'You are by far the best designer we have used for any of our hotels' is more like it. If you get a really brilliant one, it will do your advertising for you. Put it on the front page of your website – on its own.

Brochures

Put your brochures in your clients' places of work, and if you have the contacts, on their intranets. Send all your marketing materials out to your prospective clients' places of work – they may even agree to advertise your service on their intranet, if you can give them a good enough reason.

> **Lucy**: I was two years into my business before I had the brainwave of targeting law firms with my literature. 'Hello, I used to work with you and now I run a nanny agency' opened the door to a flood of new business. So keep in with your old colleagues – they could become very useful.

Sponsoring events, raffle prizes, competitions

Set up an award for .... of the year and publicise it. Sponsor a school prize or community venture, launch a competition relevant to your business area.

Speak at conferences

Find out what is going on that is appropriate to your business and contact the organisers well in advance – often up to a year, if you want to be considered as a speaker. The next best thing to speaking is attending, and making friends with the movers and shakers. Get your voice heard, even if you just make an interesting comment during a workshop, and see how people come up to you afterwards – you are suddenly someone people want to talk to. Wear bright colours so people can pick you out in the crowd. Dress to impress.

Explore and build media contacts

Are any of your school friends working in TV? Anyone else you know as a 'friend of a friend'? Get onto Friends Reunited and find out. Make sure everyone knows what you can offer, what you are an expert on and how keen you are to take part. The more contacts you can develop in the media, the more chance you will have of becoming their first port of call when they need industry comment.

Are any of your school friends working in TV? Get onto Friends Reunited and find out.

Use existing communities

Can you pinpoint where your customers are? Is there a place they all go to? Is there something that unites them? This works very well on the internet, where you can advertise your business on the sites your customers are likely to visit, but it can work in society in general as well.

Karen Mattison and Emma Stewart set up Women Like Us to satisfy the need employers had for staff and harness the energy and brains of women whose children were at school and who needed something else in their lives.

In our role as freelance business development consultants, we saw that businesses looking for people on a part-time or temporary basis weren't using recruitment agencies. From our experiences as playground mums we could see the solution very clearly — tell the women about the opportunities, not through advertising but through their existing community — the school.

By paying a school rep a nominal monthly fee to communicate with the parents through the bookbags, we have avoided the need to spend any money at all on marketing. The local PR followed on as we were a media novelty, and cost nothing. The really great thing is, when we analyse the figures, 45 per cent of our business comes through the school rep, and another 35 per cent comes through word of mouth — don't underestimate the chatter factor (or in this case the level of need). Your customers should be doing your marketing for you!

> **Don't underestimate the chatter. Your customers should be doing your marketing for you!**

Build links with other businesses

Have you thought about whether the service you offer could be offered as a package with the service offered by another business? Could you be working on a number of joint ventures as well as your own business? If you open a nursery, could you hold children's parties in there at the weekend, using your favourite party organiser? If you are a massage therapist, could you go into partnership with a make-up artist or stylist to provide pampering days for women (and men)? Weddings

> **Weddings organisers always need cake-makers and florists.**

organisers always need cake-makers and florists.

CASE STUDY *Jo Haines of Cake Magic makes wedding and christening cakes and found that the networking possibilities were endless: 'At each wedding I cater for, I meet the wedding organiser, who puts me on her list of contacts, the florist who puts me on hers, and we all refer to each others business. Once this has happened a few times, I am so busy I can't take on any more work.'*

PUBLIC RELATIONS

PR is closely linked with but different from marketing. It means using the media to get yourself interviewed, written about and talked about. If you get it right, in addition to impressing your friends and clients, it means that your intended message reaches prospective customers – for free.

Do your research

- Find out what your clients and customers read, and find out the contact details of the editors of those publications.

- Find out whether there might be an opportunity to contact the editor specialising in a particular area for the publication, who might be looking for an expert or spokesperson on that area (this is you).

- Think of publicity opportunities that might be interesting stories – your starting up, your taking on staff, expanding your business, producing a new product, your background story or some interesting triumph or setback.

- Are there any national weeks devoted to your area of business which might give rise to an opportunity?

- Is there a particularly topical issue that your product or service relates to? When it comes up in the news, be ready to approach editors with your ideas.

- Have photos ready to send out to accompany any written piece.

Then think big

Cultivate and build on relationships with the media people you meet. Make a note in your diary to keep in touch with useful contacts on a regular basis. Consider yourself an expert industry commentator and it is more likely to happen. Act 'as if'. Be committed to being visible.

Target press and media contacts with a press release whenever you have something newsworthy to report. Getting mentioned in an article or on a radio programme brings instant credibility, not to mention free advertising for your business. Target yourself carefully – a national magazine may reach more clients than a local paper, but if your business is local, as opposed to an internet business, that won't help you much. Remember that 'newsworthy' for *The Times* is going to be a more exacting requirement than it will be for the Acacia Avenue Parish circular. For maximum appeal, the media often cover things from a personal angle, so make sure that you are comfortable with that. However brilliantly you write, and whatever fascinating stuff you have got to say, they will be looking for a hook to hang it on. They also might like to get something other than a feature out of it, such as discounts for their readers.

Examples of hooks and incentives:

- It is national coaching week and you are a coach – you offer a free session to a journalist and they do a piece on the experience.

- There is a sudden trend for eating Russian dumplings and you use Russian dumplings as part of a homeopathic course in curing asthma.

• Gay marriages are made legal and you are a wedding organiser specialising in gay weddings.

Hacks are not in the habit of coming back to you to check the facts, so be extremely careful what you say and how you put it.

The great thing about PR is that it should cost you nothing. The worst thing about PR is that the businesswoman unversed in the wily ways of journalists could find herself grossly misrepresented – hacks are not in the habit of coming back to you to check the facts, so be extremely careful what you say and how you put it. See the Resources section in the Appendix for more information on doing your own PR but note the following:

• Target your article or contribution and do your research. Make sure you know as much as you can about the publication, programme or interviewer. Be ready to talk about how your contribution can help their message and format.
• Be clear, concise and accurate and keep your message short.
• Keep it topical, as per the hooks and incentives section above.
• Practise your introduction, pitch, anticipate questions and have your responses prepared.
• Don't just talk about what you want – more business or referrals – offer something that the readers or viewers will find informative, interesting or enticing – an offer or 'ten top tips' is a particular favourite for most magazines and newspapers.

COMMUNICATIONS TIPS

Every time your phone rings, or a customer comes into your restaurant, shop or consultation room, talks to you in the street or logs onto your website, some form of marketing has worked. It is easy to assume that you have already succeeded in getting your client (and you have to a certain point), but there is still a lot to play for. Good, confident communication skills are everything when it comes to getting and keeping clients.

Remember your USP and your key sentence from Chapter 1? You need to become an expert in writing and speaking that message whenever you are called upon to do so.

Telephone techniques

In business it is likely that you will spend a lot of your time on the phone. When you make or receive phone calls, follow these guidelines to make your customer put down the phone and say 'Wow!'.

> *Make your customer put down the phone and say 'Wow!'*

- Always answer the phone promptly and enthusiastically, saying your first name so they know who they're talking to.

- Speak clearly, and listen patiently, however much you may want to jump in.

- Make sure there is always a voicemail message in the event that you are out of the office or otherwise engaged – include your hours of opening and an email address if possible.

- Always take as much information as you can about a client on the phone – and don't forget the phone number.

- Do whatever you need to do to sound professional, including dressing the part, standing up (useful when you want to end a conversation or inject some energy) or speaking in front of a mirror.

Writing the message

Most businesses rely on written communications at one level or another. Whether you type letters, send emails, or write articles and press releases, stick to these guidelines to maximise the impact of what you produce.

- Be confident in your approach – don't underplay your

achievements – where you shy away from self-publicity, another business will be very happy to storm in and take the spotlight.

- Be clear and concise in your message – depending on where the text is appearing, adjust the length of sentences and use of vocabulary to maximise the impact of the message.

- Tell your reader what's in it for them, make it irresistible reading to your target audience.

- Get advice – as with all writing (apart from diaries), it is only as good as the reader thinks it is, and your work may benefit from a second opinion and more objective viewpoint. Find someone you trust in your business network who you could barter your skills with. We found this happening a lot at Wimbledon Women in Business – one member's personal shopping experience was paid for by her advice on website copy for the personal shopper.

> *Tell your reader what's in it for them, make it irresistible reading to your target audience.*

- Include photos – people buy people, and if they can see your smiling face as they read your article, press release or web page, they will feel closer to you and the business, which has to be an advantage.

- Include testimonials – it lets your reader know that people like them have been delighted with your service.

- Make it easy to be contacted. Have you ever received a letter without a return address, or found a website but without a Contact Us button. How infuriating is that? If you include all your contact details at every reasonable opportunity, more business is likely to come your way. Of course if you are producing a very small advert, you may not have the space to include your address and all your numbers, but one number and one website address is essential for most businesses.

Face to face

Talking to your clients on the phone, you might be safe (if not at your best) in your pyjamas with a fag hanging out of your mouth, but you need to take a lot more care when meeting clients in person. Here are some general guidelines:

• Do your research beforehand.

• Look and act the part.

• If you have control over the meeting venue, choose carefully – not too noisy, busy, dull, seedy…

• Offer a firm handshake if appropriate – resist kissing on the cheek unless he/she initiates it, or you're in France.

• Explain at the beginning of the meeting what you intend to cover and summarise at the end with allocated action points if appropriate.

Body language

Body-language expert and author **Judi James** has the following advice for businesswomen who want to make an impact:

• Make a good entrance, stand up straight, walk in as though you have come into the right room, not the wrong one.

• Iron out your facial expression.

• Speak as soon as you can – get your voice out there.

• When sitting, drop your shoulders.

• Don't fiddle.

• When speaking, drop your voice if you want to be heard; no one listens to a high pitched squeak.

• Keep your hands at waist level, don't flap.

Remember that there are some gestures which will automatically 'mean' something to your audience – grooming gestures tend to imply that you fancy the person you are speaking to; leaning your chin on your hand with your thumb upwards says 'I'm listening', whereas when your index finger is pointing upwards on your cheek, you are questioning what you are hearing. Covering your mouth when you talk can give the impression you are lying. Pit-baring (holding your hands behind your head, often accompanied by ankle on opposite knee (crotch-baring) says 'I'm in charge'. Beware of tapping your feet, rattling jewellery and rummaging in your bag – all these give a disorganised impression. Walk as if you were someone famous.

> *Women tend to shuffle out of the way and make space for others, which is very honourable on a crowded bus, but in business it will give other people the message that you are backing down, that you don't want to rock the boat, that you don't want to be in the competition.*

Women tend to shuffle out of the way and make space for others, which is very honourable on a crowded bus but in business will give other people the message that you are backing down, that you don't want to rock the boat, that you don't want to be in the competition. Be aware of what you are trying to achieve and sensitive to the impression you give to others – if you are physically small and/or want to lead a meeting, you may need to take up lots of space and volume in the room. If you are physically large and/or want to take a back seat, give others space.

Making presentations

Unless standing up in front of people was part of your job, or comes naturally to you, this could be something you are not looking forward to. It's that British reserve popping up again (or rather still hiding behind a bush). But remember those teachers you really listened to? Have you ever been to a lecture or a talk that was particularly effective or memorable? Most of us have at some time or another been on the receiving end of a really good presentation, and most importantly, remembered what was said. It is that kind of presentation that you need to learn to deliver.

There are a number of situations where you might have to or want to present to a group: explaining your services to the board of a large organisation, demonstrating how a new product works, introducing yourself and your business to a networking group, or speaking at a conference in front of hundreds of people. Thinking back through your life so far, have you ever had to do this before in a work or education context? Teachers should be natural presenters, and usually find a room full of adults much more amenable than a class of 30 ten-year-olds ... Lawyers and accountants often have to chair meetings and give talks; anyone with a background in training or HR will have had to speak to a group at some point. It's just the same now, except you are selling something, something that you feel passionately about, and that is what makes it so much easier.

> *Selling something, something that you feel passionately about, makes it so much easier.*

Lucy: My first experience of presenting my business was talking to a group of childcare students at a local college. As soon as I arrived in the room I suddenly remembered I had done this before, years ago when I stepped in and taught my mother's law students when she was ill. Remembering how much I enjoyed it, and having the added bonus now of feeling much more into my subject, I was imbued with confidence, and it all went incredibly well.

Bella: I used to hate doing presentations for the company I worked for. I felt very anxious about speaking to any group of people, but was told I just had to grit my teeth and get on with it. I did almost literally that, and delivered it in a rather dull, factually correct monotone (which at least didn't betray my churning nerves) but didn't engage people either – I'm sure you've been to presentations like that. Now that I'm talking about something that I really care about, and I can use my own words, I'm much more comfortable, although not entirely nerve-free. I don't fear getting things wrong like I used to, as I'm talking a lot from my own experience, and am so comfortable that I'm not even concerned about being challenged. In fact I'm best with questions, so I try to get a conversation going with my audience or group as quickly as possible. The talks where I have spent ages preparing — perhaps a whole day for a ten-minute talk — are the ones that go best.

The way that it feels different for me is that rather than having all my energy focused in the back of my head and throat, painfully squeezing all the right words out, I'm throwing it out through my eyes, looking and connecting with my audience. I would like to lighten my style more, so I'm still learning. I'll never be the kind of inspirational speaker who 'motivates' 1,000 people in a central London hall, but neither do I aspire to be.

When you present your business for the first time, you will probably need to do a bit of homework to ensure it all runs smoothly. Doing that homework is one way to reduce your nerves. Other tips for feeling less nervous include:

- Rehearse what you're going to say in front of partner or a friend, and reduce your talk to a series of key words on cards.

- Speak slowly and avoid words like 'umm', 'you know' and 'stuff'.

- Arrive early to make yourself familiar with the room.

- Rhythmical movement, like passing a tennis ball from one hand to the other (or something less obvious perhaps) can greatly reduce nerves, and has successfully settled people with serious conditions such as agoraphobia — but choose one that your audience won't notice or they'll get too distracted.

- Make sure you are familiar with any technology so you are not left floundering and embarrassed.

- Don't hold pieces of paper which will draw attention to any shaking!

During your presentation, stick to these rules to make sure things run smoothly:

- Introduce yourself – it's amazing how many speakers rush over this bit.

- Limit the background info – you may feel it is relevant, but unless it is fascinating, you will lose their attention.

- You've heard it before, but it works: say what you're going to say, say it and say what you've said – and build your key points into the beginning and the end, as this is when most people listen hardest.

- Be excited about your message. You might have said it all 100 times before, but this is their first time hearing it.

- Involve your audience – ask them questions, listen to them and use humour to draw them in.

- Connect with your audience – look at them as a friendly and kindly bunch even though they may not be smiling. Don't overlay the image of a bear-pit onto them.

- Keep handouts in case the technology fails you, but only distribute them at the end or you will find everyone reading and rustling during your talk.

- Give them something to go home with, a phrase, a mantra or some other memory of your message.

- Smile occasionally.

Networking

However Machiavellian it may sound, networking is something you are probably already doing every day. Since you first had the idea to set up this business, you have been talking to people about it: your family and friends, other mothers, work colleagues, neighbours, anyone who has shown interest, or who you think might be able to help you in some way. They may have offered you advice, sympathy, the loan of their garden shed, money (if you're really lucky) but most of all, they will have thought of someone they know who needs your services. When the phone rings the next day and your new customer says 'I was given your name by…', you will know that, whether or not you were consciously out to get business leads, your networking is working.

> *Be excited about your message. You might have said it all 100 times before, but this is their first time hearing it.*

When we say 'networking', we mean meeting people, usually with a view to getting business, information or friendship from them or their contacts, at some point in the future (not necessarily on the spot). This can be through a business networking group (of which there are hundreds across the UK) business and professional organisations (like your local chamber of commerce) or through less contrived circumstances (at events you attend, conferences, parties, social gatherings, etc). It's not about thrusting your business card at every Tom, Dick and Harry – it's about making real, meaningful connections with people – getting them to like you, and building up a set of professional contacts who you like and trust.

> *When the phone rings and your new customer says 'I was given your name by…', you will know that your networking is working.*

The formal networking groups range from local to national networks, all with different rules, arrangements and cultures, so choose one that suits your personality and is convenient (or you could always set one up). The first networking event you go to may feel unnatural and embarrassing, but as you go to more and more, you'll become more practised and sophisticated at saying what you want to say, meeting people you want to meet, and you might surprise yourself by enjoying the whole process. Everyone is there for the same reason as you. Just being at an event is often enough to absorb the atmosphere, feel less isolated and see what others are up to. It's a great place to do your research as well – ask what others are doing, watch how they introduce themselves and their businesses, what they wear, and see what works for you. Dress and present yourself with care. Being seen at a networking event time after time builds your reputation and creates trust and a feeling of community. If you're feeling adventurous, you could always offer to speak about what you do (after all, that's the whole idea).

Ellen Kerr is a Merseyside business advisor, and told us:

A lot of women I have assisted have had an unpleasant surprise when they actually get to the point of trading as they have expected everyone to just knock on their door and want what they are offering. Then they invest in a few hundred leaflets and are disappointed when they do not get a massive response. I always promote networking as a major route to sales and marketing as you never know who you will meet at an event. People buy from people they like and trust and women are excellent at building relationships and remembering detail. But there is always a danger of 'networking and not working' so it has to be a balanced and specific approach.

> **Women are excellent at building relationships and remembering detail.**

Entrepreneurs can be very independent by nature, and don't feel the need to seek out membership of new groups as soon as they set up in business, but there are lots of interesting opportunities out there. At worst, networking is free marketing and, at best, it is all about making new friends and winning new clients.

Chambers of commerce are a great place to start, and most organise networking nights where you will meet other local business people. Through the chamber, you might also find out what other networking groups exist in your area – most of these will charge for membership, but allow guests one or two free visits. But meeting other business people can become a rather dry and thankless pursuit after a while, so sprinkle your networking calendar with some more interesting relationship-building exercises like these:

1. Go where your customers are – if you run a nanny agency, go and meet mothers and childcarers at playgroup sessions or at story time at the local library; if you are a physiotherapist, try hobnobbing with local sports clubs – you will be surprised at how much people value a friendly face over a company name in the Yellow Pages. Physiotherapist **Katherine Watkins** developed a specialisation in dance medicine, treating injuries to which dancers are particularly prone. She found that making contact with local dance schools and liaising with sports medicine practitioners was key in developing a network of referrals.

2. Join a group that's nothing to do with business – following your own hobby or pastime, whether it's rambling or salsa dancing, will get you talking to like-minded people, while you have fun doing what you love. You need that relaxation time, and this way you are promoting your business and getting to know more people at the same time.

3. Create your own group or event – we set up Wimbledon Women in Business back in 2003 and have seen it grow beyond recognition. If you think there is a need for a group in your area, chances are someone else does too. Throw a party for everyone you know who has helped you or could help you with your business.

4. Look at who you know already, and find out who they know – a great deal of business can be generated by your existing address book when you start up in business but you don't always realise that. Start looking at your Christmas card list in a new light. It's fine to ask friends for help – sensible in fact.

You may find that all this comes naturally to you, or you may find it one of the more challenging aspects of business building. This will depend partly on your personality type – the more outgoing, open and relaxed you are, the easier it will be. To help you get through it, especially the first few times you find yourself out there stumbling over your 'elevator pitch' with a glass of warm Chardonnay in one hand and a clutch of business cards in the other, here are some tips.

Top tips for networking

- Always carry business cards, in all your bags, your purse, your car, and keep them handy, so your new friend doesn't fall asleep while you're rummaging in your handbag.
- Give two cards away at a time, one for them to keep, one for them to give away.
- Always dress comfortably, and don't wear painfully high heels – you may get a good view of the room but not for long if your feet are in agony.
- Repeat a name to remember it and/or find a link in your mind that triggers the association.
- Don't forget to present yourself as a rounded person, not just interior designer or accountant – they may end up asking you about your business because they like you and want to be useful to you, which is a much more effective process.
- Remember to think about what you can do for them, not just what they can do for you – generosity will automatically make new contacts warm to you.
- When you get home, write notes on the business cards you have collected to make sure you remember who you met.
- Follow up new contacts – make that introduction if you said you would; send them that article or phone number you promised.
- Enjoy making new friends.

> *Always carry business cards, and keep them handy, so your new friend doesn't fall asleep while you're rummaging in your handbag.*

IS IT WORKING?

It is all very well engaging in an extensive marketing campaign, but if your tricks aren't working, you will be wasting your money. To find out how well your marketing plan is succeeding, you can use the following tactics:

- Get feedback from clients – where did they hear from you, what did they think of your newsletter?

- In your adverts, ask readers to quote a promotional code.

- If word of mouth works, spend time asking clients for referrals.

- Measure the hits on your website or other internet presence.

- Keep a record of the effectiveness of all your different techniques, and act on it. For example, if you find word-of-mouth referrals really work for you, concentrate on getting more.

- Keep up the market research – undertake a regular review of your competitors' marketing strategies, prices, websites and promotional activities.

SO, HOW READY ARE YOU TO GET YOURSELF KNOWN?

☐ What are your business name and strapline going to be?
☐ Who are your target customers?
☐ Why will they buy from you?
☐ How are you going to go about branding your business?
☐ How are you going to win business?
☐ How are you going to keep those customers coming back?
☐ Where and how will you advertise or become known?
☐ Who do you know in the media – can you gather their contact details?
☐ What is on your marketing and PR shelf?
☐ What changes do you need to make to your wardrobe/appearance?
☐ Who are you talking to – coach/friend/partner? What feedback are you getting?
☐ How are you feeling about your business at this point?

6

DEVELOPING AND MANAGING
YOUR BUSINESS

After all the effort of planning and launching your new venture, this is where the reality of owning and running a business really hits you, but hopefully not too hard. Your business is no longer the idea you have been thinking about and working on, it exists in its own right and even receives post. This is all very exciting, but when your business takes on a life on its own out there in the big wide world, it can leave you feeling very exposed and vulnerable. There is no 'apprenticeship' for this new role of leader that has suddenly been thrust upon you, but don't worry. Running a business is the best training course there is, and you're now on it.

> *Running a business is the best training course there is, and you're now on it.*

The journey that you take from here will be unique to you. You may experience sudden meteoric growth and take it all in your stride, or you could find there's still a long way to go before you get where you want to be. You may deliberately restrict the expansion of your business to accommodate your other responsibilities and priorities, but however your business evolves, there will be plenty of issues to contend with along the way. It is the development of your business that this chapter focuses on, and how you are going to manage and lead your business forward.

HOW WILL YOUR BUSINESS EVOLVE?

You will be aware through your market research and your experience of dealing with your first customers, of the potential of your business, and this will inform your overall aims and vision once you are up and running. The reality of running a business can lead you to revisit your original goals, and reassess whether they are still what you are aiming for. A lot of start-ups begin trading on a small scale to try out a product or service on a sample group of customers so that they can make any adjustments before casting the net wider. Your first weeks of trading will also give you an idea of how popular your idea really is, in a way that isn't always completely predictable from your market research. Many a new business has failed because when it came down to it, there simply wasn't the demand for what they offered. Equally, many a new business has been thrown by an unexpected take-off in sales. Demand needs to be more than your friends and relatives buying from you; it needs to be considerable, public and constant if you are to succeed.

So with that in mind, and now things are up and running, how do you think your business will develop? Take a look at Figure 7.

Growth patterns

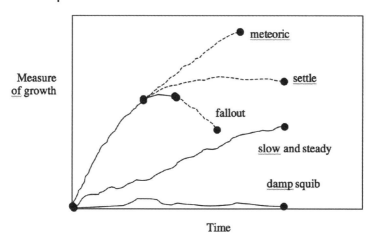

Figure 7: Growth profiles

Assuming you want to avoid damp squibs and fallouts, which profile suits you best? Take a moment to sketch the kind of growth you want for your business in Figure 7, and fill in the timescale on the bottom axis. Of course, neither life nor business is as tidy as a graph (thank goodness) but yours will create its own pattern, depending on:

• how you want it to grow

• what infrastructure you put in place

• what the market is like.

What growth profile do you want from your business, and are you prepared for it?

1. How much would you like your business (empire) to grow in the next three years?
   World domination •————•Things ticking over nicely

2. Would you like your rise to be meteoric or slow and steady?
   Shoot for the stars •————•Easy-she-goes

3. How flexible can you be and how much hard work can you put in?
   Whatever it takes •————•Within constraints

4. What infrastructure do you (plan to) have in place
   Fully equipped •————•Kitchen table
   and efficient, staffed premises

5. Attitude to risk
   Ready to risk it all •————•Need to protect myself

If you have leaned more towards the constrained, kitchen-table, protected, ticking-over kind of business, have you asked yourself why this is? The most common reasons women cite for restricting growth are:

- family and caring responsibilities (and associated guilt)

- lack of access to finance and business advice (don't know how to grow)

- risk-averseness/fear of the unknown.

If, you play 'little old me' while secretly you want to build a huge empire, you may end up feeling resentful and confused when other businesses overtake yours.

If you can be honest with yourself from the start about what you want and why you want it (or don't want it in this case), you will be more comfortable with the outcome. If, on the other hand, you play 'little old me' while secretly you want to build a huge empire, you may end up feeling resentful and confused when other businesses overtake yours.

Having said all that, staying small is a perfectly acceptable format, and suits some women very well.

CASE STUDY

Rebecca Exley is a self-employed hydrogeologist working in rural Wales. Among her many activities, which include lecturing at Cardiff University, she works for clients who are not served by the mains water supply. Commercial clients and householders rely on her to ensure the safety of the water they get from wells and springs. Rebecca says:

I'm quite happy not growing my business for the moment. My business is based totally around me doing the work to my own high standards, so if I did ever want to grow, I'd need to clone myself! I need to know that the tests carried out on site are performed thoroughly and legally, and I want to know that I stand by every word in every report I send to a client. And anyway, I like getting my hands dirty. That might change in the future, but at the moment, my children are at school, and my business revolves around them – I can't count the number of times I've told clients I have to be back for a three o'clock meeting!

Geetie Singh, founder of Sloeberry Trading, felt disillusioned with the unfair practices and lack of sustainability in the hospitality trade she came from. Having grown up in a self-sufficient commune with strong values, she was determined that her business would be ethically run. She consciously chose not to expand her business beyond what she could realistically control, because she didn't want to risk compromising her values and priorities.

If Gita or Rebecca did ever want to grow, their first step might be to find a partner or employee whom they trusted to carry out work to their standards, which is what Lucy did:

Lucy: I used to be firmly of the opinion that no one was going to be as efficient and effective as I was at running my home and nanny agency. Cloning myself seemed to be the only way to stop me being overwhelmed by all my commitments. But then I woke up to the fact that I was spending considerable time on things that did not demand my personal attention (mainly tidying up my house and sorting out washing) so I brought in someone to do that. On the business side, I got talking about the pressures to an old colleague. We discussed the business in more and more detail, and within a short time were discussing the possibility of her becoming my business partner. We signed an agreement, and she walked into the job and exceeded my expectations from day one. Never mind cloning me, I want to clone her!

Evolution and/or expansion?

All businesses need to evolve; not every one needs to expand. Evolution can involve expansion, but doesn't necessarily mean world domination in two years' time. It can mean any or all of the following:

> **All businesses need to evolve; not every one needs to expand.**

• getting new customers

• bringing in new partners

• coming up with new products or services

- becoming known as a market leader

- making more money

- hiring people to satisfy the demand for work.

Notice that the above list does not include new premises, shiny new equipment or the latest mobile phone for all your staff. New premises and gadgets are not a sign of growth, but a cost to your business. You may need a new building and more telephones to make more sales, but make sure you don't confuse spending with earning. You need to have the systems, people, products and processes in place to sell and deliver whatever your business does, but you could be wasting valuable resources on a rented office full of staff and expensive computers if there is not enough work in the pipeline.

CASE STUDY

Halos 'n' Horns experienced a meteoric growth – from being an idea to a product stocked on the shelves of Tesco, Somerfield, Asda and Morrisons within just one year. Founder **Leila Wilcox** says:

Many people imagine me at the top of a flashy office with an entourage of staff. The reality is that we work from my business partner's kitchen table, and there's pretty much just me, my business partner and my PA. We keep our overheads to an absolute minimum, and cleared all our debts in month one. Obviously we can't do everything ourselves, but we didn't want to pay massive rent and salaries when the product is at such an early stage of development. We subcontract the manufacturing and packaging and our Finance Director, Operations Manager, PR Manager and other important people are consultants, rather than staff, and they're all fantastic. Being freelance, they have the entrepreneurial streak that is so important for us to work together. They enjoy the work, we speak the same language, I keep costs as low as possible, and don't have to do all the recruitment and administration of managing staff.

When you mention your plans for your business, you have probably found that people are quick to offer advice, which may be anything from 'make sure you don't grow too quickly' to 'seize the moment'. A period of growth, or planning that growth, can be a very exciting time, but also one in which you need to be seriously focused to absorb all the changes around you and keep moving forward. It's not a time to take the reckless advice of a spendthrift acquaintance who is here today, gone tomorrow. Other dangerous sources of advice are the friends who only know you as a mother/colleague/karaoke addict, and haven't seen the other side of you. They can be too stifling, too anti-change. After all, there's nothing in it for them if you go off on this new tangent and they lose their karaoke partner. They need reminding that you can be everything you want to be, not just what you are at the moment. So, find some really solid support for yourself and the business.

> *You can be everything you want to be, not just what you are at the moment.*

Common barriers to growth

Put simply, the most common difficulties that most small businesses run into during the growth phase boil down to one of the following.

1. **Over-trading** – committing to deliver something you can't deliver properly (or at all). This is especially common during a period of fast growth. Putting yourself in the bargain-basement price bracket, for example, can lead to problems keeping up with demand for whatever you offer, not to mention feeling resentful and overworked.

    Solution: Only promise to deliver what you know you can deliver – this includes promises you make in your marketing material and in person. If the shelves are empty, or the advertised goods are unavailable, or if the staff are too busy or not ready to deliver your service, you will be missing out on opportunities. Put time and effort into building an infrastructure that can cater for this scenario – it will be worth it.

2. **Overspending** – paying more to keep the business afloat than is coming in. This could be to do with overestimating demand and underestimating marketing, bad financial planning or unforeseen events – equipment failure, staff sickness, supplier problems, etc.

> **Solution**: Stop spending. Only spend on essentials. Concentrate on getting business in without spending money. Talk to people. Network. Your business plan should cater for as many disaster scenarios as possible, and you should have a clear and workable proposal for how to deal with each one.

One way to avoid both problems is to invest in people, to devote your energies to finding and keeping the human beings that support your business, and talk to them. Your business success relies upon people – the people who buy from you, the people who work for you and the people who help you do that: your customers, your employees and your suppliers.

CUSTOMERS

It goes without saying that you should treat your customers well. How strange then that we all have experiences of appalling customer service – from surly waiters who probably spat in our food, to the builder swearing down the phone and hanging up. Clearly it doesn't come naturally to everyone to go all out to please the client. So what does good customer service mean?

Customer service

Do they need champagne? Do they need sympathy? Give them that, in bucketfuls if necessary.

To get and keep customers in an increasingly competitive marketplace, you need to really know them, and show them that you know them. Put yourself in their shoes. What need do they have that you are fulfilling, and how does it feel to have that need? Customers may come to you with a spring in their step (if you are selling luxury holidays) or with their head in their hands (if you are a dentist). Do they need champagne? Do they need sympathy? Give them that, in bucketfuls if necessary. Send them home with something to remember you by. Chartered physiotherapist **Katharine Watkins** sends her customers home with a bottle of spring water and a miniature bottle of aromatherapy oil so that her treatment has an impact long after the client has walked out of the door. Go the extra mile and you will be an extra mile ahead of the competition.

You will have heard it said that people buy people. The bank First Direct has run a whole publicity campaign on the basis of its friendly 24-hour telephone banking service; the AA man was always 'a very nice man'; Currie Motors (if you can remember that far back) were always 'nice people to do business with'. With the choice that is available to consumers these days, your customer service skills will be one area where you can really distinguish yourself from the competition and stand out. The extent to which you embrace this concept will depend on the kind of person you are.

Extroverts are generally thought to be good at dealing with customers. If you are shy and retiring, you may baulk at having unnecessary contact with your clients, but approach clients in a way in which you are comfortable, and your sensitivity may be an asset. Most of all, customer service is about being thoughtful. Here is one businesswoman who can really push the boat out:

CASE STUDY

Claire Alexander of Ad Hominem makes luxury suits for her male clients, often overworked high-flyers:

Personal service is absolutely the most important aspect of my business, and the future of all commerce. There are very few barriers to entry in many businesses, mine included, so what sets me apart every time is my total commitment to personal service. Everyone wants to feel special, and I ensure that all of my clients are made to feel like they, and their individual requirements, are of utmost importance to me. In this way, virtually all of my clients repeat order and have become loyal to me. This is essential as I rely solely on word of mouth for new business, and so their testimonials are the future of my business. I go to great lengths to make sure my customer service is of a very high standard. This may mean sending them for a deluxe massage when they have had a long week, sending a Cuban cigar and a bottle of Bollinger to recognise their birthday, or delivering a suit by express limousine to their office if they need it for an event in the evening. I always take a great interest in all aspects of their lives — not just those that relate to the business — and make a point of treating them as valued individuals, not just another client. Great customer service doesn't have to be grand gestures. Sometimes I simply send them a newspaper cutting that I think might be of interest to them with a note attached saying 'saw this and thought of you'. My business without this level of customer service would, in many ways, be just another generic business. My individual service is my point of difference in an increasingly competitive marketplace.

Be friendly . . . but professional

Women are remarkably good at customer service because their ability to empathise enables them to see things from others' point of view and react accordingly. But a common pitfall arising from this is over-friendliness. Don't forget while providing all this extra care and attention that your customers, like your employees, are not and should not be your best friends. You have a professional relationship with them that may develop a personal element to it, but that needs to be kept in check if the professional side is to flourish. You might think of them as 'more than just a customer' but to them you might still be 'just a supplier' who they will pay, and then forget. Customers can become friends, but generally of the 'will tell what I did at the weekend' variety, rather than the 'could borrow your knickers in an emergency' variety. You have your reputation to think of.

> **You might think of them as 'more than just a customer' but to them you might still be 'just a supplier' who they will pay, and then forget.**

Paula Lamb, aka Mrs Fixit, a builder and carpenter whose clients range from landlords to old ladies, finds that her relationships with clients vary from extremely formal to much too friendly. Her own helpful and approachable manner have occasionally landed her in complicated situations reminiscent of a TV sitcom:

> *I was in one house for a while where every day I was made cups of tea, cake, a hot lunch, and heard lots of stories about this and that grandchild, so much so that it became difficult to extricate myself and I ended up spending longer on the job than I wanted to, then felt guilty on leaving her on her own again. On another job, where I was working while the family were on holiday and feeding the cat, I ended up having to pay for emergency vet treatment when the cat got taken ill. Another unforeseen event in the time-management department…*

Don't be afraid of asking for feedback from your customers. You can do this after the job is finished, or if you are in an ongoing relationship with customers (coaching, consultancy, accountancy advice), you can check regularly with your client that everything is going OK for them – whether that's through asking a question at a regular meeting, or through a formal survey of customers' experiences. With any luck (and your superb customer service skills in place, of course), feedback should be good. But as soon as you become aware of any negative issues, do your best to resolve them, and try to understand how they may have arisen, so you can prevent them happening again. (See the section below for further guidance on dealing with complaints.) You don't have to badger your clients for feedback, but if someone asks you to phone them in a few months, then do just that (and if they don't volunteer that, ask them if you can). One businesswoman we met uses a 999 rule – after doing some work for a client, she phones them 9 days, then 9 weeks then 9 months just to see how they are doing.

Be interested, and interesting

The lives of your clients are likely to be as busy and varied as your own. Most women are experts at remembering the names

Most women are experts at remembering the names of their clients' children, and where they went on holiday last year, which is a valuable skill in business – the person at the end of the phone will warm to you instantly.

of their clients' children, and where they went on holiday last year, which is a valuable skill in business – the person at the end of the phone will warm to you instantly. Keeping in touch with what is happening in your customers' lives is part of the professional relationship you have with them, and also enables you to react to their needs.

As well as being interested, be interesting. Being interesting doesn't mean regaling your client with your fascinating views on climate change policy in Europe – it's just about being yourself and sharing information about things you've been doing, observing and thinking. Doing this provides a welcome balance to showing interest in others, and helps them trust you. Customers who trust you will use you again, will recommend you to their friends and forgive you when you make a mistake. Customers who don't trust you won't come back for more, will say nasty things about you to their friends and find fault with everything you do.

CASE STUDY

Carla Boulton runs Naughty Mutt Ltd with her husband Nigel. She provides web design, graphic design and printing services, often to start-ups who are looking for new brochures and websites. We spoke to Carla on the sixth anniversary of the company's launch she runs with her husband, Nigel. Over the years, Carla has seen the launch of countless new ventures and has developed a sixth sense for what works and what doesn't:

I like to help people with their new ventures as much as I can, so I set aside a good chunk of time for the first meeting. Obviously graphic design or web development is the focus of our conversation, but I use the experience that I've gained over the years to help clients with anything I can to do with starting up.

Dealing with complaints

Excellent customer service can turn a complaining, unhappy client into a delighted one, and even the people who don't buy from you will recommend you if you delighted them or resolved their complaint in a really outstanding way. If you do make a mistake, the first thing to do is own up, and sort it out. You will be surprised how an apparent disaster can turn into a publicity spectacular!

CASE STUDY

Catherine Green of CG Scrubbers Cleaning Agency had exactly that experience:

One of my clients had a cat which had given birth to kittens in the conservatory. The cleaners (or 'scrubbers') went to go 'ahhh' at the new arrivals, but the main door of the house slammed and locked and they couldn't get back into the house. The back garden was fenced off with iron railings. The thinner scrubber managed to squeeze through the railings but the larger one couldn't fit through. Her colleague called me and I suggested calling the fire brigade. At the prospect of this, the bigger, horrified scrubber literally wrenched the iron railings apart to escape. Of course I apologised profusely and offered to pay the client for the damage to be repaired but he just laughed and said he actually preferred to leave it as it was — it would make a great dinner party story for years to come!

Top tips for good customer relations

- Don't commit to anything you aren't 100 per cent sure you can deliver.
- When you're committed, deliver 100 per cent or more.
- Exceed your customers' expectations wherever possible.
- Be friendly, but professional.
- Make buying from you a pleasure and a delight.
- Ask what else you can do for your customers, and do it.
- Get to know your customers and win their trust.
- Listen to and react to feedback from customers.
- Make sure all your staff follow and believe in your customer service policy.
- Manage customer relationships using a database and update it regularly.

EMPLOYEES

So the tables have turned and you are about to be an employer. If you are a first-time employer, your experience of being an employee will be valuable in thinking about the relationship from the other perspective. You will have learnt how to be a good employer from all the good bosses you have had, and all about what not to do from the bad ones. What may be new to you is the concept of being partly responsible for someone else's wellbeing, career and livelihood. Will you embrace this responsibility, or does it fill you with dread?

CASE STUDY

Veronica Sarkhels runs a chain of four restaurants in London providing Indian and Chinese food.

My challenges are different to someone who employs UK staff. I do employ some people locally, but I need chefs who are trained in the authentic ways of our cuisine. I employ them for that reason, but also because part of the raison-d'être for my business is to provide my employees with the opportunities that I have had to work overseas. I always set staff up legally and provide them and their families with accommodation. That hasn't stopped immigration officers raiding my premises and carting my employees off because they can't wait five minutes for me to find the papers they want, which is totally infuriating. My staff need a lot of support when they come to this country — they need to learn the language, the culture and way of life, and they have so much to offer in terms of authenticity and gastronomic education. Often one of the first things they need to learn is what our pounds and pence look like! They don't have anyone else here, and my mobile phone is always on to help them and their families get settled and cope with the huge cultural adjustment to a new country. Of course I have to keep an element of professional distance, but I have found a way to be able to laugh and joke with them, and provide the practical and emotional support they need, without reducing the authority that I have as their boss. I learnt how to be an employer (or rather how not to be one) through my experiences as an employee. My father encouraged me to work for someone else before I could join the family business so I could understand both sides of the coin.

Veronica is an inspiring example of a woman who goes the extra mile for her employees. She recognises that she probably doesn't make as much money as her restaurant chain could make, but the satisfaction she gets from being able to provide human contact and a good living for her employees and their families is part of her reward, and is an essential element of her definition of 'success'.

Taking on this level of responsibility for employees is not everyone's ideal, and isn't always necessary, but it is good practice to recognise your employees as individuals with their own goals and dreams in life, and often their own families to support. As Veronica says 'When I employ just one person, I become connected to their whole family, and I have 45 employees as well as my own family. If an employee is happy at home, they will be happy at work, and that's what I want.'

> *Recognise your employees as individuals with their own goals and dreams in life.*

Catherine Green, who we met in the last few pages, is unusual because she employs her cleaners, rather than subcontracting them. This means that she pays them for holiday time, sick pay and so on, but, as a result, she has a team of loyal and dedicated staff, all of whom are hand selected to live up to her motto of 'perfect is standard'. It also means that she really knows the people she employs as people, not just as 'scrubbers' as they are affectionately known. She told us:

CASE STUDY

I really get to know the girls I employ. I hear and sympathise with their stories (and I've heard some horrific stories of abusive backgrounds and violent husbands). I know that for many of them, coming to work is a release and a pleasure. My cleaners go out in a band. They love the team spirit and it makes it seem less like drudgery. We did have warring factions on one occasion in the past, but generally the team thing keeps spirits and standards high.

Recruiting people

The first employee for most small businesses will usually be some kind of a 'business manager' — either a PA (personal assistant) or an MD (managing director) and, for small businesses, the roles may not be a million miles apart. Of course you may be recruiting for a more specialist role, or for more than one role.

So, if you decide to employ someone, how do you go about it?

1. Decide what assistance you need.
2. Draft a job description including terms and conditions.
3. Advertise or engage a recruitment firm.
4. Shortlist applicants or review your recruiter's shortlist.
5. Interview applicants (maybe more than once).
6. Check qualifications and technical ability.
7. Take up references.
8. Make an offer and agree a contract.

There are many ways to advertise your vacancy, from word of mouth to using a recruitment agency. Whether you use assistance or not, it's vital that you draft a job description yourself, and that you engage fully with the shortlist and interviewing process. If you do use a recruitment agency for any part of the process, spend all the time you need telling them what you want. Use them as a route to contacts — don't let them make your hiring decisions for you (certainly not until they've proved they know what type of people you want in your business). Use your gut feeling about people, but always take up references personally, even if the candidate is part of your network or has come through an agency. Use the interview process to ask as many questions as you can and really explore whether the person in front of you is right for your business. Ask all the questions you want, and invite them back for interview as many times as it takes (within reason). Do they fit? It's always useful to ask someone you trust to sit in on the interview, whether that is an existing staff member or a professional contact that you trust. Finally, take up references and find out all that you can about potential employees' ability, performance and attitude and check attendance and sickness history.

Different employers apply different tests when interviewing potential new staff. Here's a good one:

Claire Owen of Stopgap told us:

> *Whenever I recruit someone, whatever level they are, I use the 'lunch test'. I ask myself, 'would I want to spend an hour or so having lunch in the company of this person.' If the answer is no, then they are not going to be right for us. Cultural fit is so important, with teamwork and friendship being essential ingredients for a successful business. I believe giving someone a job just because they have the right 'technical' skills is a huge mistake; we only want people to join us who are going to get on with everyone else here – and I find my lunch test is a very easy barometer for us to use to gauge this.*

Stopgap recently came tenth in the *Sunday Times* list of Top 50 Best Small Companies to Work for.

I ask myself, 'would I want to spend an hour or so having lunch in the company of this person.

Cultural fit is so important, with teamwork and friendship being essential ingredients for a successful business!

Managing people

Management and leadership (which we discuss later in this chapter) are closely connected but not necessarily the same thing.

- **Leader**: sets the direction of the business, makes key decisions relating to the 'big picture', inspires staff and embodies the business.

- **Manager**: organises how the work is to be done, organizes the workforce and timescales, implementing the plans of the leader and making sure they are adhered to.

If you are a sole trader, or run a small business, it is likely that you will be playing the role of both leader and manager. The more your business grows, the more likely you will be to separate the roles:

CASE STUDY

When **Jocelyn Ashton** set up Building Blocks Nursery in 2000 she paid her staff better than the competition, ensuring that she had the choice of the best people. By concentrating on training them and enabling the more entrepreneurial girls to take on more responsibilities in different areas when they showed interest or aptitude, she has succeeded in fulfilling her dream of having a loyal and happy staff team. Nursery assistants, through training and experience, have been allowed to progress up to managerial roles, and one particular member of staff, who came originally on a temporary placement just after finishing her degree is still there five years later, managing the nursery's second branch where they operate sessional care and the after-school and holiday club. Building Blocks is about to open a new nursery and Jocelyn is looking forward to the challenge of taking on staff that are already in place: 'I love getting the most out of people. I love seeing how good they can be. That's what excites me most.'

I love getting the most out of people. I love seeing how good they can be. That's what excites me most.

The relationship you have with your employees is one of the closest professional relationships you have in your business. Like all relationships, its success relies on common expectations, mutual respect and good communication skills. Your team will rely on you to provide them with direction and guidance on an interpersonal level as well as simply telling them how to do the job. If you are a parent, you will be accomplished at this already, or on the well-trodden learning curve. But transferring the skill to the adult world can be more intimidating.

A mentor or role model can help you find your own management style. A good starting point is to consciously review the style of all the managers you have had in your life. In each case, think about the dynamics of the relationship. How did they make you feel generally? What effect did this have on your performance? What particular positive and negative moments can you remember in your relationship? What do you feel about them now – resentful, grateful? What does this make you want for yourself as a manager? What are you going to be like? What are you not going to be like?

Lisa Coles, an ex-employee, doesn't miss being managed at all:

I remember very clearly my first day as a trainee. My 'boss' was a terrifying and unapproachable middle-aged man whose reputation went before him. He took me to meetings at investment banks (at least I think that's what they were) where another bunch of intimidating middle-aged men ignored me and talked in code about things I didn't understand. I told him afterwards I hadn't understood a word of what was going on. He rolled his eyes and barked that I should go and see one of his colleagues, who would help me decipher my notes. I emerged none the wiser, wondering what I was doing in this job. It just didn't make sense and I felt very unhappy and undervalued. Despite my good education, I felt about as clever and confident as a dormouse.

Understandably, many women new to management who have experienced this kind of casual mistreatment in the workplace fall into a common trap of wanting to be liked first and foremost. Being nice is obviously crucial to getting your employer to like you, and to like coming to work, but over-befriending your employees, as with your customers, can have negative results for the business. Using your power wisely and responsibly is a crucial first step in getting the most out of your employees.

Assertiveness

Assertiveness, though a commendable personality trait in management and leadership, has had a lot of mixed press over the years. Being highly assertive can easily be misinterpreted as aggression, especially for women, but the trap we more commonly fall into is passivity: the apology-ridden monologue where we end up having achieved nothing and simply confirmed our unworthiness to ask for what we want. The trick is to learn to communicate with people, and to lead them, without either dominating them or manipulating them. Table 3 highlights the qualities of an assertive manager.

> *The trap is passivity: the apology-ridden monologue where we end up having achieved nothing and simply confirmed our unworthiness to ask for what we want.*

Table 3: The assertive manager contrasted with aggressive and passive managers

Aggressive manager	Assertive manager	Passive manager
Example: 'Why can't you ever get the report done on time?! Well, if I want something done properly, I guess I just have to do it myself!'	Example: 'John, can you complete your report by the end of today so that I have a chance to read it before we meet? Thank you.'	Example: 'I'm so sorry, maybe I didn't give you enough time to do the report – I didn't realise that ... and if I had known maybe I could have ... and ... do you think you could possibly...'
• Angry, fault-finding, superior, bullying, patronising, judgemental • Thinks people need to be put in their place • Shows no consideration of others needs or feelings • Has no time to listen to other people's needs	• Straight, honest, open, fair, relaxed • Strong • Able to disagree with someone and retain their friendship and respect • Self-aware and aware of others • Comfortable expressing needs • Win/win	• Weak, inactive, indecisive, indirect, victim, pouting, sulking • Thinks others' feelings and thoughts are more important than her own • Fears offending or upsetting anyone • Is uncomfortable expressing needs
This manager seems to have staff jumping to fulfil her needs, but she is isolated and unpopular and often generates feeling of anger, resentment and subtle resistance in others	Considers the thoughts and feelings of others without discounting her own. Characterised by both fairness and strength. Assertive individuals are able to stand up for their rights, but remain sensitive to the rights of others. People who choose this style are usually relaxed and easy-going, but are honest about their feelings. This is the best style for gaining people's respect, minimising stress and maintaining long-standing relationships	On the surface, this person may appear easy to get along with, but there is a lot left unsaid that can fester beneath the surface. Other people's needs, and being liked, are seemingly more important than her own needs and judgements. Her feelings are suppressed or denied, and resentment and anger can build up, producing stress and tension and over a long time – depression and physical illness
Body language: rigid, tapping fingers, slamming down papers, shaking head, raising eyes, closing eyes, sighing, pointing finger, threatening	Body language: upright, direct appropriate eye contact, respectful, strong, 'grounded', open, relaxed, friendly	Body language: blank, eyes downcast, fidgeting, hair twisting, quiet voice, hesitant, stammering, permanent half-smile, frozen, unengaged

The two prerequisites for assertive management are that you are honest and that you know what you want. An assertive manager negotiates with her employees as equals, even though she may make a request or decision from a position of authority.

If you ever feel that your staff are managing you, rather than the other way round, some personal development work in this area could help. Assertiveness is a big topic best dealt with in a supportive environment, so if it feels right get yourself on a course or get some coaching sooner rather than later.

Tips for assertive behaviour
- Use the right body language.
- Be honest.
- Prepare for the conversation and know what you want.
- Say:
  - the person's name
  - what you want
  - why you want it
  - when you want it
  - stop.

What gets in the way of assertive behaviour?
- Passive and aggressive behaviour.
- Fear of being wrong/looking bad/not being perfect.
- Not being assertive where it counts – no good being assertive to the postman if it is your clients or partner who need to hear it (but good practice).
- Emotional baggage – blocks, anxieties, patterns of feeling/thinking.
- Taking things personally.
- Starting assertively … then giving in.

Getting the best out of your staff
Your employees look to you for their work direction and a

salary, but also need you to create a pleasant, challenging and enjoyable working environment. Having a working partnership with a motivated and interested team can be a pleasure and reward in itself, as well as enabling your business to grow. Staff dedication and loyalty are something that you earn through good management and relationship building, and it's important that you model the qualities you want your staff to have.

If an employee sees you as someone who uses power responsibly, you are more likely to get buy-in when it counts.

You will need to find a philosophy of management and decision-making that works for you and your team. At some points you will need to make hierarchical decisions that might not be popular, and this is where the trust that you have built up counts for a lot. It is easier to take on board decisions from on high if we trust the person who has made them, and we understand some of the reasons for the decision. If an employee sees you as someone who uses power responsibly, you are more likely to get buy-in when it counts.

Tips for treating employees well
Do the right thing
- Pay a fair salary for the role.
- Provide a clear job description and boundaries of responsibility (see the legal aspects of employment in Chapter 3).
- Comply with legislation governing pay and conditions, and exceed legal minimums wherever you can afford to.
- Provide pleasant working premises and conditions.
- Show appreciation for what employees do for your business.
- Be aware of their personal circumstances. There's no need to cross any relationship boundaries, but show you are interested in them as a person and a colleague/employee, not as a workhorse.

Develop staff
- Take time to provide feedback on performance.

- Provide guidance, support and training on areas of development.
- Develop your coaching skills.

Motivate staff

- Make the job something they wouldn't want to leave.
- If you ask for more than the role demands, e.g. ask someone to stay late, then be flexible to them in return. Allow them to go early or give them a gift or bonus to say thank you. Never take employees for granted.
- Find out what motivates your staff – a meal out with the team, or a trip to the health spa they can do on their own. All of our motivation flags from time to time, and everyone appreciates a boost.
- Have parties or other events to celebrate anniversaries or big wins. (But remember those excruciating office parties you used to go to where no one really had fun, but pretended they did before sneaking off to the pub? Don't make yours like that.)

> *Model the behaviour that you'd like to see around you.*

Inspire staff

- Model the behaviour that you'd like to see around you.
- Use your power, but use it responsibly.
- Be positive.

Managing difficult people

It is inevitable that there will be some people you deal with, employees or even clients, whose behaviour drives you to distraction. It can seem that no matter how you behave towards them you just can't figure out how to communicate effectively with them. Dealing with that type of person quickly becomes stressful, anxiety-provoking and undermines your confidence and energy. Keeping the relationship professional and healthy (or healthy enough) can be difficult when they 'get to you' personally. This is a situation where there is really no substitute for exploring what happens from your perspective with a good coach or on a management development course.

Almost always, there is a pattern to the type of person we find difficult. Maybe we just can't tolerate someone who is superior, manipulative, or unprofessional in some other way – lazy or unreliable. The first thing to look at is to make sure you are not the bigger part of the problem. Reflect on your behaviour, solicit feedback from trusted friends and close family or colleagues to see if they can enlighten you about the part that you might play in the drama. Here are some further tips:

> *If you confront the behaviour, be clear, direct and as assertive as possible.*

- Book yourself some time away from the situation to try to understand what is going on both externally (what happens, what is said) and internally (how that makes you feel).

- Develop an 'uncensored' view of what is going on. Give clarity to the situation through spoken or written words – using strong language is perfectly acceptable at this point.

- Understand what part you play in the situation and be prepared to take responsibility for that part of the difficulty – use the 'Rule of three' (see below).

- Choose whether or not to address the behaviour with the person – you do have a choice, and either decision has consequences.

- If you confront the behaviour, be clear, direct and as assertive as possible.

- If you choose not to confront the behaviour, try to understand how you can avoid a similar situation arising in the future.

The rule of three

The rule of three helps us to figure out where the responsibility for an issue resides, and is a simple list of questions answered with a percentage figure:

- Is it me?
- Is it you?
- Is it someone else/bigger than either of us?

So, for example, if A expects B to produce a weekly report, but B never does, there are several possibilities:

– A has never actually told B what to do (100 per cent responsibility of A)
– B never does the report, despite agreeing to it (100 per cent responsibility of B)
– the report was defined by C and is impossible to do (responsibility split between A, B and C).

In most situations, 'me' and 'you' categories both take a share of the responsibility for difficult communication, and there is often a percentage for the third 'environmental factor', e.g. there are not enough hours in the day, or the train was late, or someone was ill.

Once you've done the exercise, make sure you do something with the bit that is your responsibility. Don't use 'it was partly their fault' as an excuse not to do anything. Equally, don't use it an excuse to beat yourself up – the purpose of this exercise is take hold of the bit you can control and change things for the better.

The Rule of Three was developed by the **Global Resonance** consultancy.

SUPPLIERS

All businesses need suppliers but your degree of reliance on them will depend on the type of business you have set up. Recruitment agencies, coaching organisations, PR consultants, therapists and copywriters all deliver a service that does not necessarily involve the provision of any physical product. Your suppliers will be mostly providing office or business products (stationery, IT equipment, massage table, etc.) and office-related services (printing, IT support, marketing).

On the other hand, if you are opening a restaurant, an interior design business, a shop or a construction company, you will be heavily reliant on products; in fact you won't be able to do a day's work without them. Whereas the services-based businesses are using suppliers to hold up the business, you will be actually selling the products you have sourced (somewhat altered). Your suppliers are therefore crucial to the success of your business, and the quality of what they sell you will directly affect the quality of what you sell to your customers.

You may need to do lots of research and pavement-pounding to find suppliers who offer the product you want at the price you want. It can come as a shock to you to find that not all suppliers are falling over themselves to do business with you.

Sahar Hashemi, co-founder of Coffee Republic, says she started off knowing nothing about coffee, but applied herself to learning everything there was to know. When she eagerly approached coffee suppliers with a very clear idea of what she wanted, she was amazed at how many couldn't be bothered to deal with her, and how unpleasant and offhand some could be about potential new business. Her response was to find suppliers with the same 'spirit' that she and her brother had. 'What we needed were suppliers who were entrepreneurial and thought like us. Suppliers who believed in our vision and would go that extra mile to meet our needs.'

Getting your suppliers exactly right at the start can be a challenge, but finding new suppliers when things go wrong can be a bigger problem – once you are up and running, you will have much less time to shop around for a better deal. Most businesses do change suppliers for one reason or another at some point. Businesses evolve and the products and services they use will change as well. The most common reason for changing supplier is cost – businesses are more likely than consumers to shop around for a better price. The cheaper they can get the product, the bigger their profit margin. So bearing this in mind, and also to cater for any potential disasters in the supply arena, always keep a second supplier lined up in case the first one lets you down. This also provides an insight into how you are seen as a supplier to your customer. It is a reminder to make sure you know what your customers are looking for, and offer it to them before they presume you can't and go elsewhere.

Suppliers have an annoying habit of needing to be paid. Whether you are dealing with a food wholesaler or your local printer, try to strike a balance between keen-as-mustard prompt settlement of their bills (your cash is much better off sitting in your bank) and being late paying up. Your relationship should be one of mutual trust, and you may be called upon to produce references from suppliers at a future date for credit rating purposes. Try to resolve any disputes with suppliers amicably before jumping ship – it can be a lot less painful.

> *Try to strike a balance between keen-as-mustard prompt settlement of their bills and being late paying up.*

MONEY

It may not be your main reason for setting up your business in the first place, but managing money and keeping on top of your cashflow is important if you are going to *stay* in business. We explored your relationship with money earlier in the book in the context of pricing. What we go on to deal with here is the nitty-gritty of what is happening in your bank account, how to monitor it and what to watch out for.

Cashflow

Cashflow is a critical aspect of all businesses, small and large, and monitoring cashflow (and trying not to worry about it) may occupy a large part of your working time. If you are in the service industry you may be less affected by cashflow issues in that you can keep your costs low, but you will still have to make sure there is money in the account to pay the bills and make it worth your while.

Teresa Owen and Martin Abel run Fairwind Trading, a fair trade gifts business, online. Martin offered us a simple view of cashflow:

If sales are good and outgoings are low, then you become 'fat and happy'.

The cashflow dynamic is comparable to our diets; what goes in (food or money in this case) take away what is used (exercise or spending) = what is left. Keeping to our ideal weight levels is notoriously difficult for most of us. Cashflow is exactly the same, but our desire is in the opposing direction – to get fat! If sales are good and outgoings are low, then you become 'fat and happy'; if sales are bad and outgoings are high, then you become 'skinny and unhappy'.

Fairwind Trading is a cash-intensive business. As importers of goods from overseas, they have to pay for buying, shipping and storage long before they can sell their gifts, recover their money and make a profit. On the other hand, most shops can benefit from getting customer payment at point-of-sale – i.e. you pick up a product and have to pay for it before leaving rather than within 30 days of the invoice date. So if you are not importing goods, you may find you can arrange a long payment period with suppliers, which allows you to get paid by customers before you have to settle your own bills.

If you are in the Fairwind category and have to buy before you sell, you may find yourself reliant initially on a loan to bridge the gap between money going out on supplies and money coming in from customers. Loan repayments are another outgoing for your cashbook and your bank's credit system will rank your business according to how well you run your account. If you go over an overdraft limit or become overdrawn without a facility, this will knock down your credit rating, which in turn will affect your ability to borrow later.

Leila Wilcox of Halos 'n' Horns found that negotiating 30 days' payment terms with her customers, and 60 days' payment terms with her suppliers, meant that she kept the cashflow largely under control. **Claire Owen** of Stopgap, whom we met as a great employer earlier, has never had a loan or debt in her personal life, or for her (now) multi-million pound business. Cashflow was one of her three main focuses for business success (the other two being customer and employee satisfaction). In the early days of her business, Claire made sure they always had enough money in the bank to survive a month where no new business came in. Taking that solid approach to cashflow could mean your business takes longer to grow, but Claire's priority was being true to herself, rather than shooting for the stars.

Your cashflow can be broken down into four elements:

- **The easy bit – regular debits**, e.g. rent, rates, monthly fixed bills, loan repayments.

- **The scary bit – variable large debits**, e.g. VAT, wages, stock purchases.

- **The sneaky bit – 'sundries'**: numerous small amounts that come and go through your account, e.g. stationery purchases, fuel, bank charges, petty cash top-ups.

- **The good bits – credits**: what goes into your account can vary even more than the debits, making it difficult to match the two up. Monitor your sales closely and take predictions with a pinch of salt. Follow up and learn from late payers and think twice before doing business with them in the future.

Cashflow often has seasonality, so it may be helpful to map out your predictions for the whole year. Most businesses are broke at some time of the year and cash-friendly at others. Woolworths is a good example of a cashflow extreme: they take something like 80 per cent of their revenue during the Christmas period.

If you get your cashflow under control, you are in a good position to predict any trouble. You will also be able to get figures together quickly to present to the bank if you need an overdraft or loan. Your monthly bank statement (or internet bank statement) shows the playing field, warts and all. Beware the rogue cheques drawn on your account. Someone cashing a large cheque very late when you've forgotten about it is a nightmare. Make sure you know what's due to be cashed from the cheque book and factor that amount into the figures.

Getting paid

Getting the business is only half of what your business needs to do – getting paid is the other half. Learning to get paid can be a steep learning curve for newcomers to self-employment. It's something most employees don't have to deal with, but is the dirty work done by the rather shadowy invoicing department. Well, you are your invoicing department now, so here are some tips for getting paid.

Top tips for getting paid

- Agree payment terms upfront and in writing before you start work.
- Take on clients that you believe can and will pay – if necessary do credit checks, or speak to other suppliers.
- Make sure your invoices are professional-looking, accurate and add up correctly.
- Invoice promptly and state clearly the payment terms and time for payment on your invoice.
- If appropriate to your cashflow situation, take a deposit upfront or ask for payment in instalments.
- Monitor payments in, and if you don't get paid on time, don't stew, pick up the phone, ask for payment, and agree when that will be.
- If someone hasn't paid you when they should have done, don't do any more work for them until you have been paid.
- If all else fails, consider using debt factoring services who take the hassle of collection off your hands in return for a percentage of the profits.

GETTING THINGS DONE

'More peaks than Derbyshire and more troughs than a pig farm' was one business woman's summing up of the highs and lows of running her own show. When you were tucked away behind the scenes of a big organisation you barely noticed how well it was doing financially. Most of us were too busy taking advantage of lulls in workload by having a sneaky afternoon off, and whether we were off sick or working our socks off late into the night, we never saw a change in the number of pounds going into our bank account.

When it's *your* business that's having a quiet time, on the other hand, it's a different story, and the last place you'll be found is getting a manicure at the nail bar. Women are always accused of 'over-reacting' and you may well live up to this reputation when the pace of your business slows – you'll be panicking that the business has failed, that it's all over. When things busy up again you'll think you've hit the jackpot and can retire at Christmas, or more likely you will panic again that you've got too much on. Both busy times and quiet times bring their own particular stresses and anxieties.

> *When the pace of your business slows – you'll be panicking that the business has failed, that it's all over.*

Charlotte Fuller, an independent PR consultant, says:

CASE STUDY

What you need to realise when you set up in business is that it's not all going to be controlled by you. Much is made of the benefits of work–life balance and flexibility offered by self-employment, but in reality your schedule is dictated by your clients and their deadlines, which often all coincide with each other. Then there are quiet times. There is no magic solution. Being single and child-free helps, but there are still only 24 hours in a day...

All of us need a balance between being too busy and too quiet, and this applies as much to life as it does to work. When we haven't been out of the house for a while, we may get 'cabin fever', but if we have a week where we are out night and day, we may crave some

Women are so keen to admonish their menfolk for not being able to ask for directions but suffer the same incapacity when it comes to asking for help with family and other responsibilities.

quiet time to recover at the weekend. This is an area where people's preferences differ hugely, and it is important to get the balance between 'out in the world' and 'in your own space' right. It helps to know your own personal rhythm and, as much as possible, to design your business to support that.

Here are some tactics to deal with the overload and the underload.

Busy times

- Prioritise – put to one side everything that can wait, and concentrate on the most urgent work, the most important client, the most valuable task. Make a list of what you are going to do and in what order. Making lists takes time, but calms and focuses you when you start getting into a tizz.

- Call in help – whether it's childcare or a temp to answer the phones for a few days, don't be afraid to ask. Women are so keen to admonish their menfolk for not being able to ask for directions but suffer the same incapacity when it comes to asking for help with family and other responsibilities.

- Don't over-promise – without actively upsetting your customers, be as honest as you can about when they are going to get that document, that bookshelf, that chat on the phone. All clients like to feel like they are the centre of your universe, so they may not be impressed if you are too elusive. By all means switch the phone to answerphone all day if you have to, but try to return the most important calls as soon as it is reasonably possible.

- Don't routinely over-deliver – the over-delivering habit can soon land you in trouble with time and cost management, and routinely causes businesses to fail. It's a nice idea, but be realistic about your limitations.

- Look at your email less often, and don't spend hours forwarding jokes to all your friends.

- Relax – if only for a moment. Close your eyes and put your head in your hands (if you aren't already doing that with the stress of it); walk outside, look at the sky, go into another room, do a yoga class. A moment away from the problem can ease the situation.

- If you can bear the thought of more work, let people know you are busy. It's that gang culture again – people want to go where the other people are and if you are the busiest juice bar in town everyone is going to think you serve the best juice.

- Don't show off about it too much – next month might be awful.

Quiet times

- Prioritise – don't let this quiet time slip away without having used it to get on with things that need doing. Make a list again.

- Keep focused and energised – don't let the lull send you to sleep. Get exercising, revisit your business plan, your business vision, your marketing plan. Are you sticking to it? What more can you do?

- Talk to people. Remember this is something you don't have time for when you're busy. Remind your friends you still exist. Go to a networking event. Call up someone, just on the off-chance. Get in touch with your customers. Being the last person they spoke to is always good for business.

- Plan your leisure time – it will give you something to look forward to when things seem very flat at work.

- Go shopping. Yes, really!

- Tidy up, sort out your email folders, do that thing you keep putting off. Have a folder of things to do in quiet times, and do them.

- Get out there in the community – it's people that make life worthwhile.

CASE STUDY

Portrait photographer **Jackie Frost** said:

When I started my business, it was very much a case of pounding the streets with my portfolio, visiting schools, nurseries and toddler groups. Very quickly, my efforts paid off and I had a viable business. Like any business, I have ups and downs, but whenever there is a lull in business, I'm out there as I was on day one – pounding the streets with my portfolio. After many such cycles over the years, I don't worry any more that I'll go under during the quiet times, or during the busy times. I've learnt that's just normal.

CASE STUDY

Kelly Chandler and Britt Armstrong-Gash of the Bespoke Wedding Company found, perhaps not surprisingly, that most of their work was between April and September:

There is the odd winter wedding, but not really as much as we'd like to keep us going. So, we are in the process of setting up a sister company, the Bespoke Event Company, to arrange corporate and private celebrations including Christmas parties. A lot of the skills and contacts we use will be the same as we'll concentrate on the same type of high-class, sophisticated clientele as we do for weddings. It will be nice to balance out the seasonal nature of our business, and to do slightly different events too.

Both quiet times and busy times are a useful and inevitable part of business, so don't panic when the phone doesn't ring – enjoy the quiet. And don't feel snowed under when it doesn't stop – ride the wave. Ups and downs are normal part of business life, as are setbacks and breakthroughs.

Ride the wave. Ups and downs are a normal part of business life.

Setbacks

Setbacks range from losing a key client and having a difficult few weeks, to serious events that inevitably have an impact on your business. One newcomer to our business group lost all her office equipment and business paperwork during a move that went wrong, but we're glad to report she was back in business after a few painful months.

Often women are motivated to start a business by their setbacks, in some cases serious and tragic ones: **Nicola Horlick** set up Bramdiva after losing her daughter after a long illness to leukaemia, not to mention a divorce and a series of well-publicised challenges in her city career.

Sandy Eifion Jones of SEJ Consultancy set up her business after a divorce which left her a single mum, but finds her teenage daughter a great help with research, decision-making and IT. Sandy, formerly a champion swimmer, has been a wheelchair user for the last 16 years, but turned this setback into her latest business opportunity. She realised that she was uniquely placed to help small companies make their premises suitable for disabled people, which they need to do by law:

I had a lot of information on disability, 16 years of personal experience, was highly articulate and I knew how small and large companies worked. I felt someone like myself — who was once able-bodied — could bridge a gap between the two worlds — thereby helping both sides ... I think everyone should see what cards they have in their hand and play them to their best advantage. Being female is part of that — I think women should learn to use their femininity in a positive, natural and non-confrontational manner. I'm quite sure many men envy the power that a woman can exert — just by being herself, being at ease with herself as a woman and accepting her female role. For me there is a parallel lesson in being a wheelchair user — by being myself and allowing my personality and

> **I think women should learn to use their femininity in a positive, natural and non-confrontational manner.**

> *talent to shine through in a natural way, most people say they forget I'm sitting in a wheelchair and don't notice it after a while. This is the best compliment I can have. After all, it's me and my business and talent I want others to recognise — the rest is irrelevant. Though setting up a business has been challenging, I have developed as a person. My self-esteem and confidence are both higher — I recognise my potential and am sharper, more wary and questioning. My personality is more positive and brighter. I am becoming more aware of and interested in current issues and I am happier.*

Everything is much easier when you feel confident, but confidence is something that comes and goes. Women seem to be more prone than men to extreme swings in confidence, because they don't always know how to 'not worry about it', which is the tactic men always seem to recommend (and deploy) when faced with a problem.

When your confidence and self-esteem are low, that's precisely when insecurity and critical thinking (of others as well as yourself) come marching in the door. We wrote in Chapter 1 about the need for resilience to deal with setbacks, but that doesn't mean you have to do all the coping on your own. What we find useful is to have someone to call at difficult times, or just when you're doubting yourself or feeling blue. Call your mum, your friend, someone you met at a networking event, anyone who can help you feel grounded and powerful again.

Chief Executive of Merton Chamber of Commerce, **Diana Sterck**, told us:

> *When things start going wrong — and they inevitably do — women are generally very good at asking for help. They are willing to speak to one of our business advisors and listen carefully to the advice they get. Of course, it's their decision what to do, and their business to make a go of, but women don't suffer too badly from being too proud to accept help.*

Stephanie Butland set up haveyouthoughtabout.com to help women decide on career changes and remarked upon women's resourcefulness: 'the less they have, the better they use it'. **Amar Basra**, Women's Enterprise Project Officer from the Business Skills Department at the University of Bath in Swindon, adds: 'often the setbacks faced by women give them grit and determination to succeed and not to be dependent on others'.

> **Setbacks faced by women give them grit and determination to succeed and not to be dependent on others.**

Of course, being a woman, one major setback you may have to deal with is pregnancy, which doesn't always run smoothly.

Bella: Two years after setting up my business, I became pregnant. I was excited about the turn of events, looking forward to taking it a little bit easy, having some interesting cravings to amuse my husband with, and planning for our new arrival. A long piece of work had just ended and I had lots of ideas about what to do next. My plan was to work for the first six months of my pregnancy, and to spend a few months winding things down before the baby arrived. But it was not to be. Almost from the moment I saw the blue line, I felt totally sick and exhausted, some days not even able to go down the stairs because I was too weak and tired. I spent the little energy I had cancelling everything in sight and was laid up for almost the entire pregnancy. It was definitely not the time of blooming health and happiness that I had envisaged, and, with so much time to stare at the bedroom ceiling, it was easy for me to spiral into worries about my baby, my health, the future and money. Good health is something that I'd previously taken very much for granted, but my experience of pregnancy gave me a taste of how debilitating health challenges are, physically and emotionally. Thankfully this is all behind me now, and we have a beautiful, healthy son. Being laid up for so long gave me a very real understanding of what it means to have a long-term illness, which I draw upon in my work, and, on a different scale, it will help me relate to my son during the inevitable chicken-pox years. I think he was pretty clever to have taught me that.

Breakthrough

The early months, even years, can feel like a long hard slog, where more things go wrong than right, you struggle to break even and wonder whether it's all worth it. But one day when you least expect it, you may suddenly find you have turned a corner. Be prepared (one of the better male mottos), and keep putting the make-up on because at any moment you might find the spotlight is on you as you break through to the next level of business success.

This breakthrough may not be your dream multi-million pound client – it may just be that your partner turns round and says how happy and relaxed you look now you are self-employed, or that a national newspaper writes about your product and you are flooded with enquiries. Either way, it can be a defining moment when you suddenly see how all your hard work has paid off.

CASE STUDY

Judy Bell set up Shepherd's Purse in 1989 from the family farm in North Yorkshire, because, in her words, 'the future of farming looked gloomy, and farmers were being encouraged to diversify'. While working as a receptionist for an alternative therapist, she became aware of the number of people with an intolerance to dairy products made from cow's milk, and decided her sheep could help. Undeterred by a lack of knowledge of milking sheep, making cheese or running a business, she threw herself into doing everything she needed to do to produce an award-winning cheese. She worked hard to create a product that looked attractive, had lots of information on the label – not just nutritional information but it also suggested recipes. She sold it at country fairs and entered her cheeses for prizes at competitions – her first breakthrough came after winning just such a competition: 'I came off the podium from receiving an award, clutching my trophy, and was literally surrounded by representatives from Tesco wanting to supply the cheese in their stores. We struck a deal in which I got to work with their deli staff directly to share my experience of how to sell fine ewes' milk cheese.' She now sells to all the major high-street supermarkets, and the company is growing 20 per cent year on year.

Once you have had one major breakthrough, you may find the next one comes more easily, and suddenly you are doing business.

Leila Wilcox's strategy with Halos 'n' Horns was to use each success as a springboard for the next, spurred on by her business partner, Ivan: 'We'd finally got a meeting with Somerfield and they'd agreed to take our products and give them a big launch. Ivan and I were pulling out of the car park, both grinning from ear to ear. He said "Fantastic! Now dial 118 and get the number for Tesco's."' Halos 'n' Horns products are now stocked in all the major supermarkets.

So don't be scared of fast growth, or of setbacks and break-throughs. If you keep your wits about you, and keep learning, it's an exciting time.

Project management and SMART goals

Once you're up and running, with your filing system working a treat, and daily business a breeze, you might like to think about a change to your business. If it is a largish change, and perhaps has some complexity to it, you should designate it a 'project', and manage it as a professional project manager would do (because that's what you are for your business). An example of a project for a small business might be to implement a new computer package, to redevelop a website, to develop a new product, or to find new premises.

Here are some top tips for managing your business project:

- Spend time planning – set a start date, end date, budget (time and money).

- Decide what goal your project is going to achieve – this should be a SMART goal (see below).

- Plan the major steps you are going to take to achieve your goal.

- Don't have too many projects 'live' at once – two or three major projects are probably quite enough for one person to handle, especially if there is day-to-day business to do as well.

- If you subcontract your project delivery to someone, make sure they know the grand plan, and give you regular updates, especially if things aren't going to schedule.

- Review your plans regularly to see how you are doing against the plan.

- When a project has finished, close it down properly – reflect on what you've learnt and what you'd do differently, file all papers away, go back to 'business as usual'.

SMART goals

You will no doubt have goals for your business, but the mistake that many people make it to have big plans ('one day I'll be a big business') but no SMART goals – **S**pecific, **M**easurable, **A**chievable, **R**ealistic, **T**imed. One sure way not to achieve any goal you have is not to have it properly defined. So really think about how you set that goal, and once you've written it down, make a photocopy of it and pin it somewhere you'll see it every day.

Make sure all of your goals are SMART goals.

Make sure all of your goals are SMART goals, defined in the following way (using the example of **Jackie Abey and Jill Smallcombe,** who are launching a range of protective workwear for women).

Example of a SMART goal
- **S**pecific, e.g. to develop protective clothing to be used by women on construction sites.
- **M**easurable, e.g. three new garments for head, body and foot protection.
- **A**chievable, e.g. you have experience of equipment design and knowledge of Health and Safety legislation.
- **R**ealistic, e.g. it is something that you have the wherewithal (know-how, premises, etc.) to do.
- **T**imed, e.g. within one year.

LEADERSHIP

Entrepreneurs are natural leaders. But what does that mean? Many women we talk to don't see themselves as leaders, even though they may:

• be the main influence in the lives of their children

• be responsible for appraising and developing a team of people

• teach, train and coach

• inspire their friends

• give talks – either formally, or speak their views to a group of people

• initiate social and community events

• influence people's thinking

• run a business.

What is difficult for many of us, in thinking about leadership, is that the role models we have around us as 'leaders' aren't often the type of people that we want to follow, or the type of people that we aspire to be. The stereotypical leader is the powerful man or bossy woman who 'leads' by saying, 'This is how things are to be done because I say so and I know best' (i.e. hierarchically) and not through seeking or creating consensus (i.e. co-operatively).

Carol Daniels is a self-employed consultant, working with organisations on gender issues, and undertaking a PhD in gender and leadership at Bath University. Carol told us:

> *Both men and women have been victims of the traditional leadership role models of middle-class white men: able-bodied, heterosexual,*

decisive, opinionated, autonomous and individualistic. Organisations recognise that 'pale-male-stale' doesn't work anymore for either gender

> **Organisations recognise that 'pale-male-stale' doesn't work anymore for either gender.**

— partly because women continue to leave in droves, but also partly because of globalisation and decreasing job security that affect men just as much as women. It makes us all question what we're doing and why we're doing it, and makes us more accepting of what doesn't fit the accepted model. If you add to that the success that women are finding in leadership roles — their networking and relationship skills are perfectly suited to these changes — it seems that the leadership role is changing to encompass more of what women have to offer.

A research report from Aurora and Caliper supports this:[vii] 'We're looking at a different paradigm of leadership and it plays naturally to the strengths of women. The tide has turned. The leadership skills that come naturally to women are now absolutely necessary for companies to continue to thrive.' The study showed that women leaders had 'significantly higher' levels of empathy, flexibility, sociability and urgency than men. Interestingly, women leaders feel the sting of rejection more than men but 'rapidly learn from adversity and develop an "I'll show you" attitude'.

> **Women leaders 'rapidly learn from adversity and develop an "I'll show you" attitude'.**

Women have a different style of leadership from men. They tend to be more co-operative, more inclusive, more consensus-seeking and more willing to forgo some personal gain for the good of the group. In the old model, asking for help or giving anything away was weak. Leaders were expected to have all the answers, all the power and pots of money, and many of them were only to happy to meet this expectation.

Alan Sugar built Amstrad up into an enormously profitable business, motivated almost entirely by money as a result of childhood poverty. He found public fame after his recent appearances on BBC's show 'The Apprentice' and epitomises what could be kindly described as an aggressive hierarchical style. 'I'll shove it right up your bloody a**e if it doesn't work … I don't like bulls******s, schmoozers, liars or cheats!'

We know from (bitter) experience that this bullying style of leadership does not produce contented followers. In fact, much of the stress, depression, anger and resentment that seethe beneath the surface of corporate life could be put down to bad leadership. And yet, we are very reliant on our leaders, and place mighty expectations upon them and their egos. There are, necessarily, more followers than leaders, so what about them?

A survey carried out by Jo Owen, author of *How to Lead*,[viii] revealed that most people wanted their leaders to be positive, professional and people-focused. Leaders were expected to have:

• the ability to motivate others

• vision

• honesty and integrity

• decisiveness

• ability to handle a crisis.

Interestingly charisma, intelligence, organisational skills and inspiration were not on the list.

What is becoming clear is that leadership is not about being a bossy know-all, but rather about personal qualities – in fact the ones we discussed in Chapter 1. This definition of leadership as something that comes from within and relies on personal qualities is easier for women to identify with.

Jenny Cook, an accredited facilitator for the Institute for

CASE STUDY

the Development of Human Potential (IDHP), said:

Having been quite confused about leadership in the past, despite being a leader, I have become a lot clearer about it in the last few years. There are two important things about leadership for me. Firstly, it is a never-ending journey, and secondly, it is something that happens internally (developing the qualities you need for leadership) and externally (manifested in the way you use those qualities out in the world). I worked for many years as a manager for the NHS, progressing from nurse and midwife to the management of over 400 staff. I managed people intuitively, in the style of my family, which was pretty co-operative, and it worked — I was even awarded Welsh Woman in Leadership Award. Later on in my career through personal development courses, I began to see how important it was to own my own power and use it responsibly, and I was challenged about assumptions and judgements I didn't even know that I had, by people from all walks of life. I don't think it matters whether it is the internal or external that starts the journey, but sooner or later they need to be integrated — that's what it means to be who you are. The next step for me on my journey is that I'm about to lead the IDHP course that I found so inspiring as a participant, and so important for the development of my leadership skills.

The fact that you are an entrepreneur, or considering setting up your own business, already shows that you have a great instinct for leadership. One of the reasons you may have left your previous job is that the opportunity to use your leadership skills simply did not surface, leaving you feeling that you had an untapped energy source. Business ownership is likely to provide you with an outlet for that energy, but real leadership skills (as opposed to just being very bossy) emerge through a continuous and conscious process of self-reflection, training and experience. It will be a personal development journey in itself, where you have the opportunity to discover your own style and round off any rough edges. You are bound to make mistakes along the way — all part of the

> *Real leadership skills emerge through a continuous and conscious process of self-reflection.*

occasionally painful process – but the outcome will be a noticeable increase in self-confidence, power and self-belief, which will show on the outside as well and be useful in all areas of your life. One (anonymous) businesswoman we spoke to told us how a hopeless crush she had on a married man gradually evaporated, as she became more and more sure of herself and the direction her life, and business, were taking.

Business ownership provides the ideal environment to develop as a leader because it not only allows you, but actually requires you, to be who you really are – to harness the resources around you and the personality within you to their best effect. You have the opportunity to build a business that you want to lead, and choose the people you want to lead. Eventually, by setting an inspiring example and letting go of the reins when you feel it appropriate, you will find yourself passing on the skills you have learnt and empowering the people around you. This is how businesses grow 'organically', and is a tried and tested method of keeping good staff.

Claire Owen of Stopgap, whom we met earlier as a good employer, is, unsurprisingly also, a great leader. She recently won the Sunday Times Award for Best Leadership, an achievement made even more meaningful for Claire because it is awarded on the basis of staff feedback. We loved this quote about Claire, from one of her employees:

> *'What makes Claire special? She's a lady! Strong yet caring, nurturing but not scared of confrontation. She is not shy of being girly – which a lot of businesswomen are: often women in business associate their femininity with weakness – which is what causes so many of them to become hard, uncaring and miserable. No female employee can respect or associate with that. I can, however, associate with and respect a woman who has not 'sold out' and become some sort of androgynous super-creature. Claire is transparent, she admits when she needs help, never treats her*

Often women in business associate their femininity with weakness – which is what causes so many of them to become hard, uncaring and miserable.

employees as subjects but rather as helpers, and encourages those around her to be the best that they can be.'

That's leadership.

RELATIONSHIPS AND RESPONSIBILITIES
Yourself
Throughout this book we have talked a lot about the importance of being who you are, developing a work–life balance that works for you, and having quiet times to balance the energy required to run a business.

Our plans often take good health for granted. When you are responsible for your own livelihood, with no corporate health plan or gym membership, you need to actively take charge of keeping yourself fit and healthy. It is up to your personal philosophy whether you guard against sickness by preventative medicine, eating well, exercising, medical insurance, or a combination of these.

A good starting point for mental and physical health is to decide what holiday time you need and keep this time precious. It is easy to start to sacrifice holiday time, or, on a daily basis, even mealtimes and gym time to keep up with clients' demands, but you and your body are in fact the main resources of your business. Look after that precious resource.

Couples
In this section, we talk mainly about relationships between men and women. The same principles may apply to same-sex relationships, but it seems that a particular dynamic exists in couples of a man and woman, to which men bring 'man stuff' from their biology, upbringing and society, and we bring our 'woman stuff'.

Without falling too deeply into the trap of 'men are like this and women are like this' (largely because the people who are making a difference are the ones who are challenging the stereotype and conditioning), it is difficult to talk about relationships without making some generalisations. Here, we share what we've learnt from real women in their own words, to show that, what really matters is not the big picture but the personal relationships in your life.

If we had a penny for every woman in business who has told us that their husband, or ex-husband, wasn't coping well with her success, we would be rich. Without laying all our interviewees' private lives on the line here, it is safe to say that there are a fair number of divorces where the wife's career success appears to be the reason for the relationship failing. Why is this? How often do women throw the towel in because their husband works too late or too hard? What is it about women fulfilling their potential, achieving their dreams, that drives men away in their droves? Whether it is entrepreneurship or employment that keeps women in the office and out of the kitchen, the same dilemma crops up again and again, as described by **Fiona Price**, who founded Fiona Price & Partners, a financial advisory service for women.

If you look at the type of woman who is succeeding as an entrepreneur, what you find is a woman who has vision, who is a leader, who makes decisions, who takes responsibility and who knows how to pick herself off the floor when things go wrong. And has charisma as well. The problem is that when a male successful entrepreneur goes home, he doesn't have to make a step change from his work persona to his family persona. The dilemma facing entrepreneurial women is: should she 'dumb down' this bigger person that she is at work or does she have to change the kind of relationship that she is looking for ... or the type of man?

> **The dilemma facing entrepreneurial women is: should she 'dumb down' this bigger person that she is at work.**

Mary Corrie, a former senior executive at Shell, who founded internet business Cityorganiser, adds:

A successful businesswoman today doesn't need a man for the same things that women did in the past — she's pretty self-sufficient financially, used to making decisions, doesn't need a shoulder to cry on in the same way, and therefore what is it that she actually needs? To me it's the little things that mean so much and probably cost virtually nothing, which is love and caring. It's about somebody listening, doing nice things like buying me flowers, opening car doors — I like that, I surprise myself! I love the fact that my partner probably knows me better than I know myself — he looks after me and takes me on holiday, which I never did for myself. They are the things that for me add value when I can provide the basics for myself.

Liz Nelson, OBE, co-founder of Taylor Nelson Sofrès plc, points out that to play that wifely role, you have to want it in the first place: 'I am someone who loves my work more than living with a man … two husbands couldn't take it…' Twice-divorced **Catherine Green** of CG Scrubbers says that she has found a real sense of freedom, control and happiness since being single for the first time, and it makes her a better businesswoman. She adds: 'I lay the blame for the failure of my marriages firmly at my own door. I'm such a mixture of a free spirit and a Cancerian who wants to settle down and make a lovely home. I have found that doing both, properly, is virtually impossible.'

As we discussed in Chapter 2, paying someone to look after the children or the house is still a real taboo for a lot of women. Here's Lucy again with even more to say about delegation.

Lucy: From my Gina's Nannies experience of taking calls from overwrought mothers, what it comes down to is that guilt thing again. Women feel guilty about delegating their traditional role in the family. Even if they are running an international business, some women feel they have let everyone down if they are not there at teatime spooning food into baby's mouth, with a homemade pie in the oven for the hubby. It's a hard lesson to learn, that you should spend your time on what you are (a) good at and (b) where your personal input is most highly valued. The carpets don't care who hoovers them, and, shockingly, my children don't mind if I'm not there at teatime. Knowing this doesn't make me feel redundant, it makes me feel free. I think there are plenty of women who don't feel entitled to this kind of freedom. Men have had it for centuries.

> **Spend your time on what you are (a) good at and (b) where your personal input is most highly valued. The carpets don't care who hoovers them.**

Over the last 30 years or so, we may have picked up extra roles (Barbie got her first job as a surgeon in 1975), but it doesn't feel like we've changed the old ones to suit, or dropped any of them (in 2006, only one of Barbie's 65 outfits is work attire).

The definition of 'family values' has been distorted over the years. What it should mean is equal partnerships, but somehow just the putting the word 'traditional' before 'family values' means that women end up doing everything. This inequality, and the overload imposed on women who may have jobs as well as family responsibilities, is no better for men than it is for women. Going back to the old model of men at work and women at home is neither possible nor desirable at this point, so there really is no option but to find a new way forward for family relationships and responsibilities.

We have met women during our research who genuinely didn't want to work and who did want to stay at home and look after children. Some of our best friends are stay-at-home mothers. (We have found that they also tend to devote more time to friendships, which is another lesson to us.) What we sometimes found too, though, on further questioning, was that they hated their old job, and, at least partly, saw having children as an escape or excuse. And why wouldn't they, if they had a bad experience at work or an unfulfilling career? In a civilised Western country, women should be able to work alongside men without experiencing unacceptable practices or harsh environments, and with a real prospect of being rewarded and valued for what they do. Men should be able to be more involved with family life without their careers suffering. It seems that we aren't quite there yet. We get back on our soapbox and write more about women, work and responsibilities in Chapter 7.

One solution to the family being torn in different directions by conflicting responsibilities is to get your husband or partner to join you as a business partner. **Jocelyn Ashton** of Building Blocks Nursery took her husband on after a few years on her own and is still very much not divorced at the time of writing. If hiring hubby is not an option for you, make sure you still see each other. **Mary Corrie**, who has been in a happy relationship for the last eleven years, says: 'In my first marriage, I probably displayed tunnel vision and I missed the warning signs. I spent too much time at work and didn't notice that my alpha male at home felt that his ego was being badly bruised by that. So now it's a question of making sure that the focus is on the marriage.'

Top tips for keeping your relationships intact while your business develops

- Keep talking – men don't always say what they think, and women don't always say what they mean. Ask him how he feels about you running your business, listen to the answer, tell him your point of view, try to understand each other.
- Be clear at the setting-up stage and beyond about the bottom line concerning the things that affect your time together, like travelling or working at evenings/weekends – these will really affect your relationship and your capacity to do business.
- Go on a regular date together – chances are your business won't collapse in your absence, and you may even find you have other things to talk about than your latest defaulting customer.
- Get his dinner on the table, or pay someone to make that happen.

- Have sex (with him).
- Get him involved. He may be happy in his own job and not need to apply for your post of office manager, but keep him entertained (not bored) with the interesting parts of what is going on.
- Ask for his advice. Listen to it and then do something completely different (he won't ever know until you come asking for some tips on how to sort out the mess you've made later).
- Let him see the fruits of your labours, pay for the kitchen extension, or send him off somewhere in a hired Ferrari.

Being single

The word on the street, and in women's magazines, is 'it's tough being single' (subtext: go out and find someone, and here's the best lipstick for the job). Actually, there are tough things about being single while you're setting up and running your business. No one to come home at night and be the first friendly person you've spoken to all day. No one to share the financial burden with, or to inspire you at home. No one to pick up something for dinner. But enjoy the green grass over there for what it is – a chance to work wherever and whenever you feel like it, peace and quiet, no one to interfere while you're inventing the new you, no one to question that or hold you back, no one to check with before you go out networking. No one to cramp your style.

Lone parents (90 per cent of whom are women) are a group who are particularly likely to want to set up a business that works around their children, and gives them financial security. **Linda Lloyd** set up Homeopathy Resource around her three children, training for many years and setting up her business during school hours and in the evenings, and using her school and family connections to build and develop her business.

But if you don't want to go it alone, take inspiration from the women we interviewed earlier: from Eugenie Harvey in

Chapter 1, who wanted to meet someone and did that as a result of her transformational success; and from Catherine Green and Liz Nelson, who found they were better off alone. Or Claire Owen and Fiona Price (below), who split up with their partners largely due to their success, but later found men who loved them for it. (In Claire's case, she treated it like a project and interviewed potential candidates she met on the internet.)

Fiona Price says:

> *I think I was a fairly typical women in business – I lived and breathed work until my mid-30s, and at 42 my longest relationship was six months. I attracted men who saw me as strong, who either wanted mentoring and emotional support, or who quite fancied the challenge of dominating me. I got to the point where I either had to resign myself to being single, as my list of requirements was becoming more precise, or I had to throw away the list altogether and ditch the stereotype. I managed to do that somehow, and at the age of 43 I met a man who wasn't the stereotype and I wasn't his, and we've been living together ever since. He is a very strong character in his own right – he's a successful businessman but he doesn't need to be better than me at things, and he quite likes me being better than him at some things. There's a lot of parity and we rub along extremely well.*

The truth is that it can be lonely setting up a business on your own whatever your situation, whether you are married, dating or single. Find yourself support, whether that's a trusted friend, your new business network or your internet dating partner.

And keep the home fires burning.

CHAPTER

7
THE BIGGER PICTURE

There is huge interest in women-owned businesses. You may have noticed the buzz around, or if not, and you are setting up a business, you soon will. In this chapter we look at why that is and how it affects you. We also look at what is happening in society around us – at places of work, in our schools, colleges and universities, in women's business networks, government and in our communities.

WOMEN AND WORK

Women have always worked. They have not always been paid for their work, and despite advances in women's rights, that is a pattern that continues today. Early in the twentieth century, women worked at home for the most part. While local exchanges of services were widespread – a woman might look after a neighbour's children or take a lodger who would do a few odd jobs – most of their jobs were domestic, caring and community roles, carried out quietly behind closed doors. Women did not go out to the labour market in force until the wars. Then, Britain needed women to drive trains, mine coal and run companies to literally keep the home fires burning. When the Second World war was over, and the men returned, women stopped running the country and went back indoors.

In 1975, a flurry of new laws were passed, and a new women's movement was born. There was a huge amount of optimism about the future and a lot of progress was made in the ensuing years, but there is still work to do. Although today's men take on more housework and caring responsibilities than our fathers did, and despite the rise in career opportunities for women, the labour market is still set up around the old-style model of men as breadwinners and women as carers. Most women adjust their careers to fit around their children, and most men don't, and the cycle continues. Children see that their mothers do the bulk of caring, and conclude that this is the norm. It is, in feminist terminology, a 'half-formed revolution'.

Taking responsibility for the bulk of the caring role means that women are only available for part-time jobs which are, for the most part, low-pay, low-status roles with little prospect of progression – the so-called 'sticky floor'. Women's employment is concentrated in the lower-paid industries, called the 'five c' sectors – caring, clerical, cashiering, catering and cleaning.

> *Women are consistently pushed into jobs which are below their potential and it's a real loss to our economy that we aren't letting those people contribute.*

Jenny Watson, chair of the Equal Opportunities Commission (EOC), says: 'While the Sex Discrimination and Equal Pay Acts have done much to tackle discrimination, the scandalous inequalities that women endure today show that (those laws) have reached the limits of their usefulness.' She talks about women as a pool of wasted talent: 'Women are consistently pushed into jobs which are below their potential – four out of five people working part time are working below their potential, and it's a real loss to our economy that we aren't letting those people contribute.'

In her book, *Hard Work*,[ix] **Polly Toynbee** shows how the pay gap for these low-paid jobs has widened over the last few years, with the equivalent job at a local hospital earning £36 less per week than it did 30 years ago. 'Not so much sticky floor, as nailed to the floor and pushed down the floorboards', says the *Guardian* journalist.

Relatively few professional or management jobs are available on a part-time basis, although north London organisation, Women Like Us, is attempting to change that by promoting the benefits of flexible, part-time work to employers, and recruiting mums to fill the resulting positions. **Karen Mattison**'s inspiring and innovative idea uses reps, like Avon Ladies, to talk to women at the school gates about employment opportunities that fit around families. **Alison Pearson**, journalist and author of *I Don't Know How She Does It*, says on their website:

> *Women Like Us is a brilliant and timely idea, a characteristically pragmatic, female solution to a dilemma that affects millions of mothers. Every day in the playground, I witness how hungry women are to carry on some kind of working life while having the time and energy to be good mums. Women Like Us offers practical help and inspiration on the route to that promised land.*

For women with an education, the picture is rosier than for those lacking qualifications or work experience. Women are more likely nowadays to be accepted into senior positions, but that does largely depend on them not having children and working full-time, or having fewer children later in life and using full-time childcare. Many organisations including political parties now want to have senior women among their ranks, and not just for the sake of political correctness. But the changes over the last 30 years have not been radical or wide-ranging enough to create a level playing field and haven't gone deep enough to address gender equality in a serious and lasting way. Women are still leaving corporate institutions in droves.

Bizarrely, there seems to be an impression in the UK, among both men and women, that gender inequality is not an issue that affects them. This is despite the facts in the box below, not to mention that in our daily life we see women pushing kids up to school in the morning to be taught by low-paid teachers (mostly female) or looked after by low-paid nursery assistants (mostly female), and men (mostly) shaping the world and reaping the rewards on the nightly news. Girls and boys emulate this model, and the cycle continues.

A frequent response to the question *why is the world so different for men and women?* is the biological differences between us. **Sandra Bem** puts this argument firmly in its place, in her ground-breaking book, *The Lenses of Gender:*[x]

So, yes women might turn out to be biologically more nurturant than men on the average, but that should make them psychiatrists, not secretaries.

No matter how many sex differences are someday shown to have a biological component, that knowledge will add little to our understanding of why women and men have universally played such different and unequal roles in virtually every society on earth … So, yes women might turn out to be biologically more nurturant than men on the average, but that should make them psychiatrists, not secretaries.

The reality of being human beings is that women are pregnant for nine months, give birth and then may breastfeed. Women often want to work part-time, or not at all, to accommodate their changed life and their babies' needs, but find that the part-time jobs are low paid and/or career dead-ends. This might explain why men and women don't often both work part-time around their families even though many parents would find this arrangement ideal. The burden on men to earn the family's daily bread and to stay firmly on the career ladder is greater if they are the main provider. So suddenly, from being equal partners at work and home, the pressure on both parents is different, they are less able to relate to their partner's circumstances and they often don't have time to talk anyway.

The facts
- Women receive on average just 54 pence for every £1 of income received by men.
- Women working full-time receive 80 per cent of men's full-time hourly wage.

- Women working part-time receive 60 per cent of men's full-time hourly wage.
- 80 per cent of part-time jobs are held by women.
- Women pensioners receive just 32 pence for every £1 of income received by a man in a pensioner couple.
- 5 million women (43 per cent of all women employees) earn less than £5 an hour.
- 30,000 women a year are sacked or forced out of their jobs because of pregnancy, and 200,000 more face discrimination. Of the 30,000 UK women a year who lose their jobs because of pregnancy, only 1,000 take their cases to a tribunal.
- Three out of four recruitment agencies said they knew of businesses that had blacklisted young women. More than one in ten said pressure from employers had stopped them putting forward women who were pregnant or likely to have children.
- 78 FTSE 100 companies have female directors, but only 11 have female board level directors, and only one has a female chairperson.
- 33 per cent of managers are women, i.e. there are two male managers for every female one. Mind you, in 1975 it was 1.8 per cent.
- 80 per cent of women compared with 17 per cent of men are responsible for looking after the children or arranging childcare facilities.
- People from a black or ethnic minority (BME) background are statistically four times more likely to be working below their potential, and BME women are three times more likely to be asked about their marriage and children plans than white British women.

Facts courtesy of Fawcett Society, Equal Opportunities Commission, FTSE report, BBC Money Programme, Barclays 2000, Women in London's Economy Conference 2006

The reasons that so much discrepancy exists are complex. The story starts with education – girls choosing subjects and degrees that lead to less lucrative careers, young women making wrong choices early in their careers and ending up in dead-end part-time jobs when they have a family. The pay gap becomes a chasm if a woman does go on to have children.

A consequence of the sudden divergence of roles after parenthood is that for men, the gender issue is largely invisible. It does not affect them in the same way as it affects women. At home, their partner is doing what all mothers do when a baby comes along, so that's normal isn't it? At work (now surrounded by fewer and younger women) many men benefit from a patriarchal system, and many others would suffer by opposing it, being discriminated against or ostracised as a result. Men are also victims of the narrow stereotype of power that is around us – the white, middle-class, heterosexual, able-bodied male – and challenging these stereotypes is as difficult for men as it is for women.

> *Men are also victims of the narrow stereotype of power that is around us, and challenging these stereotypes is as difficult for men as it is for women.*

Women are becoming more vocal about their needs, and are leaving organisations where those needs aren't being met, but in order for their concerns to be truly validated and acted upon, men need to do the same. **Jenny Watson** of EOC says: 'It's time for fathers to come out. We know that dads want to spend more time with their children. We need to hold up a mirror to society and show men that they are not the only ones in this situation. There are thousands of others like them, a whole generation of men, all wanting the same thing.'

All of us, men and women, need to find new models of behaviour that are powerful (power with) but not dominating (power over). The gender gap represents a significant inequality of power, but still the greatest power gap exists between the rich and the poor. This is mirrored by the global power of rich Western countries – Europe and America – over the poor countries in the rest of the world, and women are as much part of that picture as men. While women in the West move into employment and away from caring and domestic responsibilities, their place in childcare and domestic work is taken up by immigrant workers, often women who are leaving their children and other dependents behind in their own countries.

The gender equality movement has a big challenge on its hands – it needs to take into account these global inequalities as well as addressing the diverse situations in which women, rich and poor, find themselves. Alongside the fact from the Fawcett Society that women in the UK are twice as likely as men to live in poverty is the Inland Revenue fact that among the 18–44 age group there are more women millionaires than men. Many of these newly rich women are entrepreneurs.

Women-owned businesses

Developing a reliable picture of female-owned businesses in the UK is hampered by a lack of reliable data. This is partly because the data collection agencies do not disaggregate this information by gender, and partly because small business figures rely heavily on VAT returns provided to the Inland Revenue. Many women-run businesses fall below the VAT threshold, so they do not appear in official statistics.

The overall picture is one of women being under-represented in the self-employed labour market, as a result of cultural factors ('nice girls don't do deals') and also specific barriers such as lack of finance, inaccessibility of childcare, inappropriate business support services and difficulty of making the transition from benefits to self-employment. (One in five women enter self-employment from unemployment, compared with around one in fifteen for men.[xi]) Here are some other differences:

In contrast to self-employed men, women:

- Own smaller businesses in terms of employment and turnover.
- Are more likely to operate from home and on a part-time basis.
- Are more likely to have entered self-employment from part-time work or after a career break.
- Spend less time at start-up engaged in acquiring finance.
- Start business with lower investment.
- Are more likely to use credit card debt as a source of start-up capital.
- Are more risk-averse regarding business funding.
- Are more likely to have female customers than male customers.

From ACCA Research Report no 90, February 2006

Professor **Sara Carter**, co-author of the ACCA report quoted above and Professor of Entrepreneurship at Stirling University, was one of the first academics to recognise female entrepreneurship as a growing and important social trend, and one that she wanted to research and promote. She has huge amounts of experience of this area, and is driven to address the inequalities that exist between women's and men's enterprises.

She is ideally placed to describe and explain the relevant trends, and to do so, we include below the core of her speech to the Women's Financial Advisory Group in January 2006:

Twenty years ago, as a young researcher starting a career in academic research, I was part of a team that undertook the first ever study of women entrepreneurs in Britain. So little was known of this area, that our job was to 'find and explore' female entrepreneurs, in much the same way as an anthropologist would seek out a rare tribe in the Amazon rainforest. To do seventy case studies, we travelled the length and breadth of the country, looking under stones, trying to find some of the very few women who had started their own business. What we discovered was a small group of women business owners, with a common experience of under-capitalisation, constantly challenged credibility and an acute lack of confidence.

I vividly remember one interview with a textile manufacturer in Nottingham, whose husband – who had nothing whatsoever to do with her business – insisted on being present, standing next to her throughout the interview. What I realized was that his presence represented not her lack of confidence, but, rather, his lack of confidence in her. His loitering at the door appeared to symbolise his suspicion of her business life – constantly looking over her shoulder, silently judging her endeavours. I admit this had a huge resonance for me. As a lowly research assistant, I was expected to contribute the greatest effort, but there was an ever-present male professor who similarly loitered at the threshold, constantly looked over my shoulder and silently judged my endeavours.

What we discovered was a small group of women business owners, with a common experience of under-capitalisation, constantly challenged credibility and an acute lack of confidence.

The issues we identified twenty years ago: a lack of capitalisation, constantly challenged credibility and isolation from business networks, represent inequalities that separated businesses owned by women and those owned by men. These inequalities underpin all research into female entrepreneurship. If there were no differences and no inequalities between male and female businesses, there would be no interest in researching women entrepreneurs.

So what has changed in the last twenty years? Firstly, women entrepreneurs have become more visible. There are nearly a million women business owners in the UK today, a much larger number than ever before. Women have a direct stake in fifty per cent of all businesses in the UK. They own fifteen per cent of businesses outright and co-own, with male partners, a further thirty five per cent.

Despite these great strides and the fantastic predictions for the future, it is still the case that women, on average, are poorer than men. Women earn less than men, women own less than men and women inherit less than men. This is both a fundamental inequality for women and a distinct disadvantage for women entrepreneurs. Businesses started by women, on average, start with only one third of the capital used by men. Women are less likely to use bank

Businesses started by women, on average, start with only one third of the capital used by men.

finance and tend to rely on personal savings and credit cards. The reason this is important is because under-capitalisation at start-up has an enduring and negative effect on business survival, performance and growth of female owned businesses.

While the number of women entrepreneurs has increased dramatically in the past twenty years, their experiences of business ownership are rather different to those of men. Women owned businesses still tend to be younger and smaller. Women are more likely to start-up on their own, rather than with partners, and women tend to have fewer employees. Women are also more likely to operate in traditionally 'female' sectors: retailing and services, and to operate business from their home. Crucially, women entrepreneurs are still being charged more for bank borrowing. A survey by Warwick University last year, found women entrepreneurs are charged one per cent more than men for term loans: two point nine (2.9) per cent over base, compared with one point nine (1.9) per cent over base. I'd like to dwell on the Warwick report for a minute because when I was reading the study, I noticed that on five separate occasions the report stated that they had found 'no evidence of discrimination' but couldn't explain why women were being charged more. I don't know what their definition of sex discrimination is, but in my view it's being treated unequally and unfairly.

> **A survey by Warwick University last year, found women entrepreneurs are charged one per cent more than men for term loans.**

In addition to the fundamental inequalities that characterise some aspects of female entrepreneurship, it is also clear that women often have a different approach to 'doing business'. This became clear in my latest research project, which looked at gender, entrepreneurship and bank lending. This project looked not just at differences between male and female entrepreneurs, but also differences between male and female bank loan officers.

We found no overt differences in the way that male and female bank loan officers appeared to treat male and female entrepreneurs. However, I was taken aback by the marked differences in how male and female bank loan officers approached the internal processes of handling loan applications.

Male bank loan officers tapped into a fertile network of business and social contacts which were a source of lucrative and juicy business deals. Though, with days apparently devoted to playing golf and evenings spent in lap-dancing clubs, it's a wonder they were able to get any work *done at all. Women bank loan officers found it difficult to access good deals from their introducers and brokers and, while they understood the importance of networking in theory, rarely had time to do it in practice. The deals they were given were low value and often tied them up in paperwork for weeks on end. The result was that almost all of the male bank loan officers achieved their year-end bonus, but none of the women did. Not a single one.*

Once the deals had been supported by the bank loan officers, proposals were sent to the Bank's credit controllers for sanctioning. The women loan officers relinquished control as soon as the proposals had been emailed to the bank's credit controllers. The men, however, continued to negotiate through the Chinese wall and attempted to exert influence on the decision making process. We all know how this is done: they phone their friends in credit control, and they say, 'Did you watch the game last night? Great goal! By the way, I've got a proposal coming through. Watch out for it, it's a great deal'. Football is the universal language of men, and is becoming the universal language of business.

The men succeeded by cultivating networks, using tacit, unwritten knowledge and watching football. Women often fail because they're isolated from networks and follow the rules, rather than their mates.

The banks we looked at aren't unusual in any way, and our findings, I think, are typical of how men and women operate within all types of organisations. The men succeeded by cultivating networks, using tacit, unwritten knowledge and watching football. Women often fail because they're isolated from networks and follow the rules, rather than their mates.

There are lessons here for all women. Perhaps, however, we need to start emulating men by using our tacit knowledge. In my professional life, I am surrounded by women who are far too busy, who work far too hard and who obey all the rules — and not a single one of them gets promoted as quickly as men do. This is a common experience for many women. We are so busy being busy, that we fail to appreciate that men are leading very different lives to us. Men threw out the rule-book years ago, and trust their contacts, instinct and judgement.

My research has been concerned with exploring and exposing the disadvantages faced by women entrepreneurs. Researchers are, by nature, idealistic people. By exposing inequalities, we want to remove them and bring about a fairer business environment.

Creating a fairer environment is often one of the key motivating factors for women setting up businesses. A survey commissioned by the East of England Development Agency found that women are significantly more likely than men to want to start a business that tackles social exclusion. Women seem to be leading the way as social entrepreneurs – identifying practical solutions to social problems, and defying the traditional profit/not-for-profit, work/life, manager/worker, male/female, western world/developing world pigeonholes.

Women seem to be leading the way as social entrepreneurs.

CASE STUDY

Stella Thomas, a global water consultant, was deeply affected by the statistics that 1.3 billion people have no access to clean water, 2.4 billion people have no access to sanitation and that women and children in developing regions regularly travel 10–20 km a day for clean water. She says, 'All statistics have a human face attached to them.' She set up the Global Water Fund to 'create an awareness of the world's water situation and to bring clean water and sanitation to all'.

Engineering, building, manual trades and construction are traditionally male domains, but there is encouraging evidence of female successes in this area, exemplified not least individuals like Stella Thomas above, and Mrs Fixit who we met earlier, but also by the creation of organisations such as the National Association of Women in Construction and the Women and Manual Trades organisation (see the resources in the Appendix for contact information).

CASE STUDY

Jackie Abey and Jill Smallcombe are builder-designers who have worked together in the south of England for ten years. They see a growing number of women entering the construction industry, where health and safety codes are necessarily strict. After years of wearing ill-fitting equipment – high-visibility jackets, hardhats and steel toe-capped boots – all designed for men, they are planning a range of protective clothing for women who work on construction sites. This includes architects, surveyors, planners, plumbers, painters, electricians, builders – none of which are exclusively male professions any longer.

WHAT THE GOVERNMENT IS DOING

Let's look first of all at who our elected representatives are. In the House of Commons, House of Lords and the Northern Ireland Assembly only 20 per cent of representatives are women. Wales are right on the nose with 50 per cent female assembly Members, and the Scottish and Greater London assemblies are making great progress, both with 36 per cent female representation.

So Wales and Scotland are leading the way and reaping the benefits of representative representatives, as it were, but in our main UK elected body, the House of Commons, female representation is still absurdly low (after the 2005 election, a *Guardian* columnist joked that at this rate, there would never be more women than Davids in the House of Commons.)

> *There would never be more women than Davids in the House of Commons.*

No surprise then, that despite making up 52 per cent of the population and the majority of the voting public and being courted by all the major political parties, the female interest level and female voter turnout at elections remain low.

Fortunately, a number of high-profile organisations such as the Fawcett Society and Equal Opportunities Commission are working towards a fairer society. Pressure from groups such as these has led to the report of the Women and Work Commission asking why the gender pay gap still exists, 30 years after the Sex Discrimination Act and the Equal Pay Act.

The Gender and Equality Duty, part of the larger Equality Bill coming into force in 2007 will require public-sector employers, such as the police, NHS and local government to actively promote equality. Unlike the 1975 legislation which requires individuals to make a stand against their employer if they are unfairly treated, this duty puts the onus on employers not to discriminate.

The body with the most potential to support future women in business is the National Women's Enterprise Task Force. The new group aims to increase the start-up rate of women-owned businesses by making information, childcare and finance easier to obtain, and by reaching out to the regions nationwide. The new group is being launched as a result of the work of the DTI Small Business Service and Prowess, both of which are working towards the government's targets to increase the number of women in business.

Although recent tax-credit schemes have helped some low-income women, they are complex in their nature and aren't taken up by all those eligible. A great area of concern is the lack of a clear relationship between benefits agencies, job centres and the various regional schemes to get women into business. As **Nina Sian** (who won the 2006 Prowess Business Support Professional of the Year) from Slough Enterprise Gateway told us:

> *At the moment, women who are on benefits but want to set up a business are allowed to keep their benefits for exactly six months, but after that time they don't get a penny. As anyone who has set up a business knows, it takes months to do the research and planning that a new business needs, so it's unlikely that any new business is going to be thriving after just six months. It takes a while for the first client to walk through the door, and often much longer for that to be a steady and reliable stream of clients. What would be much more helpful is some kind of top-up benefit so if a woman has a good week in her new business, the state pays her less, but if she has a bad week she can still afford to eat. Or businesses should be able to trade for three months before being registered. If a woman on a low income is motivated enough to use her precious little time and money to set up a business, isn't that great for everybody — her, her dependants, the tax payer, the*

community? That's why we've got to encourage it, not make it a jump off a cliff. Also, we need a much more co-ordinated approach between agencies, and consistency of funding. There are so many agencies that need to work together in this environment, and the mixed public/private system we're in is so complex, it's difficult to make positive and lasting changes, despite the fact that we all want to do that.

So even though efforts are being made to help women in business, the messages and experiences on the ground are mixed.

Why does the government want more women to set up businesses? Well, it's mostly because the country as a whole would earn more money if more of us became entrepreneurs. Here are the facts.

How women-owned businesses make a difference

- If the UK could achieve the same levels of female entrepreneurship as the US, Britain would gain three-quarters of a million more businesses. (Chancellor of the Exchequer Gordon Brown, Advancing Enterprise Conference, 4 February, 2005)
- A pound invested in developing women's enterprise provides a greater return on investment than a pound invested in developing male-owned enterprise. (Chief Executive of the Small Business Service, Martin Wyn Griffith, Speaking at the National Dialogue for Entrepreneurship, Washington, DC, March 2005)
- If women started businesses at the same rate as men, we would have 150,000 extra start-ups each year. (Rt Hon. Jacqui Smith, Minister for Women and Equality, speaking at 2nd Prowess conference)
- Women starting up in business will tend to provide a more immediate contribution to the economy: around one in five women come into self-employment from unemployment, compared with around one in fifteen for men. (SBS Promoting Female Entrepreneurship, March 2005)

> *A pound invested in developing women's enterprise provides a greater return on investment than a pound invested in developing male-owned enterprise.*

WHAT BANKS AND FINANCIAL INSTITUTIONS ARE DOING

According to the women's organisation Prowess, fear of debt is the single biggest barrier to entrepreneurship for both men and women. Women are less likely to borrow money and borrow up to a third less than men. This may be because generally women do not tend to 'think big' at the outset, and are more risk-averse than men when it comes to borrowing money. It's also a language issue. There has always been a real lack of clear, jargon-free information about financing options available to businesses in general, and the use of obscure language is cited as one of the principal obstacles between women and the fulfilment of their business dreams.

> *The use of obscure language is cited as one of the principal obstacles between women and the fulfilment of their business dreams.*

It is important for banks to recognise the differences between men and women, as well as the fact that women want to be treated with respect and understanding, just as men do. Also it is important for us to recognise that entrepreneurs, especially the female ones, are different animals from bank managers. **Anita Roddick** says, in her irreverent manner, 'Most bank managers are pathologically boring and don't understand your pathological enthusiasm.' But if you are looking for funding, you need to understand the bank's position, and realise what they want from you – inevitably return on their investment, and security for their loan.

Thankfully, some banks meet us halfway. **Clare Logie**, Director of the Women in Business Team at Halifax Bank of Scotland, says:

> *We have had the Women in Business team in place for over two years now and in that time, we have seen the dedicated resource and effort applied to understanding the women's marketplace reap great benefits for us. The key has been in ensuring that women are not patronised or segregated but that the subtle differences of their requirements are genuinely appreciated and handled effectively – women know the*

difference and our increasing numbers of female customers is proof positive that it works.

Surely more banks will follow their example as time goes on.

Not everyone gets the green light from a lender, though. Single mothers and women on benefits have a particularly difficult time applying for business loans. Often they will have no credit rating (if, for example, her house is in the husband's name only), and can find themselves dismissed out of hand by lenders who haven't looked further than that. In fact, if a woman has made it this far as a lone parent and has the gumption to draw up a business plan and approach a lender for funding, surely this in itself shows that she has qualities worthy of some attention.

Generally women don't feel as comfortable in the banking environment as men do. If we had designed them, they would probably look and feel very different. A number of women we spoke to talked about how they felt they had no choice but to drag their husband or male colleague to the bank with them in order to get the attention of the frowning man in the suit behind the desk; and predictably, the man in the suit talked to her man in his suit, believing him to be in charge. This all sounds quite alienating, but what you have to remember is that once you have set up your own business and are doing very nicely, the banks will be bending over backwards to lend you money. If you can do whatever you need to do to get through the macho bank thing, and come out with what you went in for, the job will be done.

Emma Reid of Grey Sells told us that 'learning to love debt' was one of the biggest lessons she has learnt in business:

CASE STUDY

There are huge anomalies in the financing industry, and actually a real gap in the market for female-friendly access to money at tolerable conditions. Every bank I approached wanted my house as security for my business, which I wasn't prepared to consider. I didn't see why I should, given that I have an excellent credit record, and my hallway is regularly overflowing with offers for unsecured loans and credit cards. But if I want to use the money for work – an investment in my future – then why should my home suddenly be up for grabs in a way that it wouldn't be if I wanted to blow a few grand on the high street, or buy a new car?'

Men and women do things differently when it comes to seeking finance, and are treated differently, as Professor Sara Carter explained above, and as the following facts illustrate further.

But if I want to use the money for work – an investment in my future – then why should my home suddenly be up for grabs in a way that it wouldn't be if I wanted to blow a few grand on the high street, or buy a new car?

Men, women and finance

- Both male and female owned businesses require on average around £20,000 to start up. (Prowess)

- Women tend to rely more on their personal savings to set up a business – women's personal savings constitute between 80 and 99 per cent of initial capitalisation, while the figure for men is 30–59 per cent. (Everywoman)

- Women tend to fund growth through turnover, rather than new investment.

- 33 per cent of female compared to 20 per cent of male businesses have used government programmes to fund their business start-up. (*Achieving the Vision*, Female Entrepreneurship British Chambers of Commerce, July 2004)

- Self-employed women who work full time have a mean total weekly income of £412, compared to men's of £598 – a pay gap of 31 per cent. (*Facts About Women and Men In Great Britain*, Equal Opportunities Commission 2005)

'Investor' remains a very male word. 95 per cent of business angels are men, and while male and female business angels don't seem to invest differently, the fact remains that women prefer to discuss financing options for their business with other women, and are inspired by successful female role models.

Recognising this, Trapezia, from Stargate Capital, is the first UK venture capital fund to be dedicated to women entrepreneurs. **Gita Patel**, fund manager and inspiring businesswoman in her own right, told us:

> *Women entrepreneurs are currently poorly served by the mainstream, male-dominated investment community. For the women who come to me, values and ethics are high on the agenda, intuition plays a big part in their decision-making process, but they are held back by risk-averseness and inability to grow. They are obliged to speak to men about financing, and men and women think about finance differently. Often what happens is that bank managers demand the family home as security, and women aren't prepared to take that risk, so ideas don't get off the ground. Instead, banks should ask for personal guarantees. Without investment, these businesses will not grow, and the playing field will not be levelled. But capital is only part of the picture. We need more markets, networks, mentoring for women's businesses: they need to be nurtured. They need education, especially in tax issues, and the language we use to educate them is crucial in affecting whether they understand — there is too much jargon around finance, and it's fairly simple really. There are not enough financial services specifically for women, which is ridiculous, as women own 48 per cent of the wealth in the UK — we have more services for pets than for women! We also need more government funds to be allocated to initiatives supporting women's businesses in the fields of education, support and training. Since women's enterprise is growing at its fastest rate ever despite all the obstacles, imagine how well it would be doing if the obstacles were removed!*

> **For the women who come to me, values and ethics are high on the agenda, but they are held back by risk-averseness and inability to grow.**

WHAT SCHOOLS AND HIGHER EDUCATION ARE DOING

Business studies have been part of the school curriculum for a long time, but haven't always been held in high regard, perhaps deservedly in the days that it was a bland course with few links to real businesses. The face of business education in schools, like the schools themselves, is changing rapidly. Secondary schools can now apply for specialist status in one of ten specialisms, one of which is business and enterprise. Over 200 schools in England have been awarded Specialist Business and Enterprise Status, and, through a combination of government funding and private sponsorship, aim to equip students with the business skills they need for future employment or self-employment.

Lisa Thefaut, Business Links Co-ordinator for Ursuline High School, Wimbledon, told us what the specialist Business and Enterprise Status has meant for students:

> *Learning directly from business women is opening students' eyes to the real opportunities out there for them in business. Our developing programme of business links across the curriculum — interactive talks, visits, events, case studies — aims to build students' self-confidence by giving them not just inspirational role models, but also a real understanding of the skills and qualities needed to succeed.*
>
> *This is the best kind of learning, raising and expanding aspirations. Take the 'Who wants to be an entrepreneur?' event we ran in partnership with our local Women in Business network. Students spent a day interviewing local women who run their own business, finding out about the demands and benefits for a woman of being self-employed as well as the skills and qualities needed to be successful. Students then reflected on their own skills and qualities and considered whether they would like to be their own boss. At the end of the day, 69 per cent of students said they would really like to work for themselves; running their own business had become a real career choice.*

Learning directly from business women is opening students' eyes to the real opportunities out there for them in business.

In Wales, the Dynamo project aims to develop and nurture self-sufficient entrepreneurial young people in much the same way as the Ursuline High School – through links with local businesses, role models and a focus on increasing self-confidence and encouraging imagination.

CASE STUDY

Louise Ladbrooke set up Bees Knees Day Nursery in 1996. She won the Welsh Woman of the Year, Small Business Owner Award in 2002 and is one of 250 role models for the Dynamo project, a European-funded project run by the Welsh Development Agency. She told us:

> *I've thoroughly enjoyed being able to open the eyes of young people to the fantastic opportunity of running your own business. It's not something I thought I would ever do with my life, but it's something I've been able to do very well. I can't help thinking how great it would have been to have had businesswomen come into the school where I was a pupil to talk about running your business as a career option.*

The girls at Ursuline and on the Dynamo project are lucky. The authors of the 2006 Women and Work Commission report were shocked by the poor careers advice and work experience on offer in many British schools. Girls were actually not encouraged to continue with maths and science, traditionally subjects that lead to better paid careers, despite being high achievers at these subjects. Even when they had not expressed any interest in working in the caring sectors (nursing homes, hairdressers, nurseries), this was the 'work experience' they were pushed to do. One of the many recommendations of the report was to address the quality of careers advice in schools and move away from the current blatantly discriminatory system to one where girls are given advice that could allow them to reach a higher career potential.

Even when they had not expressed any interest in working in the caring sectors (nursing homes, hairdressers, nurseries), this was the 'work experience' they were pushed to do.

In further education, the study of business is a popular area, with many colleges and universities offering courses in 'entrepreneurship' alongside and as part of traditional MBAs. Many universities offer self-employment courses and business support to women, such as the following example of a happy student of Bath University's Women in Enterprise course.

CASE STUDY

Amanda Hazell set up Making Moves in May 2005, and was several months into it when she enrolled on the course:

Doing that course was the best decision I made. For a start, I was encouraged to put my mind to a real business plan, to face the reality of the cashflow forecast, which I had really had my head in the sand about until then. The fact that a lot of us ignore when we set up in business is that it takes a long time to break even — you have to spend such a lot of money before you can actually start making money.

Luton University is pioneering a women-only MBA to try to address the imbalance between men and women business graduates. As ever, the reasons are part biological (the average entrance age of an MBA student is 28–29, the same as the average age of a new mother) and part cultural (male partners may be less willing to relocate, and the companies that MBA students traditionally study, and later join, may be 'old style', i.e. male-dominated and patriarchal).

Liz Nelson, OBE, thinks there should be an alternative to the MBA that suits women: 'women are no worse at figures than men, and certainly no worse at business. What we need is the confidence that an MBA seems to bring male graduates, and that largely comes about through easy access to the systems and processes of the business world.'

Cranfield University runs a highly influential centre for women business leaders and research and teaching work there has changed the way that government and businesses relate to women leaders and managers, as well as providing training and networking for working women.

The picture from the National Council for Graduate Entrepreneurship is rosy – they report a sharp rise in the number of female entrepreneurs and report that over half of the graduates shortlisted to work with mentors are women. For many graduates, entrepreneurship is a more attractive option than joining a ready-made career at graduate 'milk rounds'. The Oxford Entrepreneurs are an active and impressively multicultural group run by students, for students. They attract top-notch speakers to inspire their graduates into starting their own businesses.

Women and girls now outperform men and boys at all levels of education, but are we paying too high a price for this? The levels of stress and worry among girls are consistently higher than for boys, while confidence and self-esteem are lower. Perhaps this is one of the reasons that women make up less than a quarter of the total of entrepreneurs, and is another consequence of the 'impostor syndrome' described in our Introduction.

Sadly, academic achievement doesn't correlate neatly to future career success, whether in employment or self-employment (no matter what your mother told you) – so it seems that the things we are measuring and teaching at school aren't quite the right things, and that emotional intelligence education has a bigger part to play in future.

> *Emotional intelligence education has a bigger part to play in future.*

WHAT THE REST OF THE WORLD IS DOING

Women's entrepreneurship levels are lower than men's throughout the world, but the world is waking up to the contribution that women have to make. With this level of interest, women have to make sure that their needs are met, and that they do not continue to be exploited or second-class citizens as they have been in the past. **Julie Weeks** of Womenable, in a speech at the 2006 Prowess conference, observed:

> *Women are generally too apologetic when they ask for money or business support – it reminds me of the Oliver Twist way of doing things, you*

know, bowl held up, head held down … I'd like to see women around the world asking for more in the way that black people did during the Civil Rights Movement. Head held high — 'Say It Loud! I'm Black and Proud.'

The USA is the biggest success story, where women own nearly half of all private businesses, and there are over 100 Women's Business Centres providing working accommodation for women-owned business, and support services such as financial advice, coaching and childcare. The USA has been working extremely hard to achieve this, particularly in the last ten years. As recently as 1998 an American woman could not get a business loan in her own name.

As recently as 1998 an American woman could not get a business loan in her own name.

In Taiwan, the Flying Geese programme aims to increase the number of female entrepreneurs, and South Africa is working on a Strategic Framework for women in business. International bodies such as the Global Banking Alliance and the IFC are developing standards for best practice around women's requirements for small business finance. In Japan, where two-thirds of women do not return to work after childbirth, the government has unveiled a 'Female Re-Challenge' plan to increase the number of female entrepreneurs and leaders, and to make it easier for women to combine having a family with working life. But in Japan, as elsewhere, there is concern that encouraging women to work is an attack on so-called traditional values.

In most countries the general outlook and commitment to supporting women wobble every few years, with a change of government or policy, making sustained forward movement almost impossible. Sweden is one liberal country where consistent investment in public services over 70 years is rewarding its inhabitants with a top-notch social welfare system, which provides for childcare and maternity/paternity leave, a ceiling on healthcare costs, good pensions and sick leave, among other benefits. Parents are entitled to a year's paid leave, with a month of that reserved specifically for fathers, and there is provision for full-time childcare for all children between two and six, after which they attend school. Perhaps not surprisingly, childcare is never cited as a barrier to starting a business, and the number of women-owned businesses has doubled in the last ten years. A Prowess representative said, 'The Swedish approach to childcare is light years ahead of the UK and so practical it should be shipped over here in an IKEA flat pack and quickly assembled!' The situation is not so rosy in Italy, where an increasing proportion of educated women no longer want to be mothers or wives. Childcare is prohibitively expensive for most couples, part-time jobs are almost unheard of and it is not the norm for men to help around the house. Not surprisingly, Italy's birthrate is one of the lowest in the Western world.

> *The Swedish approach to childcare is light years ahead of the UK and so practical it should be shipped over here in an IKEA flat pack and quickly assembled!*

At the root of this difference is the wide gulf in attitude between countries like Sweden, who see children as a shared responsibility of society and resource for the future, and UK/Italy, who see children and non-working parents as a financial burden and education/childcare as a political football. This fundamental difference in approach is not only ingrained in the culture, but also in the political and taxation structures. Moving from where we are in the UK towards a fairer system will require huge political will and a broad shift of mindset.

WHAT WOMEN'S BUSINESS MOVEMENTS ARE DOING

There has been a huge increase in women's business groups over the last few years, from local groups such as Rural Women in Somerset, to nationwide groups such as Everywoman and Aurora. The buzz of excitement and enthusiasm at their women-led conferences is hard to beat. There are networks for particular occupations, such as the Creative Women's Network and networks for minority groups such as Black and Ethnic

Women in Business. We provide a list of groups in the Appendix, but women are setting up new networks all the time. We set one up ourselves once . . .

In 2003, Lucy had the idea to set up a women's business group in Wimbledon, now the well-established Wimbledon Women in Business Group, which is where we met and this book was conceived.

> *Lucy: I had been a member of another mixed business group (majority men) but its culture, interests and direction didn't suit me; neither did the early morning meetings or the £5 'power breakfasts' of bacon and eggs that left me sluggish rather than inspired. I knew that there were women locally running their own businesses and invited a few over to meet each other. We started off meeting in our front rooms and back gardens, either in the middle of the day or in the evening when the children were asleep. We quickly got inspired by each other, shared our challenges and successes and the group went from strength to strength. We had so many women wanting to join that we hired (very cheaply) a local village hall where we could meet in the evenings every fortnight. It's very informal – people bring wine, soft drinks and crisps to share – and we alternate between inviting external speakers and members of the group to tell us what they do. It takes a lot of organising – we had to set up a committee, bank account and constitution for the group – but there was a lot of enthusiasm and willingness to help, among a very busy group of people. The group has been very supportive to all its members, not to mention providing a social and business network. We all use each other's services, and provide practical help wherever we can. We want to share our winning formula with other groups, so we wrote a guide to setting up your own business group for other women with a similar idea.*

While male business groups have existed for years, both formally and informally, the story we hear again and again from women in our networks is that they want a group which is focused on supporting its members' wide range of needs rather than just marketplaces for business services. In one mixed business network, members are required to provide a quota of leads for other members, and are assessed and accepted on the basis of how well they do that. The atmosphere of such groups can be unpleasantly competitive, and an unwelcome return to being marked out of ten. Women tend to set up in business to get away from this hierarchical model, and often find a more genuine community in women-only business groups. However, many women running businesses could benefit from mixed networks, and often find that the supportive environment of a women's group gives them confidence to then approach a mixed group.

> *Women often find a more genuine community in women-only business groups.*

CASE STUDY

Kelly Stevens and Sarah Steele set up the Women's Networking Company from their base in Sussex. They aim to create opportunities by providing a support system for entrepreneurs and start-up businesses. Kelly told us:

> *When I wanted to join women's business networks I found they were few and far between and I had to travel a long way at times that weren't always convenient. What we do at the Women's Networking Company is to host groups in many locations around the South East, so we go where the women are rather than the other way round and we make it convenient for women in other ways, such as lunches rather than evening events and providing an online booking facility. What women find, as well as support and networking, is that they recognise in other businesses skills and ways of doing things that they don't have in their own and are motivated to find out more, and develop their own businesses. Our events often provide women with a stepping-stone to other groups and opportunities.*

The Women's Networking Company tends to attract businesswomen with some degree of work experience, from relatively well-off areas of the South East, but there are plenty of opportunities for women in low-income areas too.

Her Business is a project in Newham, east London, a lower-income area with a high proportion of ethnic groups, and is typical of many of the programmes up and running around the country. The project is supported by European and UK government sponsors and has supported many women to move from unemployment to running a business. With many success stories under their belt, they are now building a US-style Women's Business Centre, the first purpose-built new centre in the country. Project Manager **Gill Fennings** told us:

> *The Her Business Centre (HBC) will be a purpose-built centre with an appealing shop front and easy access to any woman no matter how wide her buggy! It will be bright and cheery and open and have sofa areas for informal chats and a large space for meeting and sharing ideas and expertise. Women are the best networkers so we just want to provide the framework to give them skills, support and the right environment to do their own thing and grow. There will be incubator space, administrative support, IT suites, training rooms, catering areas, and a large lounge with big sofas. The centre will provide life and business coaching, business advice, personal and professional development, counselling and group support, and training, which remove the hurdles that women face, for example in the area of finance, confidence, marketing and time management. HBC will also provide specialist monthly surgeries with lawyers, accountants, tax experts, IT designers and marketing experts.*
>
> *HBC will also have weekly or monthly cafe evenings that will be an opportunity for the women to meet and share what they are looking for or needing to find so as to develop their business. This will be a fun and relaxing opportunity to get together and to also support women who are just beginning to consider themselves as potential business women who need a safe place to explore and grow.*
>
> *Each year we will celebrate the successes of our women's business community with a conference to take them further in their own development and that of their business.*

Her Business has recently won a Prowess Flagship Award, and we hope that the success of this first centre will lead to lots of much-needed women's business centres around the country.

Prowess is not a women's network, but rather a network for the supporters of women's businesses – like a network of networks. It is a great resource for people who support women in business and also lobbies extremely effectively for changes in policy to support female entrepreneurs. Their annual flagship awards at the high-profile conference (in 2005 this was held in Cardiff City Hall and opened by First Minister for Wales, Rhodri Morgan), and their tireless commitment to promoting women's enterprises are improving the lot for women setting up business in the UK.

WORK AND COMMUNITY

The modern-day image of community is sad by comparison – conjuring up a draughty church hall serving stewed tea to depressed groups of society's misfits.

'Community' is a word that has become rather old-fashioned and seems to represent a nonexistent golden age, where women gossiped outside terraced houses in their rollers, men went to clubs where everybody knew their name, and newborn babies wore hand-knitted cardigans. The modern-day image of community is sad by comparison – conjuring up a draughty church hall serving stewed tea to depressed groups of society's misfits. Being part of a community is seen as 'sad' and at odds with the trend for independence, individualism and personal choice. It appears that with this increase in personal choice, there is a price to pay in terms of our relationship with our community.

Being part of a community is a deep human need. At some level, we are all lonely and long for that connection with people and groups where we can be ourselves, contribute something, and be understood – in an atmosphere of warmth, affection, laughter and celebration. Healthy communities develop from being together and doing things together in an environment conducive to meeting human needs. So given that so many of us congregate at work, shouldn't our organisations be the place where modern-day communities are emerging?

Perhaps they are for some people, but all too often

> *There is little opportunity to share personal experiences in a way that builds community (anyone who has time to chat can't possibly be busy or important enough).*

dehumanising factors get in the way. Firstly, the pressure of time – lunchtimes are a quick sandwich at the desk or staffroom, and there is little opportunity to share personal experiences in a way that builds community (anyone who has time to chat can't possibly be busy or important enough). Secondly, we are often reduced to job titles in our dealings with our fellow workers. All this is 'justified' by the pressures of the omnipotent global marketplace. The much-maligned team-building day might be one of the few places that we're allowed, or even required, to interact with our colleagues on a human level but it's back to business as usual tomorrow . . .

Thankfully many of us do find some sort of community at work – fellow human beings to rub along with, split the daily run to the coffee shop and share the few quid from the lottery sweepstake. Being part of a community is particularly important to women, and it's something we often miss when we leave a big organisation, or re-emerge into the world after raising our children. The good news is that business ownership is an opportunity to create community in a more healthy and meaningful way than many large organisations have managed to do.

Even the smaller businesses are never truly 'one-man bands'. We rely on the community out there for our clients, suppliers and support, and provide services to the community we live in. We become linked into the world in a much more direct way than we are by being employed, and meet people and groups we might not have encountered before. Many entrepreneurs describe a meaningful existence where they can see the effects and value of their work first-hand as well as meeting and working with interesting people. There are some really solid professional friendships developing out there through women in business networks, neighbours working from home, and some inspiring examples of women helping each other to run their businesses.

Becoming a successful business owner is a journey, and engaging with that journey leads you to unexpected and exciting places. You make new connections, get inspired, discover lots about yourself, and generally have the chance to improve your lot – none of which happens without stepping out into the unknown.

Setting up a business means coming out into the world and saying 'this is who I am and this is what I want' and that's a great starting point for living a good life. Seeing the world respond to who you really are is without a doubt the best way to live and work.

Good luck with Making It Your Business.

Notes

[i] Pauline Clance and Suzanne Imes 'The Impostor Phenomenon in High Achieving Women', *Psychotherapy Theory, Research and Practice*, 15 (3), 1978. See also Dr Valerie Young's website (www.impostorsyndrome.com).

[ii] Marianne Williamson *A Return to Love: Reflections on a Course in Miracles*, Harper Collins, New York, 1992.

[iii] Abigail Stone. 'Bye Bye Baby: On Mother Guilt and Poverty', in *Child of Mine: Writers Talk About the First Year of Motherhood*, Hyperion Books, New York, 1997.

[iv] Susan Jeffers *Freeing Ourselves From the Mad Myths of Parenthood! Letting go of the guilt and trusting who we are,* Hodder and Stoughton, London, 2000.

[v] Julia McCutchen *The Writer's Journey*, Firefly Media, Trowbridge, 2004.

[vi] Helen Edwards and Derek Day *Creating Passionbrands: Getting to the Heart of Branding*, Kogan Page, London, 2005.

[vii] *The DNA of Women Leaders* – a research study by Aurora and Caliper (2005).

[viii] Jo Owen *How to Lead: What You Actually Need to Do to Manage, Lead and Succeed*, Prentice Hall, Harlow, 2005.

[ix] Polly Toynbee, *Hard Work: Life in Low Pay Britain*, Bloomsbury, London, 2003.

[x] Sandra Lipsitz Bem, *The Lenses of Gender: Transforming the Debate on Sexual Inequality*, Yale University Press, New Haven, 1993.

[xi] Annual Small Business Service, 2003

APPENDIX

NETWORKING RESOURCES FOR WOMEN IN BUSINESS

Aurora Womens Network
www.network.auroravoice.com
Businesswomen's network providing events, training, online communities and resources

The Bag Lady
www.the-bag-lady.co.uk
Global directory of women in business (over1,500 members)

British Chambers of Commerce
www.britishchambers.org.uk
Network of all the chambers of commerce in Great Britain

DAWN
www.mydawn.co.uk
Hub for dynamic asian women entrepreneurs and professional

Everywoman
www.everywoman.co.uk
Information, resources and advice available for women in business

European Federation of Black Women Business Owners
www.efbwbo.net
Organisation with international influence that inspires black women to come together to share, succeed, learn and profit

Forward at 50
www.londonmet.ac.uk/depts/mpd/research/micro_ent/f50/
London Metropolitan University offers courses and support for women over 50 starting a business

Mumpreneurs
www.mumpreneurs.com
Providing support and ideas and inspiration for women who combine
running their own business with motherhood

Network (national)
www.topwomenuk.com
National networking group for women in business with regional divisions

Prowess
www.prowess.org.uk
UK association of organisations and individuals who support women to
start and grow businesses

Scottish Businesswomen
www.scottishbusinesswomen.com
Provides information and advice to help women develop their business ideas.

Starting your own business in Wales
http://new.wales.gov.uk/topics/businessandeconomy/startyourownbusi
ness/?lang=en
Advice and resources for women in business in Wales

Wimbledon Women in Business
www.wwib.org.uk
Women's network based in Wimbledon, London and the source of
inspiration for this book

Women at Work UK Directory of Women in Business
www.womenatwork.co.uk
Online directory of women's businesses

Women's Business Network (North-west England)
www.wbn.org.uk
Network of networks with a total membership of over 6000 women in the
north-west of England

The Women's Company (London and national)
www.thewomenscompany.co.uk
Organise networking lunches around the UK (although London-focused) – and
you can sign up to be a "lunch manager"

Women in Business (South-east England)
www.wib.org.uk
Network of business women in Kent, Sussex, Essex and Surrey

Women in Business Northern Ireland

www.womeninbusinessnetwork.org.uk
also called "Women Doing Business" on the website – a business network
for women in Northern Ireland

Women in Rural Enterprise – WiRE

www.wireuk.org
Up to date information, advice and research

Women into the Network (North-east England)

www.networkingwomen.co.uk/page/index.cfm
Network of businesswomen in the north-east of England

Women's Marketing Forum

www.womensmarketingforum.com/e107_plugins/wrap/wrap.php?1
Online club for women business owners who want to achieve more with
their marketing

The Women's Networking Company

www.thewomensnetworkingcompany.co.uk
Offering two types of networking clubs and lunches in the South East

Women Working for Women

www.womenworking4women.co.uk
global community of women-owned businesses

DEVELOPMENT AGENCIES

England

England is divided by the government into 9 regions, each managed by a
Regional Development Authority (RDA). RDAs are business led and aim to
co-ordinate regional economic development and regeneration. They mediate
associated government and EU funds and grants.

> Advantage West Midlands (www.advantagewm.co.uk)
> East of England Development Agency (www.eeda.org.uk)
> East Midlands Development Agency (www.emda.org.uk)
> London Development Agency (www.lda.gov.uk)
> Northwest Development Agency (www.nwda.co.uk)
> One North East (www.onenortheast.co.uk)
> South East of England Development Agency (www.seeda.co.uk)
> South West of England Development Agency (www.southwestrda.co.uk)
> Yorkshire Forward (www.yorkshire-forward.com)

Scotland

www.scottishdevelopmentinternational.com
Scottish Enterprise

Wales
www.wda.co.uk
Welsh Development Agency

Northern Ireland
www.investni.com
Invest Northern Ireland

Women's Business Development Agency
www.wbda.co.uk
Agency that promotes women in business and encourages women into business

GENERAL BUSINESS ADVICE

ACAS (Advisory Conciliation and Arbitration Service)
www.acas.org.uk
ACAS offers advice on almost all employment matters and operates a nationwide network of enquiry points. The service is available free of charge to any individual or organisation

British Insurers Brokers Association
www.biba.org.uk/consumer/findbroker.asp
UK independent insurance body

Business Link
www.businesslink.org

Companies House
www.companies-house.gov.uk
This is where to go to get official advice on Company formation. The 'Free Business Information' section of the site gives a full listing of company names so you can make sure yours is original and it also has a list of disqualified directors

Data Protection Registrar
www.dataprotection.gov.uk
This is where to find out what your responsibilities are under the 1998 Data Protection Act which is essential reading for small business owners

Department of Trade & Industry (DTI)
www.dti.gov.uk

Electronic Yellow Pages
www.yellowpages.com
Details of more than 1.6 million UK companies

The Environment Agency
www.environment-agency.gov.uk
Guidance, advice and information for businesses on current and forthcoming environmental regulations

Health and Safety Executive
www.hse.gov.uk
Factsheets can be downloaded free on all aspects of health and safety. You
may find 'Health and Safety in Small Firms' particularly useful

HM Revenue and Customs
www.hmrc.gov.uk
Government tax collection and providers of tax credits and child benefits

Inland Revenue
www.inlandrevenue.gov.uk
Everything you need to know about tax and national insurance

Living the Dream
www.bbc.co.uk/business/programmes/dream
This BBC Business Programmes site includes an advice centre for
start-ups

National Council of Graduate Enterprise
www.flyingstart-ncge.com
Support for undergraduates and graduates looking to start their own
business

Nominet
http://www.nominet.org.uk/
Internet registry for .uk names. They have a directory of all domain names
ending in .uk so you can search to see if the name you want is available, and
register available names through nominet agents

Office of Fair Trading
www.oft.gov.uk
The OFT enforces UK competition policy and protects the economic welfare of
consumers. Essential reading to make sure your business stays within the rules

Patent Office
www.patent.gov.uk
Information about patents and design law

The Real Deal
www.channel4.com/life/microsites/R/realdeal/
A lively, fun site providing information, help and advice to anyone wanting
to start a business or with a great business idea

Small Business Service
www.sbs.gov.uk
The SBS is an agency of the Department of Trade and Industry. Useful
information on all aspects of small business and links to relevant
organisations including Regional Development Agencies

Social Enterprise Coalition
www.sec.org.uk
SEC is the UK's national body for social enterprise. They support and represent the work of members, influence national policy and promote best practice

Startups.co.uk
www.startups.co.uk
Provides independent news, advice and guidance free of charge for anyone starting or running a small business. It also includes a host of startup and buyer guides, full directory listings and an interactive forum

IMPORTING AND INTERNATIONAL BUSINESS

Business Link Helpline
0845 600 9 006

Customs & Excise
www.hmce.gov.uk
The "Information for Business" section contains useful contact addresses, publications and advice on VAT and the euro

DTI Import Licensing Branch Helpline
01642 364 333

EU common customs tariff
www.dti.gov.uk/ewt/import.htm

Food regulations
www.food.gov.uk/enforcement

HM Revenue & Customs National Advice Service Enquiry Line
0845 010 9000

Import Licensing information
www.dti.gov.uk/ewt/ilb.htm

The trade of dangerous goods regulations
www.hse.gov.uk/cdg/index.htm

Trade Partners UK
www.tradeuk.com
Comprehensive online directory of UK products and services which is very useful when sourcing suppliers

UK Trade & Investment Enquiry Line
020 7215 8000

FUNDING AND FINANCE

See Development Agencies, listed earlier, also:

Advantage Business Angels
www.advantagebusinessangels.com
Help for small to medium enterprises to find funding through business angels

Bank of Scotland-Women in Business
www.bankofscotlandbusiness.co.uk/womeninbusiness

British Business Angels Association
www.bbaa.org.uk/
bringing together investors with commercial experience and companies looking for development capital

British Venture Capital Association
www.bvca.co.uk
represents most major sources of venture capital in the UK

Community Development Finance Association
www.cdfa.org.uk
can put you in touch with local providers of loans for a small business and social enterprises

j4b
www.j4b.co.uk
The site allows quick and simple searches of a regularly updated database of business grants and loans

The Princes Trust
www.princes-trust.org.uk/
practical business solutions and funding opportunities for young people

Shell Livewire
www.shell-livewire.org
Shell Livewire is a UK wide competition for owner-managers aged between 16 and 30. If you've been in business between 3 and 18 months its worth having a look at the website to find out about heats in your region and at national level

Trapezia
www.trapeziacapital.co.uk/homepage
fund for women-focused businesses – headed by Gita Patel

CHILDCARE RESOURCES

Bestbear
www.bestbear.co.uk
A website for parents offering a nationwide listing of recommended nanny agencies (although no indication of criteria used)

Childcare Approval Scheme
www.childcareapprovalscheme.co.uk
This site has details of how to register your nanny (which will entitle you to various tax benefits)

Gina's Nannies
www.ginasnannies.com
Founded by Lucy Martin, now in partnership with Gail Hennessey – Gina's Nannies provides parents in the London area with nannies, mothers' helps and after-school care

National Childminding Association of England and Wales
www.ncma.org.uk
This site provides information on how to find (or become) a childminder

Ofsted
www.ofsted.gov.uk/
Here you can access reports on local childminders (who are inspected in the same way schools are)

Surestart
www.surestart.gov.uk/
Here you can search by postcode for a list of your local childminders and nurseries

TRAINING

Contact your local RDA, Chamber of Commerce (see earlier) and local adult education college/university to find out about training opportunities, also:

Enspiral
www.enspiral.co.uk
Bella Mehta's company providing personal and professional development – support for starting a business.

Institute for the Development of Human Potential
www.idhp.org
Offers short personal development and leadership courses and a two-year leadership diploma

Springboard
www.springboardconsultancy.com
Offers tailored training programmes for employed, unemployed and self-employed women

FURTHER READING

The Small Business Start-Up Workbook: *A Step-by-step Guide to Starting the Business You've Dreamed of,* Cheryl Rickman, How To Books (2005)

Minding Your Own Business: *Survival Strategies for Starting Up on Your Own,* Cherry Chappell, A&C Black (2004)

Get Noticed: *How to Boost your Small Business Profile in 30 Days or Less,* Paula Gardner, Lean Marketing Press (2005)

Authentic: *How to Make a Living by Being Yourself,* Neil Crofts, Capstone (2003)

The Definitive Business Plan: *The Fast Track to Intelligent Business Planning for Executives and Entrepreneurs,* Richard Stutely, Financial Times Prentice Hall (2001)

The Financial Times Guide to Business Start Up (previously *Lloyds TSB Small Business Guide*), Sara Carter, Pearson Education (2006)

From Acorns… *How to Build Your Brilliant Business from Scratch,* Caspian Woods, Pearson Education (2004)

Secrets of Successful Women Entrepreneurs: *How Ten Leading Business Women Turned a Good Idea into a Fortune,* Sue Stockdale, Lean Marketing Press (2005)

Business as Unusual: *My Entrepreneurial Journey – Profits with Principles,* Anita Roddick, Anita Roddick Books (2005)

Creative Business Presentations: *Inventive Ideas for Making an Instant Impact,* Eleri Sampson (2003)

INDEX